Helms

D0941779

DATE DUE

B   Wright, C.
Fried-   A royal affinity.
rich   c.2
II

6.50

3

Richmond Public Library
Richmond, California

This Book

was donated to the

Richmond Public Library

By

WALTER T. HELMS

BOOKS BY CONSTANCE WRIGHT

A ROYAL AFFINITY
*The Story of Frederick the Great
and His Sister, Wilhelmina of Bayreuth*

DAUGHTER TO NAPOLEON

MADAME DE LAFAYETTE

A CHANCE FOR GLORY

THEIR SHIPS WERE BROKEN

SILVER COLLAR BOY

✦ A ROYAL AFFINITY ✦

THE STORY OF FREDERICK THE GREAT
AND HIS SISTER,
WILHELMINA OF BAYREUTH

CONSTANCE WRIGHT

A

ROYAL

AFFINITY

✦ ✦ ✦

*The Story of Frederick the Great
and His Sister, Wilhelmina of Bayreuth*

CHARLES SCRIBNER'S SONS

New York

COPYRIGHT © 1965 CONSTANCE WRIGHT

A–3.65[v]

THIS BOOK PUBLISHED SIMULTANEOUSLY IN
THE UNITED STATES OF AMERICA AND IN CANADA –
COPYRIGHT UNDER THE BERNE CONVENTION

ALL RIGHTS RESERVED. NO PART OF THIS BOOK
MAY BE REPRODUCED IN ANY FORM WITHOUT
THE PERMISSION OF CHARLES SCRIBNER'S SONS.

PRINTED IN THE UNITED STATES OF AMERICA

Library of Congress Catalog Card Number 65-13663

1–9595

Foreword

I N telling this story of the relationship of two people to one
another lavish use has been made of their confidences. As
will be seen, there are many quotations from what the brother
and sister wrote to one another, a large, though not complete,
collection of their letters having been published in Volume
XXVII of the collected works of Frederick the Great (*Oeuvres
de Frédéric le Grand*) and in the two volumes of *Friedrich der
Grosse und Wilhelmina von Bayreuth,* a German translation
of the original French. Neither Frederick nor Wilhelmina could
speak or write their native tongue correctly.

Many other primary sources—letters, memoirs, diaries—have
been mined. Secondary works, books about the two principal
characters, have been sparingly used, the most helpful being
George Peabody Gooch's *Frederick the Great,* the most ency-
clopedic, Reinhold Koser's *Geschichte Friedrich des Grossen,*
the most suggestive, Richard Fester's *Die Bayreuther Schwester
Friedrich's des Grossen.*

Wilhelmina's memoirs are often quoted—but with discretion.
They were first published in 1810, in two editions, one German,
one French. At that time Napoleon had just defeated the Prussian army and was about to set up the Kingdom of Westphalia as
part of his continental system. The lurid—and entertaining—
picture Wilhelmina gives of conditions at the Prussian court
two generations earlier was seized upon by the French reading

public as explanation for the contemporary decadence of Prussia. This point of view abraded national patriotism. The fact that Wilhelmina says unkind things of her brother irritated biographers to whom he was the hero of all heroes. Friedrich Förster, Leopold von Ranke, Johann Gustav Droysen and other less well known historians read Wilhelmina out of court as an authority; Thomas Carlyle says she is only twenty-five per cent reliable.

Evidence accruing since these judgments were passed in the early nineteenth century proves there is more truth in the *Mémoires* than supposed. The historians, for example, deny that Wilhelmina was ever courted by Charles XII of Sweden, but letters, first printed in the *Hohenzollernjahrbuch* for 1917, show a marriage was suggested, though not seriously considered. Wilhelmina's tendency to exaggerate and to paint the darkest picture possible, however, has been taken into account in drawing material from the *Mémoires*; whenever possible other sources have been checked. In Wilhelmina's defense, it should be pointed out that she never set herself up to be an historian and never intended publication of her work. As for her attacks on Frederick, excuse can be found in the unhappy circumstances, related in Chapter XXIV, under which the *Mémoires* were written.

✦ ✦ ✦

The author is in debt for many kind services from the staffs of the New York Public Library, the library of Columbia University, the *Universitätsbibliothek* and the *Bibliothek des Hauptarchivs* in West Berlin, the *Deutsche Staatsbibliothek* in East Berlin and the Bureau of Public Records in London. She is above all grateful to her home library, that of Pleasantville, New York, for much patient and successful search for rare books scattered throughout America.

✦ A ROYAL AFFINITY ✦

THE STORY OF FREDERICK THE GREAT
AND HIS SISTER,
WILHELMINA OF BAYREUTH

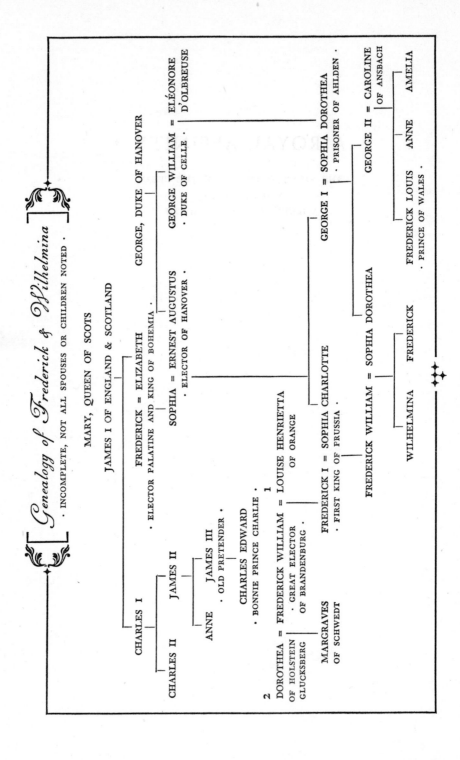

Genealogy of Frederick & Wilhelmina

· INCOMPLETE, NOT ALL SPOUSES OR CHILDREN NOTED ·

MARY, QUEEN OF SCOTS

JAMES I OF ENGLAND & SCOTLAND

CHARLES I

FREDERICK = ELIZABETH
· ELECTOR PALATINE AND KING OF BOHEMIA ·

GEORGE, DUKE OF HANOVER

SOPHIA = ERNEST AUGUSTUS
· ELECTOR OF HANOVER ·

CHARLES II   JAMES II

ANNE   JAMES III
· OLD PRETENDER ·

CHARLES EDWARD
· BONNIE PRINCE CHARLIE ·
1

GEORGE WILLIAM = ELÉONORE D'OLBREUSE
· DUKE OF CELLE ·

GEORGE I = SOPHIA DOROTHEA
· PRISONER OF AHLDEN ·

2
DOROTHEA = FREDERICK WILLIAM = LOUISE HENRIETTA
OF HOLSTEIN   · GREAT ELECTOR   OF ORANGE
GLUCKSBERG   OF BRANDENBURG ·

MARGRAVES
OF SCHWEDT

FREDERICK I = SOPHIA CHARLOTTE
· FIRST KING OF PRUSSIA ·

FREDERICK WILLIAM = SOPHIA DOROTHEA

GEORGE II = CAROLINE
OF ANSBACH

FREDERICK LOUIS   ANNE   AMELIA
· PRINCE OF WALES ·

WILHELMINA   FREDERICK

✤ PART I ✤

Some years before becoming King of Prussia, some years, also, before he had acquired his title of "the Great," Frederick II of Hohenzollern was sitting for a portrait by the most fashionable painter in Berlin, one Antoine Pesne, a Frenchman. That morning in March of 1736 may have followed a sleepless night, or a yesterday of storm and stress, for the Prince was looking gloomy. "Chin up, Royal Highness," Pesne called out from the farther side of his easel. "Think of your sister. Ah—so—the mouth is right. Now you look happy!"

Pesne and everyone else on familiar terms with Prussian royalty knew that Frederick had six sisters to choose from, but there was only one who could bring a look of relaxed contentment to his face. Frederica Sophia Wilhelmina, to give her her full baptismal flourish, was two and a half years older than her brother, and yet in the teeth of fact and physiology he sometimes said they were "born together," or they "had two bodies and but a single soul." To either it was a compliment to be told how much they looked alike. The belief that they shared a common fate was so persistent as to have at certain times a definite effect upon their lives.

A start of two and a half years, however, gave Wilhelmina certain advantages in early childhood. Of the two she was the more precocious. Born on July third, 1709, Wilhelmina learned to walk and talk at the same time. She could remember distinctly being petted by her grandfather, Frederick I, the first King of Prussia, who died before his little favorite was four years old. The splendor of Grandfather's funeral made a deep impression on one who was to have a lifetime fondness for elegance and who at a tender age was taught to resent the regime of austerity that followed.

Wilhelmina's father, King Frederick William I, having buried his parent in the style to which the latter was accustomed, drew a heavy black line down the page on which were listed the court officials whose functions were purely decorative. Those who were able-bodied were drafted into the army; those who were retained were put on half pay. Large amounts of furniture and *objets d'art*, all carriages of state, and a menagerie of rare birds and beasts were sold to pay the late King's debts. At this time building was halted on the unfinished palace of Berlin, most of its ground floor being converted into offices and the treasury installed in cellars emptied of their vintage wines.

All of these changes may not have been immediately apparent to a three year old, but Wilhelmina heard of them and of more —much more—from her mother. Queen Sophia Dorothea was a talkative woman, a woman of many grievances. By birth a Hanoverian and her husband's cousin, she had brought with her to Berlin as a bride the finest trousseau ever stitched in Paris for a German princess; its worth had been passed upon by no less an authority on woman's wear than Louis XIV of France.

The magnificence of the Sun King and the glories of Versailles had set a ruinous pattern for petty German autocrats. Sophia Dorothea, brought up in a tradition of living beyond one's means, could not be reconciled to her husband's thrift. It seemed to her as unreasonable as all his other eccentricities: his passion for soldiering, for example, his collection of giants to serve in his favorite regiment, the Potsdam Guard, his compulsive washing of himself a dozen times a day.

This opinion was passed on to Wilhelmina, who was in no position to see how hard and how effectively her father worked as organizer, administrator and generalissimo. What she could see—and hear—was that her parents often, and violently, disagreed. In these noisy battles the advantage was one-sided. Her father could not only quote Scripture and the folksaying that "women should be kept beneath the ferule," he was king into the bargain. When he was at home, which was seldom, for he was often abroad, or with his army at Potsdam, or on tours of inspection in the provinces, he showed greater affection for Wilhelmina than he did for Frederick, his impulsive hugs and kisses being no less vigorous than the blows he frequently delivered to delinquents with his cane. Wilhelmina was proud of her father's caresses and of the fact that he had no reason to find fault with her, but she was also proud of the very special attention she received from her mother.

Sophia Dorothea, whose contests with her husband had only strengthened a basic belief that women were superior intellectually and morally to men, was determined that her daughter should be well educated. The childrens' first teacher was a charming, elderly Frenchwoman, Madame de Roucoulle, who had been their father's nursery governess. Soon Wilhelmina had a tutor of her own. While on a trip to Hanover the Queen engaged the services of a Mademoiselle Letti, who was half Italian and half Dutch, her father having been a renegade monk and the author of a history of Brandenburg. Under La Letti's strict supervision Wilhelmina quickly learned to read and, what was of even greater significance for the future, to write. She was also given lessons in history, geography and deportment. Some people thought the governess encouraged her pupil to put on airs, but if this was so, she was only doing what she was supposed to do.

For a high and mighty future was in store for Wilhelmina, a castle in Spain of which her mother was the architect. Its cornerstone was laid two months after Wilhelmina's birth when Sophia Dorothea suggested an engagement between her baby and Frederick, the two-year-old son of her brother George Augustus, the Hereditary Prince of Hanover. This little boy, if he lived long enough and if all went well, would be King of England. Some eight years earlier the British Parliament had passed an act excluding the Catholic descendants of James I from the throne and assuring the succession to the heirs of Sophia, Dowager Electress of Hanover, a granddaughter of James and undoubtedly a Protestant. The old lady, the matriarch of the clans of Guelph and Hohenzollern, was in her seventies. Her great ambition immediately became to outlive her second cousin once removed, Anne of England, and to have "Queen" engraved upon her tomb. The endurance test was won by Anne, Sophia dying, aged eighty-four, in June of 1714 and Anne in August of the same year.

Midway between these two events Wilhelmina celebrated her fifth birthday. She may have found more absorbing the children's party her mother arranged for her at the summer palace of Charlottenburg, but she was quite old enough and quite sophisticated enough to realize the promotions that had taken place in her mother's family. Her grandfather, George Louis, Elector of Hanover, was now King George I of England, her uncle George Augustus was Prince of Wales, and the young cousin to whom she was more or less plighted was Duke of Gloucester.

For the past five years gifts and messages had been going back and forth between the two nurseries, and not all that came to Prussia were intended for Wilhelmina. Frederick had received a ring, made from the hair of his cousin Amelia, who was somewhat younger than Wilhelmina's fiancé. Thus a double alliance was in the making, an early example of a parallel fate for brother and sister.

On the whole, the sister's prospects were the more spectacular. Ancient Britain, with her colonies and her increased participation in European affairs now that she had a stake in Hanover, was a power of the first magnitude. Prussia, made up of the Electorate of Brandenburg, the Duchy of East Prussia, and a congery of lesser feudal entities, scattered all the way from the banks of the Rhine to the Russo-Polish frontier, had only been advanced to kingdom status at the turn of the century; it could hardly qualify as second rate.

Of this the present Queen of Prussia was very well aware—but in her children she would find fulfillment. To set a seal upon their coming greatness, Sophia Dorothea had a joint picture painted of Frederick and Wilhelmina, the artist chosen in 1714 being the same Antoine Pesne who was to paint Frederick as a young man in 1736. Pesne was already commanding high prices for his work, for he had the reputation of catching a flattering likeness. He hardly needed to flatter the two pretty, fair-haired youngsters whom he represented going out to play in the palace garden, fantastically dressed, Wilhelmina in the costume of an adult lady, low cut, tight-laced, with skirts that swept the ground; Frederick in a trailing blue velvet gown, with a feathered bonnet perched on the back of his head, the only indication of his sex and rank being the star and ribbon of the Order of the Black Eagle plastered across his chest. To symbolize royalty, a Negro page flourished an umbrella above the childrens' heads; to symbolize the lure of militarism to a Hohenzollern, Frederick had a toy drum strapped to his waist, on which he would have been thumping if Wilhelmina had not laid a gentle, restraining hand upon his wrist.

This pictured predominance of female over male must not only have satisfied the Queen, but also Wilhelmina. Wilhelmina, as her mother said, "liked to play the grown-up." Her attitude toward Frederick was that of a senior adviser and protector. That Frederick was in need of protection was a lesson early learned.

✦ ✦ ✦

A quiet child, Frederick had none of the bounce and sparkle of his sister at this stage of his and her development. Newborn on January twenty-fourth, 1712, Frederick came close to being smothered by his father's kisses. He was very welcome, two other boys, one older and one younger than Wilhelmina, having died in infancy. Frederick's chances for survival seemed good as soon as he began to reach out with vigor and determination for his nurse's breast. The successful cutting of his first tooth was an event of national importance, for one of his brothers had died ateething. The death of the other was laid to the thunderous salvos set off as part of the baptismal ceremony. True or false, this theory might account for the tenderness of Frederick's ear drums. He was acutely sensitive to noise and would wince or burst into tears at a loud explosion.

"I am afraid he is very timid," Sophia Dorothea reported, most unwisely, to her husband.

The Queen had been separated from her children for six weeks in the early summer of 1715, having followed the Prussian army on a military expedition into Pomerania. When she returned, complaining of her husband's neglect of her for his "thirty thousand mistresses," by which she meant his thirty thousand well drilled and well equipped troops, Sophia Dorothea got a joyous welcome from Wilhelmina, but Frederick, now three and old enough to know better, looked as if he were going to cry. It took several days for him to recover from his shyness.

From his father in the field had come a glut of military toys, among them a flag and tent; now a small cannon was added to the arsenal, with instructions that it should be fired frequently to cure Frederick of his unmanly fears. Every letter Sophia Dorothea wrote thereafter to her husband mentioned the success of this experiment. Wilhelmina, who also hated noise and who suffered when the drums were beaten beneath the nursery window at the changing of the guard, took up the theme. "My brother is no longer a coward," she wrote more than once in a large, sprawling hand that slanted downward across the page. Only let her dear Papa come home and see all the dangerous things that Frederick liked to do.

But when, after many months, Papa did come home, he was dissatisfied. Frederick William had wanted his son to be what he had been in early life, a bully boy, the terror of his governess, Madame de Roucoulle, of his tutors and of his father's dignified

Court Chamberlain, whom he managed to trip by the heels and throw downstairs. Frederick's fragility—he was often ill—and his lack of aggressiveness were all to the bad. He was scolded for being a milksop. He was thrust into a pint-sized uniform of Prussian blue, and his picture was painted again, this time by an artist the King preferred to Antoine Pesne because the man could reproduce so well the details of military costume.

When warm weather came a regiment of small boys was recruited and drilled in the park at Charlottenburg, with the idea that Frederick should take command after serving in the ranks. Frederick's lack of enthusiasm for the so called *Kadettenkorps* was veiled by his apologists, Wilhelmina and Sophia Dorothea. Even they could see it was inappropriate for a Crown Prince of Prussia to prefer playing with his sister to marching about in the hot sun.

For three generations Prussia had thrived on military might. She had expanded and grown strong chiefly because little Fritz's ancestor, the Great Elector of Brandenburg, had kept up an army he could deploy, first on one side and then on another, in the wars of the past century. The Great Elector's son, Grandfather Frederick I, had almost ruined the country with his debts, but he, too, had made his contribution. As a reward for armed help to the Holy Roman Emperor he was allowed to place a crown atop his abundant horsehair wig and announce to the world that he was *König zu Preussen*, a King in Prussia.

To these examples of the past could be added the success of the recent Pomeranian campaign, the finale of a prolonged attempt by the neighbors of Charles XII of Sweden to rob him of his Baltic provinces. Frederick William, a late comer to the coalition, had cooperated with Saxons, Danes, Russians and Hanoverians, and had seen how far his "thirty thousand mistresses" surpassed them all. When a peace treaty came to be signed, all the western part of Pomerania, including the important city of Stettin, would be ceded to Prussia.

At the close of the war Berlin was full of interned Swedish officers. Sweden was considered a land of magic and necromancy. One of the prisoners, who had the reputation for being a soothsayer, was called to the palace to read the hands of the Queen and her children. It took only a glance at Frederick's small palm to see he would be a great king and a great general; in addition he would be elected Emperor. The Swede shook his head over Wilhelmina's hand and was for a time silent. The Princess would be wooed by four kings, he said at last, but would marry none of the four. Only one question was asked by Sophia Dorothea. She had come back pregnant from her springtime visit to the army; what was the sex of the child she was carrying? A girl, was the answer—and a girl it was, born in March of 1716 and christened Phillipine Charlotte, Charlotte having been the name of Frederick William's deceased mother.

The advent of "Lotte," as she came to be called in the family, was of no greater moment to Frederick and Wilhelmina than that of another sister, "Eeka," Frederica Louise, who had appeared a year and a half earlier. The succession of siblings— Sophia Dorothea was to bear in all fourteen children, ten of whom survived—could not intrude on the circle drawn about brother and sister by affinity, by circumstance. They ignored their juniors; their only concern was with one another.

Standing together at the head of the family, Frederick and Wilhelmina received more than their share of parental attention. While they were still too young to realize what the choice involved they were forced to take sides in a contest between two ways of life, between two passionate and divergent personalities.

[*Chapter 2*]

FOURTEEN pregnancies bore witness to the fact that there were moments of tenderness between Sophia Dorothea and her husband, moments in which the pet names Fiekchen and Wilke were interchanged. Physical compatibility, however, was the only bond between this ill-mated pair, both of whom were short and grossly overweight. Their first serious quarrel occured only a few days after their marriage in 1706 and was due to Frederick William's jealousy of his own father.

Frederick I, ever generous, ever ostentatious, had showered his daughter-in-law with diamonds and in a pseudo-feudal ceremony had bestowed on her the Order of Purity, an order he had invented for this particular occasion. The question of female purity was a delicate one. Sophia Dorothea's mother, Sophia Dorothea of Brunswick-Celle, had been repudiated by her husband. For years she had been held prisoner in a remote manor house at Ahlden while a popular novel, using a thin disguise of pseudonym, made public her love affair with Count Königsmark. The thought, like mother, like daughter, was sure to cross the mind of a suspicious man whose religious scruples as to the sanctity of the marriage vow were buttressed by a deep-seated sexual timidity. Sophia Dorothea was neither timid nor particularly religious, but she distrusted men and was too proud for coquetry.

In vociferating her innocence, she declared, "If I am guilty, you can shut me up for the rest of my life!"

The figure of her mother, unseen for more than twenty years, had remained for Sophia Dorothea the prototype of woman wronged by man. After her marriage the Queen began to correspond with Ahlden and took into her household Fräulein von Knesebeck, her mother's lifetime companion and advocate. Sophia Dorothea hoped her father might relent on his accession to the British crown, but George I went to London queenless, accompanied by his elderly mistresses, Ehrengarde Melusina von der Schulenburg, who was homely and very fat, Sophia Charlotte von Kilmansegge, who was homely and very thin.

However much she might sympathize with the Prisoner of Ahlden, and however much she might resent a man-made world, Sophia Dorothea felt she should keep on the good side of her father and his favorites if she was to see her two eldest children married to their English cousins. Anyone who opposed this cherished scheme was her enemy. Her husband, unfortunately, only took a wavering interest in it. Marriage alliances were a well recognized way of acquiring international property and promoting international good will, but Frederick William was as uncertain and fearful in dealing with foreign affairs as he was hard hitting and dictatorial in domestic matters. His wife's relatives were anathema to him. As a child Frederick William had to be sent home from a visit to his grandmother, the Dowager Electress Sophia, for having fought, as she declared, like "a coarse little savage," with his cousin and future brother-in-law, the present Prince of Wales.

As a result of the war against Sweden, Frederick William felt even less kindly than usual toward his relatives across the water. Hanover had done too little fighting, he thought; she was demanding too large a share of the spoils. On the whole, the idea of Wilhelmina's becoming Queen of England was more acceptable to her father than that of Frederick's bringing home an English bride to look down her nose at the way things were done in Prussia. For Frederick there were more definite and more immediate plans than matrimony. Frederick William could hardly wait to induct his son into the purely masculine society in which he himself was most at ease. The first step had been the *Kadettenkorps*; the second would be taken when Frederick entered his seventh year, the age at which it was thought proper for a boy to be handed over to male tutors.

In the meantime Sophia Dorothea, who realized that she would have nothing to say about Frederick's upbringing after he had left the nursery, was given a free hand with Wilhelmina. Much to her mother's satisfaction, Wilhelmina had learned to play the clavecin very prettily. She—Frederick also—had marked musical talent, inherited, no doubt, from their paternal grandmother, Queen Charlotte of Prussia, who not only composed operas but also played in the orchestra when her works were performed at Charlottenburg. In making her next educational move, Sophia Dorothea must have had this gifted lady in mind. Charlotte and her mother, the old Electress, had carried on a learned correspondence with the philosopher Leibnitz. Leibnitz, it was said, was pressed so hard in debate with the Queen on some abstruse point that he tossed up his hands in defeat and cried, "Madame, I cannot answer your question. You always want to know the why of the why!"

There were no philosophers at present in Berlin. Frederick William, whose judgment on his mother was that "she was a clever woman, but a bad Christian," had a rude word for philosophy; it was only "breaking wind," he said. There was, however, a very learned man, a pupil of Leibnitz, who was court librarian. Mathurin Vizyierre de la Croze, an ex-monk of Saint Germaindes-Prés, could speak twelve languages, including Basque and Chinese. Just the one, Sophia Dorothea thought, to supplement Mademoiselle Letti's teaching. In the summer of 1717 Wilhelmina, aged eight, embarked on a course in world history, beginning with the creation of heaven and earth. The method used was that of question and answer, both being entered by De la Croze in a volume superbly titled *Abridged Elements of Universal History for the Use of her Royal Highness, Madame, the*

Princess of Prussia. The old Frenchman, immensely fat, even fatter than Wilhelmina's royal parents, liked to talk, and Wilhelmina liked to listen. She was a glutton for anecdote; she retained all that she heard and had a faculty for hitting off in a few sentences the personalities of the historical characters she encountered.

After a year of study, Wilhelmina had got no further than the seventh century A.D. She had hardly disposed of Adam and Eve when she and Frederick witnessed a bit of contemporary history in the making. As usual, it was highlighted for them by the sharply contrasted attitudes assumed by their father and their mother.

✦ ✦ ✦

Before marching into Pomerania, Frederick William had signed a treaty of alliance with the Czar of all the Russias, Peter the Great, the extraordinary man who, in opening a "window on the west" for his secluded, eastward-looking nation, had upset the power balance of Europe. The alliance was renewed at the end of the war. Now, in September of 1717, word came that Peter was coming to Berlin for further parley.

Except for the expense involved—it was customary to offer free transportation as well as elaborate entertainment to visiting royalty—Frederick William was well pleased. He admired Peter's vigor and his practical concern for the advancement of his people. Sophia Dorothea, who disregarded politics unless they served her personal ambition, was much annoyed when she heard of the Czar's visit. Peter disliked all ceremony; he had asked to be lodged, not in the palace, but in a private house, and the only house available was an exquisite little pleasure pavilion that was the personal property of the Queen, a gift to her from her extravagant father-in-law. Mon Bijou, decorated throughout by French artists, was the scene of the stately receptions Sophia Dorothea gave every evening her husband was away from home. Russian guests, she knew from past experience—this was Peter's third appearance in Berlin—could be destructive. Everywhere they went they left behind them a trail of smashed furniture, broken glass and trampled gardens. The Queen gave orders that all the most delicate furnishings should be removed from her house before the Czar, his wife, and his retinue arrived.

The visitors came by boat from Holland and were greeted at the river's edge by the King and Queen. Although Frederick and Wilhelmina were not among the welcomers, Wilhelmina had a full account of the meeting later. It became for her one of those borrowed memories that tend to be somewhat larger and more highly colored than life. The Czar, a mountain of a man, almost seven feet in height and clad in what appeared to be a seaman's overall, stepped from the boat to grasp Frederick William by the hand. "Brother William, I am glad to see you again," he said in gruff, but fairly coherent German. He then tried to kiss the Queen, but she haughtily retired from his embrace. The Czarina, however, had seized the Queen's hand and kissed it repeatedly—a slavish gesture.

Peter's wife, Catherine, for love of whom he had repudiated the noble consort chosen for him by his guardians, was of humble origin and was illiterate. Once beautiful, she was now a little bunched-up woman, sun-burned as a gypsy. Though splattered with diamonds, her clothes were so gaudy, so greasy, and so out of style that they looked as if they had come from the trunk of some strolling player, or from a second-hand shop. Military orders were pinned profusely to the Czarina's bosom; pictures of saints and reliquaries were attached here and there to her person by golden chains that clanked and jingled as she walked.

The appearance of the imperial suite was equally bizarre. There was a large number of ladies-in-waiting, many of whom carried babies in their arms. When asked if these children were their own, they would make a salaam *à la Russe*, and say the Czar had done them the honor of fathering their child. Sophia Dorothea, embittered by the thought of such a rabble as this invading her premises, refused to bow to the Czarina's ladies; she was sure they were only German chambermaids and washerwomen in disguise. Catherine, on the other hand, uncomprehending, good natured, and ready to do in Prussia as the Prussians did, gave great offense by ignoring the curtseys of the female members of the Queen's household.

The following day Frederick and the *Kadettenkorps* paraded for the guests, but Wilhelmina, being old enough to come to table when Peter and Catherine dined at the palace, had a more intimate view.

As soon as Peter caught sight of Wilhelmina he swept her off her feet and crushed her to him in a mighty bear hug; he all but flayed her cheek with kisses. Wilhelmina, outraged at being treated with so little deference—for was she not Madame, the Princess of Prussia?—protested shrilly. She beat at the giant with her fists and toes. Peter laughed. After he had set the child down he held her fast and for some time amused himself by carrying on a conversation with her.

Wilhelmina, though ruffled, had not forgotten what she had been told by her teachers of the Czar's career. She knew of his interest in technology and ship building, and of his campaigns against the Swedes and Turks. Her comments and questions were so intelligent that Peter was amazed. He kept turning to the Czarina, saying he would gladly give up one of his provinces if he could have a child like this.

At table the Czar was placed beside the Queen. Wilhelmina, all eyes and ears, was located somewhat farther down the board. She did not have to wait long for something unusual to happen. In the middle of dinner Peter was seized with a convulsion. His long arms thrashed about and, since a knife was tightly gripped in one of his fists, Sophia Dorothea was terrified. She tried to rise from her chair, but Peter gasped out there was nothing to fear; he had been subject to these attacks from childhood. Seizing the Queen's hand, he squeezed it so hard that she shrieked—cause for hearty Russian merriment. "My Catherine's bones are not so soft," Peter jeered.

A ball had been planned to follow the dinner, but the guest of honor would have none of it. As soon as Peter rose from the table he set off on foot for Mon Bijou.

Wilhelmina did not see the Czar again, but she shared, once more by hearsay, in an inspection he and his wife made of the royal museum. Of the collection of costly rarities assembled by Frederick I there remained only one showcase, containing, among other items, some ancient Roman statuettes. One of these that was definitely phallic in character caught Peter's fancy. He fondled it; he told his wife to kiss it, but Catherine was frightened and drew back. Peter insisted. He grew angry; he growled out something in his bastard German that sounded like "cut your head off." Only then was he obeyed.

Before leaving the museum Peter picked out this particular statue and a uniquely beautiful cabinet inlaid with amber as presents he would like to take home with him to Russia. His host and hostess, the latter most unwillingly, felt they had to humor him. When Sophia Dorothea went to inspect Mon Bijou she found that, although her guests had only been there for a few days, the house would have to be completely done over.

"It was like the desolation of Jerusalem," was Wilhelmina's later comment. A new conception and a new adjective, barbarian, had been added to her vocabulary.

✦ ✦ ✦

Only Frederick William was satisfied with the outcome of the Czar's visit, a new and more advantageous treaty, signed at Havalberg in 1718. Economical though he was, a few broken window panes and two souvenirs from the royal museum did not seem too high a price to pay for Russian friendship. Besides, the King may have guessed that a return gift would soon be on its way to him. That same autumn one hundred and fifty men, each of them as tall, if not taller, than Peter Romanov, arrived in Berlin. They had been rounded up in the Czar's domain and marched off, willy-nilly, to swell the ranks of the Potsdam Guard, Frederick William's regiment of six-foot-plus grenadiers. The Guard was the only extravagant item in Prussia's military budget, the cost for recruitment and upkeep of this one unit being treble that of an ordinary regiment.

A visitor to Berlin in 1718, after remarking how healthy the Berliners looked, how unfashionable their clothes and how few the amusements offered to the public, mentioned the fact that the Crown Prince of Prussia was being better brought up than any other prince in Europe. On January twenty-fourth the all important sixth birthday had been passed. Though for several years to come Frederick would continue to live under the same roof as Wilhelmina, he and she would have less and less opportunity of seeing one another.

Two tutors had been appointed; both were military men. Count Fink von Finkenstein was in his sixties; Colonel Christopher William von Kalkstein was in his thirties. Neither had had any personal experience of teaching. For that routine task various masters were engaged, chief among them being a Frenchman, Jacques Égide Duhan, who was born in 1685, the year in which the Edict of Nantes was revoked and a large colony of refugee Huguenots appeared in Berlin. Duhan had studied with Vizyierre de la Croze, Wilhelmina's polyglot professor of history, and had taught the sons of a nobleman, but it was not his competence that recommended him to Frederick William. Three years earlier at the siege of Stralsund in Pomerania the King noticed how recklessly Duhan exposed himself to danger.

Fritz was to associate only with men of tested valor. According to the elaborate written instructions given the guardians, he was to be taught there is nothing more glorious than a soldier's life. As a descendant of warriors who knelt to pray on the battlefield, Frederick should be strengthened in the Protestant faith of his forebears, but second only to his love of God should come a sincere, a brotherly, love for his father. No fear should be allowed to stand between them. If the boy should prove obstreperous, his mother's displeasure, not his father's, should be used as a threat. It had been a dream of Frederick William that he and his son, whom he had almost kissed to death in infancy, should be all in all to one another.

Evidence of Frederick's progress in this respect took the form of letters which he himself wrote to Potsdam, or wherever else the King might happen to be when absent from Berlin. Compared with his sister, Frederick was slow to learn. Wilhelmina had been able to write to her father before she was five; Frederick was seven when his first letter was achieved, though earlier his hand had been guided by one of the tutors. The letters were written in German, the language Frederick William used as a matter of principle—and used most incorrectly, he, as well as his children, having heard little but French from birth.

If Frederick was at a loss as to what to say to his father, as well as how to say it, the tutors were there at his elbow with suggestions. Fritz was enjoying his exercise with the *Kadettenkorps*. Fritz had been out hunting and had shot a rabbit, an act which might be taken as an exorcism, *Hasenfuss*, rabbit's foot, being synonymous with coward in Frederick William's vocabulary of scorn. In telling of the incident, Frederick mentioned the rabbit's having been cooked and eaten, thus showing he was aware of the useful purpose served in killing game. At the end of each letter, love and a longing to see his dear Papa as soon as possible was expressed.

Occasionally, but not often, a carriage was sent from Potsdam to take Frederick back for a visit with his father. Wilhelmina could not help being jealous as she saw her brother go off without her. She complained to her father of Frederick's letters being answered, while she, who had written "a hundred thousand times," had never had a reply. "I know," she protested, "my brother is more important because he is a boy—but that's not my fault! After all, I am my dear Papa's daughter, and I love him better than he is loved by anyone else in all the world."

Wilhelmina playfully suggested that since her father only corresponded with his officers, she should apply for a commission as captain of dragoons. She only meant to make her father laugh, but the fantasy of being of the same sex and enjoying the same privileges as Frederick was comforting.

Of officers in general Wilhelmina held the low opinion voiced so often by her mother. Just as Frederick William kept a hostile eye upon his wife's ladies-in-waiting and was ready to send them packing at the merest whiff of scandal, so Sophia Dorothea suspected the very worst of her husband's intimates. The Queen's receptions at Mon Bijou—so refined, so reminiscent of Versailles—were in part a protest against the way in which her husband liked to spend his evenings.

After the hard day's work was done, Frederick William looked forward to relaxing with his military friends at sessions of the *Tabagie*, or Tobacco Parliament, meetings dedicated to the smoking of long clay pipes, the drinking of wine or beer, and the exchange of hearty, masculine anecdotes. As the evening progressed, laughter increased in volume and rose in pitch about the long bare table on which were set baskets of coarse cut tobacco, bottles and dishes of such hearty hors d'oeuvres as pickled eels or truffles floating in oil. As each bottle was emptied it was set upon the floor. Soon there was a long line stretching from one end of the room to the other, the King being responsible for a large part of what was consumed.

One member of the *Tabagie* who always ended up prone and on the wrong side of the table was its official Reader of Gazettes, Herr Jacob Gundling. Gundling had never seen a battlefield; drink had ruined his scholarly career. All of Frederick William's spite against intellectuals, a spite which had been accumulating since his schooldays, was visited on this unfortunate individual. To play the fool, Gundling was paid the salary once enjoyed by the president of the Berlin Academy of Sciences, an organization now defunct, except for the training of army surgeons and horse doctors. A ridiculous scarlet uniform, topped by a helmet of nodding ostrich plumes, had been invented for the Reader of Gazettes. Often, when helpless, Gundling was a victim of the brutal practical jokes that were a feature of the *Tabagie*.

No woman was ever allowed to cross the threshold of the Tobacco Parliament, but Frederick was introduced to it on one of his early visits to Potsdam. He found it unattractive. "I would rather meet a pig than a drunken man," Frederick said coolly to a parliamentarian who was only slightly intoxicated.

"But your father would like to see you merry," the officer exclaimed in hurt surprise.

"One must obey God first, man second," was Frederick's crushing reply.

One of the first fruits of an unguided pen had been a prim little essay on "'The Way the Prince of a Noble House Should Live." It contained quotations from Scripture. Colonel von Kalkstein, who copied the composition and corrected its spelling—Frederick was and would remain a phonetic speller—added a comment of his own: "May God confirm him in these pious sentiments, for they are far beyond his age."

The piety was genuine. Frederick was at present responding as enthusiastically to the religious instruction of Chaplain Andrëa as to the music lessons he was taking—clavier, harmony and counterpoint—with the royal organist. But the uses, as well as the rewards, of religious faith are manifold. In precepts drawn from the Bible Frederick had found a safe vantage point from which to criticize his father and his father's friends. The need to thus assert himself was strong in a small boy whose courage Frederick William had underestimated. After coming upon a passage in the writings of Martin Luther which declared King David unfit to build the temple at Jerusalem because he had shed so much blood Frederick announced that he would always be a man of peace.

This, as well as other anti-militant remarks, was made to the King's subordinates, not to the King himself. Frederick might be bold, but he was not insanely foolhardy. He knew his dear Papa should be propitiated, even if he could not always gauge the parental reaction to a given situation.

One day in the schoolroom, Frederick's teacher was telling him the Latin names of various objects, ignorant of the ban Frederick William had laid in his "Instructions to Tutors" on the teaching of Latin to his son. Much of his own youth, the King felt, had been wasted in learning a dead and useless language. The subject of the case endings for Latin words had just been introduced when Frederick William entered the room.

"What are you studying today, Fritz?" he asked.

"I am learning to decline *mensa*, table," Frederick announced with pride.

A moment later he took refuge under the just designated article of furniture, quite unprepared for the oaths, the strangled shouts of rage that burst from Frederick William. "What—you dare to teach my son Latin!" The master fled from the room to escape a hurricane of blows from the royal cane.

Frederick was pulled out from his hiding place and was slapped and shaken. The mad unreason as well as the injustice of this experience was never forgotten.

✦ ✦ ✦

But it was fortunate that the teacher who was driven from the room was not Jacques Égide Duhan, the Frenchman whose bravery at the siege of Stralsund had won him his present position. Duhan would have liked to introduce Frederick to the beauties of French literature, beauties which had a special power to move the heart of an exile from France. According to the instructions, however, Duhan was to teach modern history—the history of the ancient world, as well as its languages, being taboo.

Frederick William had selected the textbook to be used, *Theatrum Europaeum*, the title being Latin, but not the text; a work in nineteen volumes, beginning with the year 1617 and continuing to the present; a crushing, an anesthetizing enumeration of dates, battles, terms of treaties, names and genealogies of kings and statesmen. There was not a single incident in it to appeal to the imagination of a child. Duhan wrote the King he was preparing extracts from the *Theatrum* for Frederick's use and received a curt reply: "*All* facts are to be memorized!"

Not to be discouraged, Duhan decided to feed the *Theatrum* to Frederick in small doses and to sweeten them with something more palatable. He chose a book that seemed to him appropriate, the famous *Telemachus* of Abbé Fénelon, who had written it for another royal pupil, the Duke of Burgundy, grandson and heir to Louis XIV of France. Just to be on the safe side, Duhan asked the King's permission and received it, oddly enough, for this was a book Frederick William had been forced to read by his clever mother.

In a gliding, pellucid prose that carries one on from paragraph to paragraph, from page to page, Fénelon tells the adventures of Telemachus, son of Ulysses, traveling about the Mediterranean in search of his father long overdue from Troy—adventures unknown to Homer and to his Latin imitators. With his tutor, Mentor, who is actually the goddess Minerva in disguise, Telemachus is shipwrecked on the island of Calypso. He visits the Underworld and an ideal republic, founded by Idomeneus, King of Crete. Implicit in the tale are many moral reflections on such questions as the duty of a ruler to consider the happiness of his subjects, the ethics of war, good faith in international relations, and the law to which even kings must bow.

Some of the ideas expressed in the book got Fénélon into trouble in his day, but his narrative is so seductive that at least one of Fénelon's readers, namely young Frederick of Hohenzollern, did not realize he was being instructed. Frederick was carried away from a world in which one had to get by heart the gritty facts of the *Theatrum Europaeum* and was beaten for declining *mensa* to a land of sensuous delights. He could easily identify himself with Telemachus. Telemachus was also a prince; Telemachus could play the flute, a skill Frederick was acquiring with gusto; Telemachus had a wise old tutor, who, when the youngster became too hotly enamored of Calypso's nymphs, threw him into the sea to reduce his temperature.

Like Telemachus, Frederick became a great traveler, if only a vicarious one. He found there were other story books that could whisk him away from boredom and routine. Duhan could supply him with some; there was a library of modern French literature at Mon Bijou. The only trouble was finding the time for reading when one was kept so busy all day long with drill and lessons.

Frederick sometimes went to bed hungry, hungry not for food, but for an unfinished book. On one occasion he could not sleep because he was halfway through *Pierre of Provence*, a tale of mediaeval derring-do in the south of France. Frederick knew where the book was; it was in the next room, where a candle was burning, set on the hearth to guard against fire.

The door between the two rooms stood open. In the dim bedchamber Frederick's bed was flanked on one side by that of a servant, on the other by that of the senior tutor, Count Fink von Finkenstein. The boy lay still until he was sure his companions were sound asleep. He then slipped out from under the covers and tiptoed into the next room.

There he remained, blissfully divorced from time, fighting the duels and rescuing the fair ladies of Provence until Count Fink von Finkenstein began to stir and snort. Before the old gentleman was fully awake he reached out his hand to touch the adjoining bed, and what he touched was cold and flat. That brought a swift return to consciousness. Frederick was startled out of his reader's trance by hearing his tutor shouting in his guttural French, "My brince, my brince, where are you?" He had just time to toss aside his book before the Count and the valet were upon him, goggle-eyed with sleep and alarm.

Frederick explained his having got out of bed by saying he had

had to relieve himself. Neither he nor Wilhelmina hesitated to tamper with the truth in an emergency. In the growing complexity of the situations they were called upon to face, secretiveness and guile had been thrust upon them.

Unlike her children, Sophia Dorothea found it difficult to keep a secret. She was forever in need of a confidante, a sympathetic female ear into which she could safely pour her troubles. Two of her ladies-in-waiting thus favored had been dismissed by Frederick William. Both had been indiscreet, but Sophia Dorothea blamed their disgrace on a pair of her husband's chosen favorites, Prince Leopold of Anhalt-Dessau and Field Marshall General von Grumbkow. It would be hard to say which of these two men Sophia Dorothea hated the most.

Prince Leopold was a professional soldier, tall, gaunt and bony, who had served under the greatest of Austrian generals, Prince Eugene of Savoy. He had invented the goose-step, the fifty-four basic movements of Prussian drill and an iron ramrod that transformed the old style musket into a rapid fire weapon. Though his estates were so poor that he needed to earn a living, the Prince was of ancient lineage, his ancestor, Albert the Bear, having been Margrave of Brandenburg in the time of Frederick Barbarossa, when the Hohenzollerns of Swabia, and even the Hapsburgs of Austria, were inconsequential folk.

When Sophia Dorothea visited the Pomeranian expeditionary force in 1715, Anhalt-Dessau told her bluntly to go home; she was in the way. His hostility was at least aboveboard. A far more subtle enemy was General von Grumbkow. Unlike his ally the

Prince, Grumbkow was handsome, suave and well educated; he had studied at the universities of Halle and Leyden. Whenever possible, that is to say whenever he was not in close attendance on the King, Grumbkow came to the receptions at Mon Bijou. He came there to spy; Sophia Dorothea was sure of that. Grumbkow was a teller of tales, forever stirring Frederick William's all too easily stirred suspicions of womankind.

If Frederick William had not had a biblical horror of "harlots" and "harlotry," Anhalt-Dessau and Grumbkow would have supplied him with a mistress whom they could manage. Failing that, they had evolved an even more diabolical scheme for getting themselves a stooge in the royal family.

Prince Leopold had a sister who was the widow of the Margrave of Brandenburg-Schwedt, a half-brother of Frederick I. Since Frederick William had had no brothers, this lady's eldest son, the young Margrave, stood third in line of succession to the throne. A marriage between Schwedt and Wilhelmina was proposed by the young man's uncle and seconded by General von Grumbkow, the postwar coolness between Prussia and England being chosen as an auspicious moment to make the suggestion.

Before the matter could be seriously considered Sophia Dorothea thought she saw a way to eliminate Schwedt altogether from the Prussian scene. In May of 1718 Czar Peter was in search of a German husband for his niece, Anna, Duchess of Courland, the narrow Baltic province dividing his country from East Prussia. Joyfully Sophia Dorothea went to call on Schewdt's mother, thinking the Margravine would be delighted by the prospect of a dukedom for her son. Instead of joy—tears; the Margravine did not want her boy to go to Russia. Not long after Peter's return from his European tour, his son by his first wife, the Czarevitch Alexis, died; now the ugly story was going the round of gossip and gazette that Peter was responsible for the death. If Peter was capable of murdering his own child, he would think nothing of disposing of a nephew-in-law if he so desired!

The mother could not be persuaded, and Schwedt remained a threat to Sophia Dorothea's peace of mind. As of February, 1719, he was eighteen years old and had the audacity to ask the King himself for Wilhelmina's hand. Sophia Dorothea told her husband their daughter was much too young for an engagement, an odd remark from one who would have signed a contract with her relatives when Wilhelmina was in her cradle. Wilhelmina would be ten in July. In spite of the difference in their ages, Schwedt had been coming to call upon her frequently of late.

"What if you had to marry," Sophia Dorothea asked. "What if you were given your choice between the Margrave of Schwedt and the Duke of Gloucester—which would you choose?"

Wilhelmina said demurely that her governess, Mademoiselle Letti, was always telling her she should marry the Margrave of Schwedt, but she couldn't bear him. He was mean and cruel. She would much rather have the Duke of Gloucester.

Sophia Dorothea had got the answer she wanted, but a suspicion had been confirmed. For some time the Queen had wondered whether Mademoiselle Letti, who had been especially imported from Hanover to prepare Wilhelmina for marriage with her cousin, had not gone over to the enemy—a case of bribery, no doubt.

Wilhelmina was asked some searching questions about her governess. Whom did Mademoiselle Letti see in her free time? Didn't she always want to know what Wilhelmina had heard from her parents?

Wilhelmina was embarrassed and tried not to give a definite answer. Her caution convinced the Queen her little girl was growing up and could be trusted to hold her tongue. Here was a confidante in the making.

"I'm very much pleased with you," Sophia Dorothea said. From now on Wilhelmina would be treated as an adult and would be with her mother constantly. "But"—this was added with an emphasis that canceled out the preceding compliment —"I will not have you being a tattletale to Letti! If she asks you what is going on, you must say you have heard nothing. Do you understand me? Will you promise?"

Wilhelmina promised. Her reward was a long and at times confused account of her mother's darkest thoughts concerning the Prince of Anhalt-Dessau and General von Grumbkow. Mysterious happenings of the past were made clear. This precious pair, Sophia Dorothea said, not only wanted to marry Schwedt to Wilhelmina, they would also like to put Schwedt on the throne of Prussia. The Queen even suspected a frustrated plot to do away with the King and Frederick. The last lady-in-waiting to disappear from court had gone to prison for slander when she tried to warn the King of his danger.

Wilhelmina shed tears of sympathy and was flattered to think she was old enough to hear of so much wickedness. She could not help feeling uneasy, however, when she thought of Mademoiselle Letti. Letti had always demanded obedience and was sometimes heavy-handed in punishment, particularly when Wilhelmina had showed her dislike of the Margrave of Schwedt by playing practical jokes on her would-be lover.

That evening the governess asked what was the news in the Queen's apartments. Wilhelmina said there was no news. Letti tried to get her usual information first by caresses and then by slaps. Wilhelmina held firm. The next evening the inquisition was repeated with greater violence. Letti threw a candlestick at her pupil's head, and blood was drawn. Wilhelmina's screams brought her old nurse, Frau Mermann, running to the rescue. The nurse threatened to tell the Queen if this sort of thing happened again, and Letti, though she browbeat Mermann, was frightened. Wilhelmina's cheek had begun to swell. A poultice was applied, and the governess came several times during the night to renew it.

When questioned, Wilhelmina told her mother she had fallen and hurt herself. She was torn between fear of Letti and yearning for her mother's favor. Letti's persecutions continued. Wilhelmina was beaten almost daily, but not to the point where bruises would be evident.

[29]

With spring there came a respite. While Wilhelmina and
Frederick went with their mother to Charlottenburg, Letti was
left in Berlin with the younger children, of whom there were
now four, Eeka, Lotte, a brother William, not yet two, and the
most recent baby of all, a second Sophia Dorothea. For the first
time Frederick and Wilhelmina would be allowed to spend the
autumn with their parents at Wusterhausen, the royal hunting
lodge. This proved to be a privilege the children would have
been glad to forgo.

Wusterhausen, the favorite residence of Frederick William,
was a small castle, complete with moat, its living space so re-
stricted that four or five people had to share a bedroom. Since
there was no dining room, meals were eaten, rain or shine, under
a tent in the courtyard, where an ill-tempered bear was chained.

Unless one was interested in the wholesale slaughter of birds
and beasts, there was nothing to do at Wusterhausen, as Frederick and Wilhelmina soon discovered. That first summer, at least,
their stay was short. They had hardly settled into their cramped
quarters when news came from Berlin of a fearful epidemic of
dysentery. People, in panic, were barricading themselves in their
houses; there had been many deaths. The first courier brought
word that brother William was ill, the second that sister Eeka
was stricken.

As if this were not enough, the King came down with an
attack of colic. Though it was midsummer warm, a fire was kept
burning in his room to guard against infection, and all the family
was forced to stay there. Wilhelmina, who couldn't get far from
the blaze, felt that her blood was beginning to boil and that her
eyes were being squeezed from her head. Twelve hours later
symptoms of the Berlin plague appeared. Wilhelmina, wrapped
in blankets, was driven back to the city and carried into the
palace. Mademoiselle Letti was waiting for her at the top of the
grand staircase.

"So here you are, madame," the governess said—Letti might
pummel Wilhelmina in private, but knew how to address her
deferentially in public—"Are you suffering? Are you very ill?

You must take care of yourself, for your brother died this morning, and they say your sister won't last out the day."

Wilhelmina was at the moment too comatose to appreciate the cruelty of Letti's words. Neither she nor Eeka died, but long after William was buried and Eeka well, Wilhelmina lay listlessly in bed. Scarlet fever had followed dysentery.

Her mother came to sit beside her, and later her father. Frederick William asked her what she would like as a get-well present. Wilhelmina chose a dress, a grown-up dress; she was sick of childhood and of the shapeless garments children were forced to wear. Wilhelmina may have had in mind a costume like the one in the painting of herself and Frederick that hung in her mother's bedroom, but that dress, if it had ever existed, would hardly fit her now.

It was New Year's Day of 1720 before Wilhelmina was able to leave her room. Her mirror reflected a small, wan face, an emaciated body clad in the new costume provided by the King. Frederick William's gift to his daughter was no Paris creation, but it was recognizably a woman's dress, with fitted waist and fullness across the front to accommodate a nonexistent bosom. Well satisfied with her appearance, Wilhelmina practiced a few stately steps and gestures.

But when she entered her mother's room, the Queen cried out, "Ah, mon Dieu, look how she has gotten herself up. What a spectacle! She looks exactly like a dwarf!"

The Queen was angry, knowing as she did the origin of Wilhelmina's finery. She scolded her now weeping daughter for having asked a favor of the King instead of coming to her. Didn't Wilhelmina realize there was no such thing as a divided loyalty?

✦ ✦ ✦

Wilhelmina's illness had not softened the heart of Mademoiselle Letti. Letti knew she had lost the Queen's confidence, but also knew why she had not been dismissed; Sophia Dorothea was afraid of giving offense in Hanover. Letti's behavior became progressively more insolent and reckless. She quarreled with everyone and complained continually to the Queen of Wilhelmina's stubbornness and insubordination. At the same time the governess was writing to an old friend, the Countess von Kilmansegge, the undernourished *belle amie* of George I, who in England had received the title of Lady Darlington.

Early in 1721 Sophia Dorothea received a formal demand from Letti to be relieved of her duties, since "a splendid position" awaited her in London. "I wish," the letter concluded, "to leave this barbarous country, where I have found neither wit nor common sense. I would like to finish my days in a land where merit is rewarded and where the sovereign does not give his favor to rascally officers while men of intellect are scorned."

Bubbling with indignation, Sophia Dorothea read part of the letter aloud to Madame de Roucoulle. Madame de Roucoulle, now that Frederick had outgrown her, was teacher to the younger children.

"Eh, mon Dieu," the Frenchwoman cried, "let that creature go! It would be the best thing that could happen to the Princess. The poor child is suffering martyrdom. I have been afraid she would be brought to you some day with all her bones broken, for she is being beaten like a sack. She might be lamed for life. Frau Mermann can tell Your Majesty more about it than I can."

Sophia Dorothea, genuinely surprised, sent for the nurse, heard her story, and gave the letter to the King. Frederick William would have liked to send Mademoiselle Letti to Spandau Prison instead of to England, but was persuaded this would not be wise from a political point of view. He let Letti know, however, that she would be a brave woman to show herself in his presence again and that she must be out of the country in eight days. Wilhelmina, whose feeling for her tormentor was ambivalent, was distressed and gave Letti all of the few trinkets she owned. The Queen contributed some farewell gifts as well, not because she was sorry for "that creature," but because she realized the harm a spiteful tongue might do in England.

Wilhelmina was still tearful when she was told a new governess had been appointed, but, as it turned out, she was forever after grateful to her father for the choice he had made. Fraülein von Sonsfeld was forty years old and had been lady-in-waiting to Queen Charlotte, the fabled grandmother, of whom Wilhelmina had heard so much, the friend of philosophers, the composer of operas. Being wise and wanting to avoid the cabals of court life, Fraülein von Sonsfeld tried to refuse the responsibility of guiding Wilhelmina, but the King insisted on acceptance. He would do much for the Fraülein's family, he said, and would give her a title so that from now on she would be addressed as Madame.

Wilhelmina was so convinced all governesses were brutes that she could hardly answer when her new duenna spoke to her for the first time. She soon discovered there was nothing to fear. Madame von Sonsfeld was always gentle and encouraging. To Wilhelmina she became "my dear Sonsine." The two had long talks on every conceivable subject, especially on the subject of books, for the governess was a great reader. Wilhelmina's education, interrupted by illness and the emotional effect of Letti's persecution, made rapid progress. At this time she began the study of Italian and, what was of more practical importance, the study of English. This, of course, was Sophia Dorothea's doing, the political climate being once more favorable to an Anglo-Prussian entente.

In 1722 Sophia Dorothea heard that a Fraülein von Pöllnitz, a friend of Lady Darlington, was coming to Berlin. Wilhelmina was told she must be sure to make a good impression.

The lady's first remark after Wilhelmina had been introduced was disconcerting. "Good Heavens, madame," Fraülein von Pöllnitz said to the Queen, "the Princess makes a very poor appearance! She is graceful and fairly tall for her age—but, oh, her clothes!"

Sophia Dorothea, chagrined, apologized for Wilhelmina's looks and said they would improve when the girl had got her growth. She urged Fraülein von Pöllnitz to talk to her daughter and to see how intelligent she was. The questions put to Wilhelmina seemed to that young lady of thirteen appropriate for a child of four and she refused to answer. Later she was bitterly reproached by the Queen for her haughtiness and, to make amends, submitted to a ridiculous memory test devised by the visitor.

Soon after Fraülein von Pöllnitz had gone, another lady came from Hanover who said it was being reported there and in London that Wilhelmina was very ugly, had a vile temper and suffered from the falling sickness. She was also hunchbacked. To refute this slander, Wilhelmina was undressed and exhibited as God had made her. Sophia Dorothea was so worried that she nagged her daughter continually.

Wilhelmina became very nervous when she learned she was about to make the acquaintance of her grandfather. In the spring of 1723 George I came for a long visit to Hanover, bringing with him Lady Darlington and his other mistress, the Duchess of Kendal—the overplump Ehrengarde Melusina von der Schulenburg. In England these ladies were known, respectively, as the Maypole and the Elephant. First Frederick William and then Sophia Dorothea visited Herrenhausen, the Hanover residence. Sophia Dorothea found a supposition she had formed correct; all the damaging talk about Wilhelmina was coming from Mademoiselle Letti, now the Maypole's handmaiden. Sophia Dorothea attached herself to the Elephant and persuaded her father to come to Berlin to discuss affairs with her husband and to see Wilhelmina for himself.

On the evening of October eighth, 1723, George arrived at Charlottenburg, where all the family had gone to meet him. Wilhelmina was intimidated by the King's coldness and taciturnity, his Spanish manners, as she termed them. She was the first to be led forward from the group of grandchildren and to receive a peck upon the cheek. "Your daughter is big for her age," George said to Sophia Dorothea.

After he had been conducted into his bedroom, the visitor took up a lighted candle and, holding it high, inspected Wilhelmina carefully from head to foot, as if she had been a work of art he was thinking of buying. Wilhelmina stood shamed and speechless. She was led by her mother into the next room where visiting courtiers were standing.

"Speak English to my daughter," Sophia Dorothea said. "You will find she knows your language very well."

Wilhelmina acquitted herself satisfactorily after the Queen had gone and she had got over her first embarassment, but she was again tongue-tied when she found herself with her grandfather. "Is she always as serious and sad as this?" George asked of Madame von Sonsfeld.

Conversation was difficult during dinner, and just as the company was rising, the visitor, who had confided to Sophia Dorothea that he was feeling ill, swayed and fell to his knees, his hat planing off in one direction, his wig in another. Frederick William sprang forward to ease his father-in-law to a prone position on the floor. There George remained for almost an hour, while various efforts were made to restore him. There was much whispering in corners: was this an apoplectic stroke, or its forerunner?

At last the old man came to himself and, though he spent a poor night, insisted on taking part in all the ceremonies and entertainments arranged for the next few days. At this time a treaty of alliance between Prussia and England was signed, and Wilhelmina was given to understand that marriage contracts for herself and Frederick were included. This was not true, though shortly thereafter the engagements were gleefully announced by the Berlin press.

Chapter 5

URING his visit Grandfather George had been much more gracious to Frederick than to Wilhelmina. Like the Czar Peter, the British King witnessed a parade of Frederick's regiment of boys. The days of the *Kadettenkorps*, however, were numbered. The youngsters had long ago outgrown their first uniforms, and some of the older members had been inducted into the regular army. The third stage of Frederick's training was about to begin. A more severe discipline was enforced as he entered on his teens. On May first, 1725, Frederick's headquarters were moved to Potsdam where he could be more continuously under his father's thumb and eye than in Berlin.

A precise schedule for the boy's day had been mapped. Fritz was to be wakened at six A.M. Without so much as turning over in his bed, he must rise and then sink down upon his knees to say a short prayer. Face and hands should be thoroughly washed, but by friction only; no soap was to be used. A half-hour was allowed for dressing and drinking a cup of tea or coffee. From six-thirty to seven there was to be another religious service in which teachers and servants took part and which included the singing of a hymn. From seven to ten forty-five, lessons. After another washing of hands and face, Fritz should run—not walk—to the luncheon table. In the latter half of the day there were three more hours of schoolwork, military drill—Frederick had been appointed colonel of an adult regiment—dinner, evening prayers, and a formal goodnight said to his father before bed at ten-thirty.

A newcomer to the Prussian court thought the Prince looked tired, as though he had just come home from a grueling campaign. He himself would be tired, he thought, if he had to follow the King about, for Frederick William expected no less from his son than he exacted from himself. He had begun to take Fritz with him on his tours of inspection, posting rapidly from province to province of his disjointed kingdom, descending unheralded upon subordinates in order to catch them idle or up to their elbows in mischief.

It was the first time that the outlying districts had seen the Crown Prince, and they were curious to know if the future promised something better than the present. At Magdeburg the City Council welcomed Frederick individually and presented him with a purse full of ducats. The city fathers were agreeably surprised when the gift was refused, the Prince saying the money should be distributed among the poor. When, however, Frederick William heard of what had happened, he angrily commanded a re-offer and acceptance of the purse. Frederick obeyed, but said he would keep the money only until he was king.

There was insult in this remark. There was also an unwelcome reference to the past and future. Frederick William saw his spendthrift father rising from the grave; he saw himself descending into it, unmourned, his place taken by an irresponsible youth, who knew how to win all hearts. Frederick William was beginning to realize that this boy with a face too weary, too mature for his rapidly growing body was a very different being from the seemingly docile child, who a few short years ago had written his dear Papa about the joys of rabbit hunting and of drill with his companions. Fritz did what he was told to do, but he did it without enthusiasm and with an ironic curl of the lip. There was none of the buoyancy his father had hoped for. There was not the slightest suggestion of the brotherly love that Frederick William craved.

"I would like to know what goes on in that young head," the King grumbled, nodding in Frederick's direction. "I know he doesn't think as I do. People are giving him ideas; they are encouraging him to be dissatisfied with everything. Rascals—that's what they are, rascals!"

But before evil influences had done their work Frederick should be warned. He was called, and when he stood at attention before his father, Frederick William said, "Fritz, you listen to me. Keep up a good big army; you can't have a better friend than that . . . Our enemies would like to shoulder us about, but I know what they are up to—and you will learn to know them too. You listen to me; don't lose yourself in daydreams. Hold fast to reality. Keep up the army! Keep plenty of money by you!"

This advice was given to the accompaniment of rhythmic taps upon the cheek, but as the speaker became more and more excited the strokes became heavier until at last they were swinging blows under which the boy staggered to left and right.

Only rarely now was Frederick allowed to come to Berlin; his father was determined to keep him away from women and their debilitating influence. Since they met so seldom, Frederick and Wilhelmina had learned to make every moment they had together count. There was so much to tell, so many ideas to interchange! Their comradeship was no longer childish; it had developed romantic overtones. After a separation of several months Wilhelmina noticed that Frederick's appearance had changed and that soon he would be a handsome young man, not the burly type so common among the King's officers, but a slender, graceful youth whom Watteau's magic brush might have summoned out of the shadows for the voyage to Cytherea. When they played duets—music was now a forbidden pastime for Frederick—he nicknamed his flute *la principessa*, the princess, while Wilhelmina's lute was *il principe*, the prince.

Each could play upon the other. They were so perfectly attuned that even when they were in company and unable to talk as they liked, Frederick and Wilhelmina managed to communicate. They had at the tip of their tongues a vocabulary of double meaning, shortcuts to expression. The Berlin palace was "Castle Bewitched"; a "labyrinth" was what went on there, the devious doings of their enemies. One of the books they had read in common was Scarron's *Roman Comique*, a rollicking tale of the adventures of a troupe of strolling players. Frederick and Wilhelmina had fitted the names of characters in the book to members of the court, reserving the name of the most unpleasant character for General von Grumbkow and that of the chief buffoon for Frederick William.

Looks were also eloquent. As brother and sister sat silent, staring at one another with large blue eyes, they commented with youthful intolerance on what went on about them. Listen to this—just look at that, the blue eyes said. How crude! How utterly ridiculous!

Only Sophia Dorothea had an inkling of what went on in the two young heads, and even she was not altogether in her children's confidence since they knew how indiscreet she could be. At this time the Queen's hopes for accomplishing her dearest wish were high, though she had had various misadventures along the road she had set herself to travel.

When King George was at Charlottenburg in 1723 he made arrangements for his daughter and son-in-law to meet him somewhat later at a hunting lodge in Hanover. On the way there Sophia Dorothea gave birth to her sixth living daughter, her twelfth child, with only her husband and a lady's maid for midwives. The baby was christened Anne Amelia and had as godparents Frederick and Wilhelmina of Hohenzollern and Frederick and Amelia of Guelph, the four young people Sophia Dorothea longed to unite in marriage. Because the birth was premature, it was delicately suggested to Frederick William by General von Grumbkow that his wife might have been unfaithful to him. There was a violent and all too public quarrel, followed by a tearful reconciliation.

Further disagreements arose when first the King and then the Queen went again to Hanover in 1725. Once more George I had come to his homeland, bringing with him his minister for foreign affairs, Lord Townsend. While Townsend and the two monarchs paced back and forth in the gardens of Herrenhausen they discussed European politics.

During the past eight years, Austria had made successful ventures in world trade, using Ostend as a base, setting herself up as a rival to the maritime powers, in particular to England and Holland. An unpublicized alliance had been formed between two ancient enemies, Austria and Spain. Frederick William was not interested in the number of bales of goods that changed hands in distant ports, but he did not like an alignment between two such important Catholic powers, even though Austria represented for him the Holy Roman Empire. To this hoary, and largely impotent institution, a Hapsburg monopoly for fourteen generations, Frederick William was strongly attached, his feeling for German unity being far livelier than that of most of his contemporaries.

Recent dealings with the Empire, however, had been disheartening. Frederick William wanted imperial support in his claim to two small, but flourishing, duchies in the Rhineland, Jülich and Berg. According to a treaty of 1666, Jülich and Berg would revert to Prussia if their present overlord, the Count Palatine of Neuberg, died without male issue. The Count was elderly; his only living child was a daughter. To Frederick William's demand for recognition of his rights of inheritance the Emperor would say neither yes nor no, the reason for his shilly-shallying being that the inhabitants of Jülich were Catholic. Protestant England, on the other hand, would be glad to see Protestant Prussia increase its holdings on the Rhine. Frederick William was promised strong support if he would join hands with Britain and with France. Before leaving Hanover for home the King had agreed to a trilateral treaty to be signed in October.

In the interval between agreement and signature Sophia

Dorothea took her husband's place at Herrenhausen and did all she could to get something in writing from her father concerning the marriages. But though George was most encouraging he said the matter would have to be submitted to the British Parliament. Since the parties to the matches were so young, there was no need to hurry; ratification could be held over until a later visit to the continent.

Sophia Dorothea thought her father's word as good as his bond and came home empty-handed, but exultant. She found Frederick William angry with her for having stayed so long without tangible result, all the more angry because he was beginning to regret the agreement with Britain. After a passionate exchange of words, husband and wife did not speak to one another for six weeks.

Wilhelmina was the chief sufferer from their silence, for both of the combatants could speak to her! She was still her father's favorite. During her mother's absence, he gave her jurisdiction over the younger children and the household; it was almost as if she were the Queen. Swift dethronement followed the return of Sophia Dorothea. Wilhelmina was lectured and abused for disloyalty. She dared not show affection to her father. If one parent told her to do something, the other was certain to forbid it.

Mother and daughter could only cooperate when it came to helping Frederick. Both of them realized how hard his life had become because of his father's growing hostility. The Queen had sent two pictures of Wilhelmina to England and wanted to send one of Fritz.

"You might just as well have a monkey painted and send them that," Frederick William growled.

Unable to catch his heir in any serious breach of discipline, Frederick William made the most of every minor fault. Fritz was untidy, his father said, his face and hands unclean, his hair too long and curly. There was a terrific outburst of rage over the wearing of gloves in the hunting field, even though the season was winter and the weather numbing cold. Fritz was given a rogue horse to ride by his father and when thrown and painfully hurt—his shoulder was dislocated—he was given no respite.

His mother thought the boy was in part responsible for his troubles. He should make some effort to better the situation. Wilhelmina one day was writing at Sophia Dorothea's dictation a letter, a humble appeal that Fritz should copy and send to his father, when the sound of the King's rapid, heavy footsteps was heard. Wilhelmina swept together her sheets of paper and hid them behind one of two small Indian cabinets that stood on the table. Madame von Sonsfeld snatched away the pens. There remained only the inkwell as a sign that anyone had been writing. Wilhelmina picked it up and just had time to conceal it in her pocket, for her father was already in the room.

After a few words to his wife, Frederick William turned his attention to—of all things—the Indian cabinets.

"They're very handsome," he mused. He was considering perhaps their cash value and stepped over to the table to examine them.

To divert him, Sophia Dorothea cried, "You have got to decide an argument that I and my daughter have been having. She says her dog is prettier than mine. I say it's just the other way around."

The two dogs in question were in the room, small, almost identical Bolognese spaniels, silky white, with brown, shading to black, across the head and ears.

Frederick William, who was in an uncommonly good humor, laughed and put his arm about Wilhelmina. "Are you fond of your dog?" he asked.

"Yes, I love him with all my heart," Wilhelmina babbled. "He's clever and he has a very good disposition." She was ready to say anything, however stupid it might sound, to keep the conversation going.

Frederick William laughed again and kissed his daughter several times. She had been holding the inkwell carefully in her pocket, but now she had to let it go. She felt the liquid soaking into her clothes; looking down she saw driblets on the floor.

As long as her father stayed in the room Wilhelmina did not dare to move. When he had gone and she revealed her inky state to the others their tension dissolved in laughter that, for its occasion, was much too loud and much too long.

✦ ✦ ✦

Just before her last visit to Herrenhausen Sophia Dorothea had heard disturbing news from her mother. The Prisoner of Ahlden had thrown what weight she could—and that was little —against the English marriages. They would be as unhappy as her own; she prophesied; they would bind together still more closely the interests of father and daughter. Now Sophia Dorothea learned from the man of business who acted as messenger between Berlin and Ahlden of a plan to escape. As prelude a large sum of money had been deposited in a bank at Amsterdam.

If the plot succeeded, it was obvious who would be suspected of having had a hand in it. Sophia Dorothea couldn't afford to antagonize her father and wrote to her mother, begging her to stay where she was until the marriage contracts had been signed. Then everything possible would be done for release. To soothe her conscience the Queen sent her mother some small keepsakes, but all the offerings were returned except a pair of family miniatures.

Though Sophia Dorothea had said that for the present letters would be too risky, the lonely woman at Ahlden could not believe this was the final word. When she heard of her daughter's being at Herrenhausen, she hoped for a visit. She sat at her window day after day, looking for a carriage to appear, a moving object in the dull flat landscape. The news of her daughter's having gone back to Prussia and of her man of business having swindled her out of the money sent to Amsterdam were blows that followed closely on one another.

In January of 1726 Sophia Dorothea heard of her mother's having suffered a stroke. Partially paralyzed, the invalid survived until late summer. Toward the end she seemed to have no thought for her children, only for her enemy, the man who had destroyed her life. When told she was dying she prophesied that before six months were over George Louis of Hanover and England would "meet her before the judgment seat of God."

Frederick William was the first in Prussia to hear of the death at Ahlden and was considerate enough to break the news gently to his wife. The court was put into mourning. Sophia Dorothea knew her brother in England would wear black and hoped, but without conviction, her father would do the same.

No notice of the event was taken at the Court of Saint James. Orders were sent for the King's former wife to be buried where she had lived in frustration so many years. Ahlden, however, was in fen country; if one dug two feet into the earth the hole filled with water. The coffin remained unburied and apparently forgotten for six months. It was then taken without ceremony to Celle to lie in a tomb beside those of the dead woman's father and mother.

Less than six months later, George I crossed to the Continent for the last time. After only a short stay in Hanover he set out for a visit to his brother, the Bishop of Osnaburgh. Halfway there the stroke, so narrowly escaped four years earlier at Charlottenburg, overtook him. Sorrow in Berlin was genuine. Sophia Dorothea saw the deferment, perhaps the ruin of her plans. Frederick William saw, and dreaded, a reshuffle in the game of international politics.

[Chapter 6]

Between the King of Prussia and the man who in 1727 became King of England no love was lost. The fisticuffs of childhood are not easily forgotten. George II, who was pugnacious, red faced and short of stature, tried to cut down all the world to his own size. He spoke contemptuously of his cousin as "the sergeant." Frederick William countered with "my brother, the comedian," or "my brother, the red cabbage."

For some time now a strong anti-British influence had been brought to bear on Prussia. Frederick William was looking out of a window in the palace of Berlin on a summer day of 1724 when he caught sight of the wrinkled face, the stubby figure of a man he had not seen for almost ten years, but with whom he had never lost contact. Leaning out of the window, the King called to his old friend, Count Frederick Henry von Seckendorf, to step in for a chat. This was exactly what the Count was yearning to do.

The two had met in the most halcyon period of Frederick William's youth, when he was allowed by his father to visit the war then in progress between France and Austria in Flanders. A second meeting occurred when Seckendorf was in command of a Saxon contingent of the allied army in Pomerania. Seckendorf had been in the pay of various governments, but he had begun life as a cornet in the Austrian army and returned to imperial service after the Swedish War. His latest assignment, undertaken at the suggestion of the Emperor's chief adviser, Prince Eugene of Savoy, was to woo Frederick William away from his friendship with Britain and to get his assent to a domestic arrangement of the Hapsburg family that for many years had governed the foreign policy of Austria.

The Emperor Charles VI had no son. He wished to hand on intact to the eldest of his two daughters the Hapsburg inheritance, which included not only all of Austria, but also the Kingdoms of Bohemia and Hungary, the duchies of Milan and Tuscany, and a large slice of the Netherlands. The Archduchess Maria Theresa, now seven years old, had been recognized as her father's heir by the principalities she would inherit, but it was necessary also to get the support of foreign nations to this so called Pragmatic Sanction. Prussia, with her strong army, stood high on the list of those to be won over.

Seckendorf set to work with caution and subtlety. His first report to Prince Eugene and that of a second visit showed how thoroughly he had looked the ground over and how carefully he had studied the personalities involved. The King, Prince Eugene was informed, could not be driven; he could only be worked upon indirectly. Before Seckendorf was formally appointed minister to Prussia in 1726 he had, in spite of a hidden distaste for tobacco, become a faithful attendant of the Tabagie, where he contributed his full share of gossip, guffaws and military reminiscence. The Prince of Anhalt-Dessau was no longer a member of the inner circle, for he had retired to live on his estates after a disagreement that nearly ended in a duel with his former ally, General von Grumbkow. The General soon became Seckendorf's closest friend in Berlin, and from 1724 on received a yearly gift of a thousand ducats from Vienna. Herr Gundling, the scholarly drunkard, and even Eversmann, the palace chamberlain, were also bribed.

Nor were the most obvious bribes to Frederick William himself overlooked. Seckendorf produced many recruits for the Potsdam Guard and, with the Emperor's permission, declared open

season for a giant hunt in Hungary. The King was often entertained at dinner. Frederick William, who could eat a hundred
oysters at a single sitting, stuffed himself with the expensive
foods that never appeared upon his own table. Seckendorf would
wait until the potent Hungarian wine had begun to take effect
before he spoke of politics.

The Emperor's man knew all about the Prussian treaties with
England. He had, in fact, sent Prince Eugene a transcript of the
latest secret agreement the day before it was signed at Hanover.
It was hardly necessary to insinuate to Frederick William that
the coalition he had joined was bent on war; Frederick William
could see that for himself and also saw England and France
protected by natural barriers while his own scattered provinces
lay naked to the aggressor.

Seckendorf was able to wangle a *sub rosa* promise of Prussia's
coming to the help of Austria if she were attacked on German
soil, a promise that was made public after the accession of the
new British King. Frederick William, however, had not got the
definite word he wanted on Jülich and Berg. He became very
gloomy when he heard of these plump Rhenish provinces being
assigned by the Emperor to another claimant, Count Sulzbach,
who was married to the daughter of the Count Palatine.

At about this time the King developed a case of gout. When
ill or when suffering from insomnia, Frederick William turned
to his only avocation, which, despite a disdain for the arts in
general, was portrait painting. The easel was set up in his bedroom. An old soldier, Bombadier Feldmann, stood by to mix the
paints. Now the subject chosen was one of the King's beloved
"long fellows," his guardsmen; now it was a sinister courtesan,
with the nipple of one of her fat breasts protruding from her low-
cut gown. Many of the pictures signed "F. W., *in tormentis
pinxit,*" were faithful and unflattering self-portraits. "God knows
what a low opinion I have of myself," Frederick William once
wrote to the Prince of Anhalt-Dessau, who, though absent, was
still a cherished friend.

By autumn the fire in Frederick William's toes had burnt

itself out, and he went as usual to Wusterhausen for the hunting season. He was still very much depressed and looked for consolation to the visits paid him severally by two leaders of the Pietist Movement, which had as its center the theological seminary and orphan asylum attached to the University of Halle. August Gotthold Francke, son of the founder of these two institutions, and Johann Anastasius Freylinghausen, their present director, were invited to the hunting lodge. Freylinghausen was the first to arrive.

The reason given for the visits was merely to become better acquainted, but there were matters that lay heavy on Frederick William's soul. Were they sins that would send him to hell? Were they minor faults that God might overlook?

When all the family and the military staff were gathered for dinner at the table that stood under a canopy in the courtyard, the King rapped for attention. "Silence, gentlemen," he called out. "Now Herr Freylinghausen will tell us whether or not it is right to go to the theater."

The Pietist said he wouldn't think of going to the theater himself, and it was not to the glory of God for anyone else to go.

Frederick William looked triumphantly at Sophia Dorothea, for he knew she would like to have a French company of players in Berlin. He himself took it to heart that he had allowed acrobatic performances and puppet shows in his capital city.

Frederick William welcomed a statement from his spiritual advisers that dancing was immoral, but when the subject of hunting was brought up he was deeply troubled. Surely hunting was permissible, because of the healthy exercise involved and the meat it furnished for the table. This point was grudgingly yielded, but the kind of hunting perpetrated at Wusterhausen, in which wild animals were driven into an enclosure before being killed, was banned as unnecessarily cruel.

"Somehow I cannot bring myself to like Jews," Frederick William sighed. He had just been reminded of his duty to love his fellow man and that Our Lord had been a Jew.

A heavier weight upon the royal conscience was revealed when Frederick William told Freylinghausen he had been sober since January; he would never drink too deep again. Later, however, when Francke had taken Freylinghausen's place at Wusterhausen the visitor was distressed by the King's staggering from the table and roaring at the pages in boozy wrath. The following day there was a penitential hangover.

"It is hard to get into heaven," Frederick William said despairingly. "I know my own weaknesses as well as any. I am a bad man. Some days I am good, and then bad again. I am well aware of this yet can't behave in any other way."

The men from Halle were interested in the King's attitude toward his children. There was no doubt who was his favorite now, his second son, August William, who, five years earlier, had come to take the place of the little boy who died of dysentery in 1719. August William was fondled and kissed and said grace before dinner, his father standing over him with bowed head and clasped hands. The elder son, the Crown Prince, aged fifteen, was given the man-sized task of carving the roast pork and serving the more than twenty people at the table with sauerkraut and baked apples. He did so in silence; only when his father was absent did Frederick speak, and then he spoke in French, a language neither Francke nor Freylinghausen could understand.

They would, of course, have liked to make friends with the heir to the throne and a prospective benefactor of the orphan asylum and seminary, but their attempts got off to a bad start. One day when Freylinghausen was sitting with Frederick William under the linden tree in the courtyard of the castle the king spoke of the doctrines which divided Protestant from Protestant. He said he belonged to the Reformed, that is to say the Calvinist, Church, but detesting the Calvinist doctrine of predestination, had brought up his children to be Lutherans. To prove his point, he wanted Freylinghausen to examine the theological knowledge of the Crown Prince.

Freylinghausen would have declined, for he saw how unwillingly Frederick came when abruptly summoned and how the tide of red rose in the boy's cheek when all present gathered in a circle about him. Freylinghausen had got to his feet in deference to Frederick's rank, but the King told him to sit down again.

"Is it true that Jesus Christ died for us all?" Freylinghausen asked.

"For all who will receive Him," was the cautious reply.

"Did Christ die also for unbelievers and the damned?"

Frederick said nothing and Freylinghausen, to fill the awkward silence, quoted some pertinent passages from Romans, 14, and Second Peter, 2.

Later in his stay Freylinghausen asked Colonel von Kalkstein for an interview with Frederick and was told that the Prince was too busy with his lessons and his attendance on the King. Francke was more fortunate, but when he tried to sweeten the occasion by reminding Frederick of how his, Francke's, father had come to Wusterhausen seven years earlier and of how he gave his youthful host a toy model of Jerusalem, Frederick said coldly he remembered the visit—and said no more. He left the room without thanks for a gift of tracts. Wilhelmina, who was also given improving literature, was more polite, but Francke noted in the journal he kept of his visit how different these two older children were from their juniors, how burdened they seemed, how melancholy.

✦ ✦ ✦

It had been a trying summer for the brother and sister. In June Frederick had had a great loss. His teacher, Jacques Égide Duhan, as dear to him as Sonsine to Wilhelmina, was dismissed and given a small government post in lieu of pension.

"I promise you," Frederick wrote Duhan, "that when I have money of my own I will give you twenty-four hundred *écus* every year, and I will love you even more than I do now, if that were possible."

Duhan had been replaced by Major Senning, an elderly, wooden-legged officer, who would teach Frederick mathematics and military science. Frederick did not object to Senning personally, but he was humiliated when, at the time of Senning's installation, four young officers were appointed to watch over him in the hours he spent outside the schoolroom. They were told by the King, in Frederick's presence, to see to it that the Prince made no unsuitable friends and had nothing to do with disreputable women. At fifteen, one's manliness is an obsession. How bitter it was to realize that, manhood reached, one would still be spied upon and held in check!

The routine of Wusterhausen, the confinement, the lack of privacy, were bad enough in themselves, but to Frederick and Wilhelmina the presence of the Pietists was an added irritation. The Prince and Princess had been publicly catechized and confirmed as members of the church, but they had begun to doubt its orthodoxies, their reading having put them in touch with the new, the revolutionary ideas of French writers whose stock in trade was doubt of dogma in every phase of human understanding. The magnificent certitudes of the past had not yet crumbled, but they were under constant bombardment.

Frederick had far less opportunity for reading than Wilhelmina, but he had begun to collect a library of three thousand volumes: encyclopedias, studies of religion, translations of the Latin classics he was not allowed to read in the original. The books were hidden in a private house close to the palace. Duhan was the purchasing agent. Money had been borrowed from bankers, quite willing to extend credit to a future king.

Almost anyone in France who was a wit and an iconoclast could claim the title of philosopher. The philosophers of Wusterhausen could not believe in the sincerity of men who spoke of going to the theater and the glory of God in the same breath. They thought Francke and Freylinghausen hypocrites. Frederick, after learning that one of them, Francke, believed in ghosts, was also certain they were fools.

When the holy men had gone, Frederick William had Scripture read aloud at dinner, a custom in force at the Halle orphanage, and held prayer meetings at which he preached a sermon while his valet led in the singing of the hymns. Frederick and Wilhelmina did not dare to look at one another during these services; the merest quiver of the lip would betray them.

The King's piety took a new, a more extravagant turn. Since the world was full of dangers to the soul, he would retire from it. He would abdicate. Only a modest income would be necessary for him and his wife and children to live at Wusterhausen. There he would till the soil and pray to God while his women-folk did the housework.

"You're clever with your hands," Frederick William said to Wilhelmina. "I'll appoint you to do the washing and mending of the linen. Frederica, who is stingy, can keep an eye on the provisions. Charlotte will go to market to buy the food, and my wife will take care of the little ones and do the cooking."

This fantasy was so much talked of and taken so seriously—the King had begun to work on an abdication document—that Grumbkow and Seckendorf were alarmed; they looked about them for a diversion. Seckendorf, having been in the service of Frederick Augustus, the Elector of Saxony and King of Poland, arranged for an invitation to come to Frederick William for a visit to Dresden during the Winter Carnival of 1728. The King was urged to accept. Of late years relations between the two countries had not been cordial, for a protective tariff had shut out Saxon textiles from the Prussian market. It might be just as well for Frederick William to have a look at his neighbor's industrial plant and at the Saxon war machine. Augustus had not yet agreed to the Pragmatic Sanction, the Austrian inheritance scheme; there were rumors of his wanting to enlarge his domain to include Bohemia, if the Emperor Charles should die. The friendly gesture now to Prussia was probably a long-term stroke of diplomacy, an insurance against an enemy in the rear if war should be undertaken in the east.

It was decided that Frederick William should leave for Dresden about the middle of January. Since there had been no specific mention of the Crown Prince, Fritz would be left in Potsdam. Only Wilhelmina could plumb the abyss of her brother's disappointment. Ever since making that imagined journey as a boy with Telemachus, Frederick had longed to travel—and Dresden was said to be the gaiest city in Central Europe, a Venice on the Elbe.

At the first of Sophia Dorothea's receptions of 1728, Wilhelmina drew the Saxon Minister aside and told him how happy Frederick would be if he could join his father. The hint brought a prompt, special invitation, but the King was ready to go and Fritz could not go with him, for he had no clothes fit for the occasion. A magnificent brocaded coat, the first expensive garment he had ever owned, was stitched up, almost overnight, and paid for by his mother. Giddy with excitement, only two days behind his father, Frederick set out to see the great world and how the other half of royalty lived.

THE Elector of Saxony was said to be the father of three hundred and sixty-four bastards. He was also said to have been suckled by a lioness and to be able to bend a horseshoe with his bare hands.

Augustus the Strong had traveled widely in his youth, in Austria, Italy, Spain and France. Soon after coming into his inherited own, the elective kingship of Poland fell vacant, and Augustus hurled himself into the race, spending large sums of money, borrowed from a firm of Jewish bankers, nosing out his principal rival, the Bourbon Prince of Conti, by a narrow margin. To win, Augustus had had to turn Catholic. He managed to keep this secret for some time from his Protestant Saxon subjects, but when it leaked out Augustus's wife, a mousy puritan, Christine Eberhardine of Bayreuth, left him and went to live outside the city of Dresden. About this time a gay little song was sung to an an unforgettable tune. Its chorus was *"Ach du lieber Augustin."* One of the few versus that were printable ran:

> *Der Mann ist versoffen,*
> *S' Weib ist verloffen.*
> (*The husband is soused,*
> *And his wife has skedaddled.*)

Possibly Augustus had waited until Christine Eberhardine was dead in 1727 before inviting Frederick William and his son to

visit him. Christine was a Hohenzollern and a distant relative of
the visitors; her presence in the neighborhood would have been
awkward, and Augustus wanted all to go as smoothly as a well
rehearsed stage spectacle.

When Frederick arrived in Dresden about noon on January
seventeenth, 1728, he was taken directly to the house of Count
Flemming, an old acquaintance who had often come to Berlin
on diplomatic missions. Flemming and his chic and charming
wife were in red dominoes and were about to set off on a round
of parties. Frederick was hastily dominoed, went with them, and
danced until midnight.

The following morning he had to be up fairly early to see the
Sleigh Parade that began before noon. It had rained on the preceding day, and three hundred wagon loads of snow had been
brought in from the countryside to slick the cobbled streets. A
procession of decorated sleighs, crammed with pretty women, in
magnificent furs and great plumed hats, swept through the city,
the Elector-King riding at its head. The ladies angled for rings
that dangled above them along the way; there were handsome
prizes for those having the highest score. The dancing then
began and lasted throughout the night. At five in the morning
Frederick, who was used to lights-out at ten-thirty, took to his
bed and plunged into the deep and deathlike slumber of adoles-
cence.

He was shaken by the shoulder a few hours later and told that
the house where his father was staying, not far from the
Flemmings's mansion, had caught fire and might burn to the
ground. "Why should I get up?" Frederick muttered. "I
couldn't put the fire out."

But he could, and must, get up to go to the Lutheran Church
with his parent to hear the chaplain of the late Queen preach a
Lutheran sermon. Even though it was Sunday, there was a play
that night at the court theater, a comedy by Molière—Frederick's first play. In the days and nights that followed there were
many firsts: Frederick's first opera, his first ballet, his first walk
through a picture gallery in which masterworks, old and new,

were hung. Above all, there was Frederick's first hearing of a full-scale orchestra. Hitherto the most elaborate music he had been exposed to was the bray of a military band or the squeaking of a couple of violins at his mother's receptions at Mon Bijou.

Dresden, 26 January, 1728. My dearest sister: In spite of all distractions I think of you all the time and will only forget you when I am dead. But wait a minute. Let me get ready for my speech by clearing my throat, coughing and spitting. What would you like to hear? All about high society? Here goes!

Frederick gave Wilhelmina a lilting, and at times a slightly malicious, account of the flamboyant folk with whom he was associating, beginning with Augustus, a mighty figure of a man, but in a state of marked dilapidation. The Elector-King had lost so many of his teeth that it was difficult to understand his speech, and he was also very lame. At his age—Augustus was fifty-seven—it was a wonder that he could still dance, ride horseback and tilt at the ring. The Crown Prince, who, like his father, was tall and handsome, but a little bit too fat, wore a blond peruke and a new set of clothes every day. His goodnatured wife, Maria Josepha, an Austrian archduchess, was equally bedizened and very ugly. She admired dwarfs, sure symptom of a dwarfish intellect.

On the whole, the sampling of Augustus's illegitimate family to be seen at court was more to Frederick's taste. There was Count Rudowski, son of a Turkish lady named Fatima; there was Count Maurice of Saxony, son of Aurora Königsmarck, sister of the man who had played such a disastrous part in the life of the Prisoner of Ahlden. Frederick passed lightly over two handsome young women, daughters of Augustus, who had Polish names, La Bielinska and La Orczelska. He did not say how much he fancied the latter, but underlined the aesthetic rapture of playing on a borrowed flute with two other flutists, an oboist and a pair if violinists, all of them exquisite virtuosi, for only the greatest artists were tolerated in Saxony.

Another time I will tell you about Holland House, and, if you are a good girl, will bring you a present. Tomorrow, *Tartuffe*. Farewell. Love me as I love you. If your ears have not been ringing, it isn't my fault, for I am always talking of you with Countess Flemming. I love you so much that I would even change places with you here. Goodbye again.

The letter was signed "Frederick, the philosopher." And even Frederick's father might not have thought it overdrawn, for the magic atmosphere of Dresden had had its effect. Frederick William was actually enjoying himself. The dinners to which he sat down with his usual wolfish appetite might offer a hundred and six main dishes to choose from and fifty-three desserts. The King's partner was usually the first lady of the land, the Crown Princess Maria Josepha, whom Frederick thought so plain. His father found her charming, even if, as he wrote to Seckendorf, she was a Catholic. The splendor, he guessed, must be equal to that of the French court in the days of Louis XIV. What would the saintly Francke think of it! If Frederick William's conscience pricked him for dancing or going to the theater, he could always tell himself that he was only a guest and not responsible for these frivolities.

Each day offered something new: a visit to the barracks; to the riding school, where the art of dressage was practiced; to Holland House, Augustus's porcelain factory, the first of its kind in Europe. Every evening there was theater, followed by a ball or masquerade.

As time went by, Frederick William's chronic restlessness and dyspepsia—he had good reason to be dyspeptic—returned. There were outbreaks of temper, as when Fritz made such a poor showing at a shooting contest that he won the booby prize. His father called him a disgrace to his country and, aiming a kick at him, told him to go home to bed. On another occasion, when the visitors were being shown about the palace, a curtain at the end of one of the apartments was suddenly withdrawn to reveal a lighted alcove in which a very beautiful and very naked woman was lying on a couch. Frederick William beat a rapid, snorting retreat, hustling Frederick, who was just behind him, out into the corridor.

The King wrote to Seckendorf that he would start for home on Wednesday. There was so much going on here he had had no time to talk politics with Augustus. "This is certainly not a Christian way of life, but God is my witness that I have taken no pleasure in it and am still as sinless as the day when I arrived."

✦ ✦ ✦

The visit had been an antidote to Frederick William's melancholia, but on his son it had had the opposite effect. For Frederick it was heartbreaking to return to Potsdam with the music of Dresden still whispering in his ears. He fell sick, lost weight, and before he was put to bed with a fever had had a number of fainting attacks. The army surgeon who examined him reported a case of incipient consumption. Frederick William, as always when illness intervened, was worried and conscience-stricken. "When children are well, one doesn't realize how dear they are," he told the Prince of Anhalt-Dessau.

But when Frederick continued to languish and the doctor suggested that perhaps he was suffering from the effects of love, unsatisfied love, sympathy with the invalid vanished. Faultfinding took its place, and Frederick's guardians were ordered to watch him still more closely. The doctor's second diagnosis was perhaps better than the first, for Frederick's symptoms began to subside when he learned that in May Augustus the Strong would pay a return visit to Prussia and that he would bring with him his daughter, the Countess Orczelska.

There were prettier women than Anna Katerina Orczelska among the hundreds Frederick had met in Dresden, but none with whom he felt such an immediate sympathy. Anna was five years older than he and a thousand years older in experience. Her mother was a Frenchwoman who kept a wineshop in Warsaw. At an early age, Anna was introduced to her father by her mother's second husband, who was immediately rewarded with the job of royal gamewarden and told that the little girl should be sent to Dresden when she was fifteen.

Augustus might have his faults, but no one could say he was not a fond and generous parent to his left-handed children. Anna was with him constantly. New debts were incurred to buy her jewels and a fantastically elaborate wardrobe, which included a large number of men's brocaded coats and satin breeches. Toward the end of a ball, when most of the guests had gone home, Anna would vanish, then reappear dressed as a saucy young man; the party would come to life again. Augustus, it was said, encouraged his daughter in this one-woman masquerade because the first time he laid eyes on her she was mounted on a horse and was wearing boy's clothing.

No young woman who had lived between the ages of fifteen and twenty-one in close proximity to Augustus could be called an innocent, but La Orczelska had inherited her father's most aimiable qualities. If her morals were untidy, her manners were meticulous. She was very openhanded. What was more unusual in one in her position, she had sympathy with poor people, having seen their infinite troubles at firsthand in childhood. After a late night, Anna might be up early on some charitable errand in the slums of Dresden.

Was it pity that made her respond to Frederick's inexpert lovemaking? Anna saw a touchingly delicate youth, thwarted and bullied by his brutal father, naive, and yet maturely sensitive to the wonders about him. It was she who showed Frederick around the museum and porcelain factory at Holland House. In spite of the rush of public festivities, the two managed to have a number of private meetings. Then, suddenly, Anna was gone. Frederick learned she had been sent away to Warsaw by her father. It was not Orczelska but an Italian actress who posed naked in the lighted alcove of the palace. Frederick was told by Augustus he could have that beauty for the plucking, but not his daughter.

Returned to Potsdam, Frederick wrote desolate and despairing letters to his mistress, for so he called Anna in the full account of his adventures given Wilhelmina. It would have been asking too much to expect Wilhelmina to feel the same emotions as her brother at thought of the Polish visit. News of Augustus's coming was brought to Berlin by Count Flemming and his wife, who, while they were there, came to call on Wilhelmina every morning.

The elegant little Countess was outspoken to Sophia Dorothea on the way her daughter was dressed. Wilhelmina's clothes, she said, would have been suitable to Queen Charlotte, dead these twenty years; the visitors from Dresden would die laughing at them! New clothes were constructed under the Countess's supervision, and Wilhelmina's waistline was reduced by several inches to conform to the current style of bouffant skirt and snug corsage. The interest taken in her appearance reminded Wilhelmina of the painful grooming she had gone through when her grandfather George came to Charlottenburg. From certain remarks made by the Flemmings, Wilhelmina conceived the idea that her father might be thinking of marrying her to their visitor, whose infirmities Frederick had described so bluntly.

There were some who declared Augustus to be so attractive to women that he was the hunted rather than the hunter in the game of sex. When at last he arrived in Berlin with his son and daughter-in-law, his four bastards, male and female, and a suite of three hundred persons, Wilhelmina could not help but admire him. No one could be more majestic or more polite. Augustus's lameness was due to diabetic sores on his feet, which made standing agonizingly painful, but he apologized for being seated, not only in Sophia Dorothea's presence, but in that of her daughters, who trooped in, all six of them, to be presented to him. He said something pleasant to each, but Wilhelmina was singled out for special attention and after dinner was his partner at cards. Her quick eye caught him once in cheating, but she forgave him, realizing that he only wanted to give her the pleasure of winning.

The other members of the party were judged severely, in particular Anna Orczelska. Wilhelmina had to admit that the girl Frederick loved had a mysterious charm, but she credited the most scandalous stories told of her: Anna was not only the mistress of her father, but of her half-brother, Count Rudowski. No wonder she was jeweled from top to toe!

It was impossible to reproduce in Berlin the luxurious jollities of Dresden, but an effort was made. There were receptions at the palace, at Mon Bijou, and later at Charlottenburg. One night the whole city of Berlin was illuminated, something Wilhelmina had never seen before. No apology, of course, was needed for the full-scale military reviews. While Augustus's courtiers were dressed in every color of the rainbow, the Prussians and their king were never seen in anything but their plain, tight-fitting uniforms.

The visitors' stay was short, much too short for Frederick, who had little chance for love-making and who realized that he and Orczelska might never meet again. Again she vanished, and the two kings went off together to East Prussia. Augustus, however, left behind him a group of the musicians he had brought from Saxony in thoughtful recognition of Frederick's love for music. Among them was a master of the lute, Wilhelmina's favored instrument, and two flutists, Bufardin and Quantz. While his father was away Frederick came up twice a week from Potsdam for lessons and a concert.

All too soon the festival was over. The King had returned, and it was time for Frederick and Wilhelmina to go to the spot they hated most, Wusterhausen. At Wusterhausen partition walls were thin. One day when Wilhelmina had been told by her father to go into an adjoining room she heard him and her mother shouting at one another on the farther side of the closed door. The battle lasted for an hour and a half. After her father's noisy departure Wilhelmina went in to her mother and found her with tears running down her cheeks. Sophia Dorothea hugged her daughter and for a long time struggled to get her breath. At last she panted out, "I am in despair! They want to marry you and the King has discovered the most wretched match in all the world."

WILHELMINA had received much polite attention during the recent festivities from a short, fat man, who had been introduced to her as Lieutenant General von Weissenfels. She had taken his bows and compliments as tribute to her vastly superior rank, for though Weissenfels was duke as well as general, he came from a minor branch of the family to which Augustus himself belonged. Yet this was the man whom Frederick William had selected as a husband for his eldest daughter, the Crown Princess of Prussia!

"A miserable poor relation," Sophia Dorothea shrilled. "All he has to live on is what the King of Poland gives him. I will die of sorrow if you stoop so low as to consent to this marriage!"

Wilhelmina said she couldn't believe her father was serious. He had only meant to tease them. A dozen years had gone by, but the prophecy of the Swedish soothsayer who promised Wilhelmina four unsuccessful but royal suitors had never been forgotten. Wilhelmina had been a child then, but already her engagement to her English cousin was an old story. She was now nineteen, and while Gloucester had taken a step nearer to the throne, having, on his father's accession, become Prince of Wales, his courtship remained nebulous, unconfirmed.

Wilhelmina realized her unmarried state was no fault of her own, she had learned to keep a poker face when the matter was discussed in public, but her pride had been pricked and pricked again. As time went on the prophecy seemed ever more credible. During the peace negotiations with Sweden a marriage with King Charles XII of that country was mentioned, but only in passing. Charles, incidentally, a morose and war-infatuated bachelor, was now dead of a bullet wound received in Norway. That Wilhelmina should have mistaken the infirm, the debauched, the Catholic King of Poland as a suitor was one of her rare, but self-indulgent, escapes from reality.

"But, oh mon Dieu," Sophia Dorothea cried, "The Duke will be here in a few days for the formal engagement! You must be absolutely firm. I will back you up, but you must back *me* up."

Mother and daughter braced themselves for shock when on Sunday, September twenty-seventh, the Duke of Weissenfels arrived at Wusterhausen. All through service in the village church Wilhelmina felt the Duke's eyes upon her from the rear and did not dare to turn her head. After church, Weissenfels followed the royal party back to the hunting lodge. He was presented to the Queen, who, though she had been ordered to be gracious, turned her back upon him. Wilhelmina slipped quietly away. She had not slept for the past two nights; at dinner she could eat nothing.

That afternoon there was even greater hubbub in the next room. When the King had gone, Sophia Dorothea called together an emergency committee, consisting of Count Fink von Finkenstein, Frederick's elderly and well disposed tutor, Frederick himself, and Madame von Sonsfeld. Wilhelmina attended, but only as spectator. Information concerning Weissenfels was pooled. He was forty-three years old and a widower. Augustus had tried to establish him in life by getting him chosen Duke of Courland, but had failed. Though far from brilliant, fat John Adolph, as he was popularly called, was said to be an honorable man.

Count Fink von Finkenstein offered to call upon Weissenfels to tell him that the Queen would violently oppose the match and that Wilhelmina felt a strong personal aversion to it. If the

Duke persisted he would only cause bickering in the family; if he withdrew, Sophia Dorothea would be grateful to him forever and would do what she could to help him.

The mission was promptly carried out. Finkenstein came back uplifted in spirit; chivalry was not yet dead. Weissenfels thought Wilhelmina "charming" and "longed to possess her," but he didn't want to marry her against her will and the will of her mother.

This speech must have been repeated verbatim to the King, for a few days later there was another *fortissimo* discussion, to which Frederick and Wilhelmina listened at the door of the adjoining room. Sophia Dorothea begged hard to be allowed to approach the English court once more. She herself would write to her sister-in-law, Queen Caroline, who was known to have such great influence with her husband that an English doggerel declared:

> You may strut, dapper George, but t'will all be in vain.
> We know 'tis Queen Caroline, not you, that reign.
> Then if you would have us fall down and adore you,
> Lock up your fat spouse, as your dad did before you.

After long, surly resistance, Frederick William agreed. But this time he must have a definite answer. "If not, I'll show them I am master here and can marry my daughter as I choose! Don't think, madame, that your tears and screams will stop me!"

Sophia Dorothea was to ask only for Wilhelmina's marriage. Frederick William could not abide the thought of an English daughter-in-law putting on airs and abetting his wife in her intrigues. Frederick, he said, was a congenital idiot, who, instead of getting a wife, should be beaten within an inch of his life. "But I know how to manage him"—this was a frequent threat of late— "If he doesn't mend his ways, he will get something he isn't looking for!"

Wilhelmina was terrified for Frederick when she learned that her mother, thinking the English court would not be interested in a single marriage, wanted Frederick to write to his Aunt Caroline, promising to marry his cousin Amelia, and no other woman in the world. Only Sophia Dorothea's letter would be shown to the King; Frederick's would be sent secretly through the English Ambassador, who was the Queen's close friend.

But what if the secret were discovered, Wilhelmina protested. Her mother turned upon her with fury. Wilhelmina was a coward, she cried. She was getting ready to marry fat John Adolph!

For his part, Frederick was willing to take the risk. "Our only hope is in England," he said gloomily. "If your engagement to Wales is broken off, we are all of us lost."

Frederick might have added that Wilhelmina was only just beginning to know what it was like to be at odds with their father. Before coming to Wusterhausen he had written to Frederick William, saying they had not seen one another for several weeks, hoping for a better understanding. He would like to know in what way he had offended.

The reply, an outpouring of Frederick William's unpunctuated, pidgin German, covered familiar ground. Frederick was a selfish "wronghead," an undutiful son, who did not love his father. "What is more he knows very well I cannot bear an effeminate fellow who has no manly traits can't ride nor shoot always dirty curls his hair like a fool and doesn't keep it cut and a thousand times I have reprimanded these faults but all in vain and there has been no improvement."

It was maddening to Frederick William that Fritz was not more affable with his father's friends and only talked to those he liked. When he did talk, he made faces, as if he really was a fool. "And in nothing does he do my will unless forced to do it. There is no love . . ."

If Frederick had been at Berlin, or even at Potsdam, he might have managed to keep out of his father's way, but at Wusterhausen there was no hope of that. At Wusterhausen, October twenty-first, the feast day of Saint Hubert, the patron saint of the chase, was always kept. A gigantic loving cup of silver and enamel, a gift from Augustus the Strong, went round and round the table. Frederick, who was sitting next to Count von Suhm, the Saxon ambassador, said ruefully he had a very bad head for wine and would probably be sick the following day. He began to talk loudly of his troubles, adding each time he mentioned his father's name, "but I really am very fond of him."

Sophia Dorothea heard and, from across the table, signaled caution. The Ambassador tried to divert Frederick, but Frederick only talked the louder.

"What's he saying?" Frederick William asked.

Suhm explained that the Prince was a little taken by the wine.

"He's only playing at being drunk," the King said contemptuously.

But Frederick, when Von Suhm put his arm about him and suggested bed, shook the Ambassador off. He lurched to his feet and shouted that he wanted to kiss the King's hand. Frederick William, laughing, stretched his hand across the table. Frederick seized it, slobbered kisses on it and repeated over and over that he loved his father, that his father loved him, that no one should stand between them.

All had risen; all were watching. Someone cried, "Long live the Crown Prince."

The shout that went up was perhaps somewhat jeering, but Frederick William, mellowed and not as tipsy as his son, was moved. Here at last was the brotherly love he had looked for so long.

"There, there now," he soothed, "that's all right—that's quite all right—only you have to be a good fellow, you know, a very good fellow."

Frederick was still babbling of love as he was helped away to bed. For a few days—but only for a few—there was peace between father and son.

✦ ✦ ✦

But between mother and daughter there was little harmony. Both were under strain. Four weeks went by before answers came from England, answers which showed Queen Caroline's diplomatic skill. The letter delivered to her nephew was filled with compliments and with nothing more; the letter to Sophia Dorothea expressed enthusiasm for two marriages, but said they both would have to be discussed in Parliament.

"They think they're going to fool me again," Frederick William growled. He took no immediate action, however, against Wilhelmina or her mother because of a new and bewildering development. In November a letter came from the Prince of Wales, who was in Hanover, who, in fact, had never been allowed to join his parents in England, saying he was about to slip away quietly to Berlin. He was ready to marry Wilhelmina out of hand.

It was obvious that the motive behind the offer was rebellion against parental neglect, but while Frederick William was pondering how this delicate situation should be handled, Sophia Dorothea exulted. "Think of the part you will play," she exclaimed to Wilhelmina. The Queen could see her daughter deciding the fate of Europe, for Wilhelmina, she was sure, was no less brilliant than Queen Caroline. If, like her aunt, she was willing to overlook her husband's affairs with other women, she could pull the strings and make him dance.

Wilhelmina was in bed with a bad cold when the news of the Prince's letter was brought to her. Though skeptical of what it promised, she did not dare express her doubts for fear her mother might blaze out at her again, and again accuse her of being willing to marry fat John Adolf. Wilhelmina did not want to stoop so low, as her mother had put it, but the picture given her of the Prince of Wales was not alluring. Tears rolled down her cheeks.

"Why are you crying?" the Queen asked. Her tone was ominous.

"I hate to think of leaving you," Wilhelmina sniffed. "All the crowns in the world wouldn't make up for that."

Sophia Dorothea embraced her daughter passionately. Tender things were said on either hand, but the reconciliation was on no more firm foundation than Frederick's drunken *rapprochement* with his father. It lasted but a short time longer.

Soon after New Year's it was learned that Wilhelmina's suitor was in England. Against his will, with tears in his eyes, it was said, he had been spirited away from an evening party in Hanover. Wilhelmina thought her mother was to blame, for, as usual, Sophia Dorothea had talked too much, and one of the people to whom she talked was the English Ambassador, in duty bound to pass on information to his government. Actually there had been a demand in the British Parliament for the heir to the throne to be brought to England. Agents had been sent to fetch the Prince before the British Embassy in Berlin could have communicated with London.

✦ ✦ ✦

In January of 1729 the two royal tutors, Count Fink von Finkenstein and Colonel Christopher William von Kalkstein, offered their resignations. They gave as their reason Frederick's coming of age, but both realized that, with the mounting conflict between father and son, the post of tutor was becoming dangerous. Finkenstein, past seventy, was old enough to be let go, but Frederick William wanted to retain Von Kalkstein for August William, the son whom he loved and who he was sure loved him. Kalkstein refused. His retirement and that of his senior partner brought but little freedom to Frederick. Two somewhat younger men, Colonel von Rochow and Count Dietrich von Kayserlingk, were appointed to be with the Prince night and day.

Only occasionally was Frederick able to escape surveillance and to make a few friends of his own. One was a Lieutenant von Ingersleben, who was fond of music and who was taking lessons from the organist of the garrison church at Potsdam. Not all the hours spent at divine service were wasted from Frederick's point of view. The organist's daughter, Doris Ritter, just sixteen, sang in her father's choir, her silvery soprano, small in volume, but deliciously precise in intonation, standing out from the rest.

The Ritters, father and daughter, were newcomers to the community and lived in an ivy-covered cottage near the Potsdam canal. Since Cantor Ritter was often away on his round of lessons, Doris was much alone. She was alone on the day when Frederick called for the first time with Lieutenant von Inger-sleben.

Thereafter Frederick came whenever he could slip away, his flute concealed inside his coat. While Doris sang, Frederick played. He brought small, inexpensive offerings, for he was always short of money: music books, scraps of jewelry, a dressing gown of watered silk he thought Doris might transform into a costume for herself. In return she gave him on demand her miniature. These gifts were exchanged on the rare occasions when Frederick and Doris were unchaperoned, for Cantor Ritter always tried to be there to add a clavecin accompaniment to flute and voice.

The responsibility of bringing up a pretty daughter in a garrison town rested heavily upon the father. Though Frederick's unassuming manners and enthusiasm for music made his visits seem pleasantly normal, the Cantor was afraid they might end unhappily. Like everyone else in Prussia, he feared the King, whom he saw frequently in church and with whom he once had a brief conversation. One day when Ritter was working in his flower garden, Frederick William, stumping by, called out to him to dig up his plot and plant cabbages and turnips instead of roses.

Frederick said nothing to Wilhelmina of his friendship with the Ritters. Ever since the visit to Dresden Wilhelmina had sensed with sorrow his growing independence. She worried that without her guidance he might get into even greater trouble than at present. She wistfully realized he had a life she could not share. Wilhelmina noticed Frederick was on familiar terms with one of their father's pages, Peter Christopher von Keith. When she saw them whispering together she wondered if they were whispering of women. She could not forbear criticism of Frederick's choice of a friend. Frederick only laughed. Keith, he said, kept him informed of what was going on around the King. Now that he and his father were on such bad terms a scout was necessary.

Chapter 9

O F the enemies to be reckoned with at present the most
dangerous was Count Frederick Henry von Seckendorf.
Frederick and Wilhelmina were well aware of this; they
jeered at the Austrian Ambassador behind his back—at his
piety, which they assumed to be feigned, at his stinginess with
all but his master's money, at his protruding front teeth, which
gave him the appearance of a rodent. To them Seckendorf's
greatest success was as yet unknown. In December of 1728 Frederick William was persuaded to sign yet another secret treaty,
one promising to uphold the Pragmatic Sanction. Prussia would
see to it that Archduchess Maria Theresa, unless married to a
Frenchman or a Spaniard, took title to all Austrian possessions
after the death of her imperial father. The *quid pro quo* was
Austrian support of Prussia's claim to Berg, but not to its sister
province in the Rhineland, Jülich. Instead of Jülich, the less
valuable principality of Ravenstein had been substituted. This
was better than nothing, but not all that Frederick William
wanted, or all that Seckendorf had led him to believe he could
get.

Seckendorf was responsible for the courtship of the Duke of
Weissenfels. He considerd Frederick William's covey of girls
an asset. He would like to see all six of them married within the
Empire; having failed in his first attempt, he succeeded in his

second. The Princess Frederica Louise, Eeka to her nursery mates, was now fourteen. Seckendorf had selected as her fiancé the youthful Margrave of Brandenburg-Ansbach, a distant relative, a descendant of the Franconian branch of the Hohenzollerns. The wedding would take place in May of this year of 1729, after the Margrave had reached his majority, he being two years older than his intended bride.

The Ansbach holdings were small. One could hardly call the marriage brilliant. Sophia Dorothea scorned it, but had made no protest. She could not fight a war on two fronts; she had to save all her ammunition for Wilhelmina, who had been given educational advantages denied to her sisters. No special tutors, no learned professor had been provided for Eeka. A daughter of Madame de Roucoulle, the nursery governess, had taught this pretty, but rather dull, girl all she knew.

In early spring the entire family went to Potsdam for the most important military reviews of the year. The exercises had hardly begun when the Commander-in-Chief was prostrated by an attack of gout in both feet at once. Frederick William suffered excruciatingly and could not suffer alone. His family had to appear in his room at nine o'clock in the morning. They were expected to follow him about all day long, for he was too restless to stay in bed and had himself pushed about in a wheel chair, using a pair of crutches as though they were poling oars.

Wife and children trooped after "like captives in the wake of a conqueror"; the simile was Wilhelmina's. She and Frederick—"that rascal Fritz," "that English scum, Wilhelmina,"—could trigger their father's rage without so much as a word being spoken. When Eeka, emboldened, perhaps, by the thought of approaching independence, ventured to criticize the quality and the amount of food on the dinner table, Frederick William picked up a plate, but, instead of throwing it at Eeka, hurled it at Frederick's head, and another at Wilhelmina's. In the King's pain-muddled mind, these two were the source of every outrage. But Sophia Dorothea, he was sure, had made them what they were.

"It's all your mother's fault; it's the way she has brought you up," Frederick William roared. He told a story he had heard as a boy from his tutor about a criminal, condemned to death for many crimes, who asked to speak to his mother before his execution. Bending down, as if to whisper to the woman, he munched off a portion of her ear. He wanted to make her an example to parents who failed to educate their children properly. Frederick and Wilhelmina were told with venom to apply the moral to their own case.

As the culprits left the room Wilhelmina had to pass close to her father. He aimed a blow at her with his crutch, which she ducked—and down the corridor she fled, the invalid's chair in hot and noisy pursuit.

Safe in her bedroom, Wilhelmina dropped, trembling, into a chair. That she felt so weak, that her face and neck were covered with red blotches she took as reaction to her fright, but the red blotches were forerunners of small pox. The patient was isolated from all the family except Frederick, who, having had a mild case, was immune to the disease.

All during her illness Wilhelmina looked for a forgiving word to come from her father and composed pathetic and punishing messages to be delivered to him after her death. She, the once favored, was now the persecuted. The broth sent up to the sickroom was salted water to her taste; the unhushed beating of the drums beneath her window was forever startling her from sleep.

Though two months later Wilhelmina was convalescent, the danger of infection was given as an excuse for her absence from Eeka's wedding. The world would not be allowed to see the older unmarried sister overshadowed and in second place. Sophia Dorothea, no doubt, was the source of the frequent and quite groundless rumors of a special envoy being on his way from England to confirm the Wilhelmina-Wales engagement. After visiting her daughter for the first time since her illness the queen announced publicly that the Princess's complexion was unblemished.

During the summer, however, it looked as if there might be an end to English matchmaking once and for all. A series of spiteful incidents occured along the border between Prussia and Hanover. Hanoverian farmers cut hay on Prussian soil; Prussian officials, who tried to stop them, were arrested. Hostages were also held for the return of ten tall Hanoverians, kidnapped by Frederick William's press gang. The King hurled smouldering protest after protest at his brother-in-law, who happened to be vacationing in Hanover, but "dapper George" returned the volley briskly.

At last, in August, all sense of the triviality of the offenses having been lost, the order for mobilization was given. The beautiful and awe-inspiring Prussian army moved toward the frontier. Fortunately there were others than Sophia Dorothea to cry halt. The English Ambassador made a hurried trip to Hanover and saw how feeble the preparations were there. He backed up offers for mediation made by the European powers which, with their cat's cradle of alliances, might become involved. Frederick William, the most unwarlike of militarists, the man who, as Peter the Great had once said, liked to go fishing but was afraid of getting his feet wet, agreed to submit all disputes to an arbitration board which would meet at Brunswick early in 1730.

The King's restraint was compensated by an increased abuse of Frederick and Wilhelmina. They were ordered to keep out of their father's sight at Wusterhausen except at mealtimes, a difficult feat in that congested spot. Once, when surprised in their mother's room, Wilhelmina dived under the bed and Frederick hid himself in the closet where the chamber pots were stored. There they remained for an hour or more, breathing dust and effluvia as quietly as possible, while Frederick William snored away the fatigues of hunting.

Their lives, it seemed, had become a game of hide-and-seek with a lunatic. Frederick could see no end to it. Wilhelmina counseled patience, but Wilhelmina was a woman and might consider it a virtue to suffer in silence. Frederick was, in his own esteem, a man; he would be eighteen his next birthday.

After the return to Potsdam Frederick performed only the

minimum of daily routine required of him. One morning, on entering the King's room, he was leapt upon, seized by the collar and thrashed by one of the cruelly efficient canes that were always ready to Frederick William's hand. Frederick struggled to free himself, but his father's grip was maniacal. He was forced down on his knees and commanded to kiss his father's feet for having failed to say goodnight the preceding evening. "I am not punishing you as an officer," Frederick William panted—officers were never beaten—"but as my child."

There were others in the room to see Frederick's humiliation. "This is more than I can bear," Frederick wrote in the note that went privately to Sophia Dorothea and Wilhelmina in Berlin. "I am too proud to submit to this sort of treatment, and am determined to put an end to it in one way or another."

But what way was there, short of murder, to put an end to it? There was flight. And the thought of flight was nothing new. Frederick had tried to get permission for foreign travel indirectly from his father, using Count Suhm, the Saxon ambassador, and Augustus the Strong as intermediaries. Nothing had come of that attempt. To leave without permission, Frederick would need an accomplice. A few weeks earlier he had asked Peter von Keith, the royal page of whom Wilhelmina disapproved, if he would be willing to go with him to France or Italy. Keith expressed acquiescence and devotion, but shortly after the New Year had to leave Berlin. A lieutenant's commission was forced upon him; he was sent away to Cleves in the Rhineland.

Frederick, with no definite plan in mind, but more resolute than ever to find one, considered his various friends. There was one rather new acquaintance who might be bold and faithful, Lieutenant Hans Hermann von Katte. Von Katte was twenty-six, eight years older than Frederick. He was a flutist, had studied law at Halle and had made the grand tour of the Continent before turning soldier; only a soldier could expect to rise to the top in Prussia. Katte could talk books and music; his manners were elegant and sophisticated. Only his appearance was against him; heavy black eyebrows overhung his deep-set eyes; his swarthy skin, unlike Wilhelmina's, had been deeply pitted by small pox.

An old song was sung in the neighborhood where Katte's family had been long established, prophesying death on the gallows, or on the wheel, for a man named Katte who had bushy eyebrows and a yellow skin. The recklessness, the ambition, that might lead to such an end, could be useful to Frederick.

✦ ✦ ✦

The news of the King's assault was more dreadful to Wilhelmina than to her mother, for Wilhelmina had been able to read between the lines of Frederick's letter. Though Sophia Dorothea was distressed for her son, all of her attention was once more concentrated on her daughter.

No sooner was the threat of war between England and Prussia lifted than the Queen was told she could write a second letter to her English sister-in-law, a fair example of how frequently, in spite of Seckendorf, Frederick William changed his mind. Only the merest hint was needed. The letter penned to Queen Caroline on December seventeenth, 1729, was brief. It bluntly asked to have Wilhelmina's fate, and Wilhelmina's alone, settled by the first of February, since the matter had been dragging on so long that "the King might want to take other steps."

After sending a copy to Potsdam for her husband's approval and after waiting for three days to hear from him, Sophia Dorothea sent the letter off, unauthorized. A week later she was surprised to hear that three of the King's gentlemen were waiting in her reception room to see her. The three were Marshal von Borcke, Count Fink von Finkenstein, and General von Grumbkow. Wilhelmina, who was with her mother when the delegation was announced, scented trouble. "I think they have come to speak of me," she said.

"What difference does that make?" the Queen exclaimed impatiently. "One has only to be firm—and I can always be firm!" A regal, and a more than usually rotund, figure, for she was once more pregnant and in her sixth month, Sophia Dorothea swept into the anteroom.

Count Fink handed over a brief that he and his colleagues had received from the King. Its tone was testy. It commanded them to call on the Queen and to tell her that her husband was sick of subterfuge; he was determined to marry Wilhelmina immediately. If a satisfactory answer did not come from England within the next eight days, a choice must be made between the Duke of Weissenfels and the Margrave of Schwedt. If Sophia Dorothea opposed this plan, she and her miserable daughter would be sent away to the Castle of Oranienburg, where they would have plenty of time to repent their obstinacy.

Before the Queen could more than glance the letter through General von Grumbkow stepped forward and delivered a little sermon on political necessity and the many passages in Holy Writ proving that children should obey their fathers rather than their mothers. Sophia Dorothea knew her Bible and was quick to catch him out. How about Bethuel, she asked? When a proposal of marriage was made for his daughter Bethuel said, "Go ask the maid herself."

"I don't deny that women should submit to their husbands, but only when the husbands are just and reasonable. The King is neither. He is trying to violate the inclinations of my daughter and make her unhappy for the rest of her life . . . I would rather see her in her grave than wretched!"

Sophia Dorothea added that she was feeling unwell today. General von Grumbkow should consider her condition. "Don't think I only blame the King," she said with an annihilating look at her adversary. "I know very well whom I have to thank for this ill usage!"

Three days later the Queen took to her bed. She was really unwell, but the word from England was sufficient reason. Queen Caroline's answer was almost identical with that of the preceding year: two marriages, or none.

Again the trio of generals called and reported even heavier

penalties for disobedience: divorce for the Queen, prison for Wilhelmina, and disinheritance for Frederick. Sophia Dorothea heard that both Schwedt and Weissenfels were in the vicinity of Berlin, ready to pop into view if summoned. One of the delegation—it was Marshal von Borcke—advised the Queen to suggest a third husband for Wilhelmina, even if she had no real interest in her candidate. While the newcomer was being investigated there would be time to make another assault on England, if an assault seemed feasible.

After several names were discussed, that of the son and heir of the Margrave of Bayreuth was chosen, the Margrave being, like Eeka's husband, a Hohenzollern of minor importance. His Franconian lands, well to the south of Prussia and adjoining Ansbach, had been coveted both by Frederick William and his father, Frederick I.

The word Bayreuth, however, failed to pacify Frederick William, who came raging to his wife's bedside, unimpressed by her illness. He would write to the Margrave, he said, but whatever the final decision might be, Wilhelmina must obey—otherwise, no dowry, no trousseau, no father present at her wedding. Sophia Dorothea's riposte was her curse forever upon Wilhelmina if she did only as her father wished. Never had Wilhelmina's dilemma been more clearly stated.

But the Bayreuth proposal had, as Marshal von Borcke predicted, gained time for one more maneuver. For eight years now Wilhelmina had been taking English lessons from Dr. Villa, the chaplain of the British Embassy. The doctor was about to go home to England and offered his services. When he came to say goodbye he was loaded with presents from Sophia Dorothea, with letters, and with verbal messages for the Queen's unfeeling relatives. If Britain failed to accept Wilhelmina for its future sovereign, Villa said, he would renounce his country forever.

It was of good omen that while the doctor was at work in London Frederick William would be absent from Prussia. The King was going on a short trip to Dresden to discuss international and military affairs with Augustus. Frederick had been ordered to accompany his father. On the February evening before they were scheduled to leave, Wilhelmina had undressed and was about to get into bed when a handsome young man, magnificently costumed *à la francaise* from powdered head to high-heeled shoes, slipped into her room. Wilhelmina squeaked with fright and hid behind a screen. Madame von Sonsfeld came running.

Not until the young man laughed was Frederick recognized, an overexcited, an overvehement Frederick. He had come to kiss his sister goodnight and to tell her of his plans. He would not return from Saxony.

"I can't bear the disgraceful things done to me here"—Frederick had again been beaten—"In Dresden I'll be able to give them the slip. I'll go to England. Once I'm there, I will be able to get you there also—so just keep calm and wait. We will meet soon in a happy place . . . We'll be together . . . at peace, no more persecution."

For a moment Wilhelmina more than half believed in Frederick's happy place, though it sounded more like the heaven promised to the pure of heart than like London. The vision faded. Wilhelmina threw her arms about her brother's neck and begged him to give up this insane idea. He would never be able to get away; the results would be frightful for him and for them both. Madame von Sonsfeld added her voice, the voice of an older generation, to Wilhelmina's.

At first Frederick would not listen to them, but Wilhelmina had dropped to the floor and embraced his knees. She would not let him go until he had promised to wait until something had at least been heard from Dr. Villa's activities in London.

While Frederick and his father were gone, word came from the chaplain. As a result of his visits to ministers and to the Prince of Wales, he wrote, a special envoy was being sent from England to discuss important matters at the Prussian court. He would arrive in early spring.

Chapter 10

CHAPLAIN Villa had let his imagination run away with him.
His championship of Wilhelmina had had little to do
with an English envoy's being sent to Berlin in the spring
of 1730. The decision for that step had been made by practical
politicians at the request of the English Ambassador and Herr
von Knyphausen, the only Prussian minister who was friendly to
Britain.

In November of the preceding year an alliance had been
drawn between England, France and Spain, its purpose being a
concerted attack on Austria. There were fire-eaters in Britain,
one of them being the high placed individual whom Frederick
William called "my cousin, the comedian," or "my cousin, the
red cabbage." There was also, however, constant bipartisan debate on foreign policy in the House of Commons. A session that
began at eleven A.M. on March fourteenth, 1730, lasted without
break until four A.M. the following day. At this time the Tories
argued that England's present alliance with France, her only
serious rival in the colonial field, was unnatural; instead of attacking Austria, it would be better to join forces with her.

Whatever shifts might occur in future, Prussia must not be
allowed to gobble up Hanover, as had so nearly happened recently. In keeping Prussia friendly, the character of Frederick

[80]

William had to be considered: his touchiness, his vacillations, his idiosyncracies. The envoy selected for the Berlin mission was the sort of man a collector of "long fellows" would be sure to like, a tall, good looking officer, a Yorkshire baronet, Sir Charles Hotham, who had had no experience in dealing with irascible foreigners, but who was well connected from a political point of view.

Hotham left for the Continent at the end of March with personal instructions from George II in his pocket. George had been much annoyed by the last letter written by his sister to Queen Caroline; he was sure his hateful brother-in-law had had a hand in it. Hotham, echoing Caroline, must insist on a double marriage. He must not allow the Prussian King to "fly out at him": he must "uphold the dignity of Britain." The Foreign Office had also supplied what was thought to be an effective lever to pry Prussia and Austria apart. It had been discovered by a judicious tampering with the mail bag that Herr von Reichenbach, the Prussian ambassador in England, was carrying on a lively correspondence with General von Grumbkow, both men being in the pay of Austria. Diplomatic secrets were going directly to Vienna while all the English news fed to Frederick William had a rank, imperial odor.

After visiting the Hague and Hanover, Sir Charles arrived in Berlin on April second. He had an audience with the King two days later at Charlottenburg, and was invited to stay to dinner, a dinner at which only men were present, the Queen having come close to a fatal miscarriage while her husband was in Dresden; though out of danger now, she was keeping to her bed in the Berlin palace.

The King seemed affable and in high spirits. During his private talk with Hotham he said he was glad his daughter was acceptable to her English relatives. Hotham, feeling it was too soon to take that for granted, said nothing. He felt he had been so discreet that he was astounded when, at table and after much wine had been drunk, Frederick William loudly proposed a health to Wilhelmina and the Prince of Wales. General von

Grumbkow also registered amazement—and chagrin. Leaning forward, he murmured, "Are we to congratulate you, sire?"

The King said yes. Everyone rose and went to kiss Frederick William's knee, or the skirt of his coat, a curious custom, Hotham thought. Tumult and rejoicing followed. The guests began to dance, and even the servants cut capers and leapt about the room. Hotham, though admittedly drunk himself, recorded later he "was not used to such vivacities." He lost no time in writing to his chief, Lord Townsend, to deny responsibility for all misconceptions.

The good news, however, had been wafted to Berlin. It roused Sophia Dorothea from her bed to greet Wilhelmina as Princess of Wales and Madame von Sonsfeld as "milady."

The following day a sober Frederick William forbade all mention of what had gone on at the dinner, but he remained surprisingly receptive to what the English envoy had to say. At later audiences Hotham made it plain that Wilhelmina alone was not sufficient guarantee; the Frederick-Amelia match would be a far stronger pledge for unity. When Frederick William asked for something substantial in return for this great concession, Hotham, prompted by Herr von Knyphausen, suggested the possibility of the regency of Hanover being given as a wedding gift to Amelia and her husband.

Sir Charles was pleased when Lord Townsend endorsed the regency scheme, for he had taken a liking to Frederick on short acquaintance. "It is impossible," Hotham wrote," to express the dejection and melancholy that appear in him. There is something so very engaging in the person and behavior of this young prince, and everybody says so much good of him, that one is the more moved by the unhappy circumstances he is under."

Kindhearted Sir Charles was just beginning to think the marriages were as good as made when a change, a change for the worse, took place in the climate of discussion. Hotham's dramatic revelation of the Reichenbach-Grumbkow correspondence fizzled. Frederick William said drily he had been intending to replace his ambassador by a man of higher rank. Reichenbach would be recalled, but would get an important post at home to make up for the one lost in London.

It was difficult for Sir Charles to understand why the Prussian King, famous for severity, should show so little concern when told of his subordinates taking money from foreign governments. Frederick William continued to be on intimate terms with Grumbkow and Seckendorf. His opinion of the marriage propositions declined after Seckendorf had branded as insults the offer of the regency to Frederick and no dowry demanded with Wilhelmina. Here were two broad hints that the King of Prussia was too poor, or too stingy, to provide for his children!

To Hotham's sense of frustration, boredom was added as days and weeks went by. The only entertainment offered the visitor were stag dinners, at which he met the same people over and over, and an occasional day's shooting. Hotham would have liked to meet Wilhelmina. He would have liked to meet the Queen, who was still invisible and still with child.

On May twenty-third, 1730, Sophia Dorothea bore her last princeling, who was christened Ferdinand. A few days later, Hotham left for what promised to be a pleasing change from the monotony of Berlin. There had been much talk of a great event, scheduled for June, a military pageant to be held at Radewitz in Saxony, to which all German princes were invited. The host, Augustus the Strong, was aiming to out-glitter the Field of the Cloth of Gold, the sixteenth century fraternization between Henry VIII of England and Francis I of France. When Hotham asked his government if he might go to Radewitz, the answer was an emphatic yes; this exhibition of German might should be observed.

Shortly before leaving for Saxony with a companion, Mr. Guy Dickens of the embassy staff, Hotham received an odd little letter from Frederick, who had only been glimpsed from time to time during the past six weeks. Frederick begged the Englishman to work for Wilhelmina's marriage and for the moment to forget his own. He hereby pledged himself once again: come what may, he would marry his cousin Amelia. "I am a person of my word," Frederick concluded, "and will be able to bring about what I promise. You can tell that to your court!"

✦ ✦ ✦

The trip to Dresden had been too brief for pleasure. If Frederick had expected to see Anna Orczelska there he was disappointed. Anna was no longer with her father. She had recently been married to Count Charles of Hesse-Beck, a man more interested in what his father-in-law could do for him than in his bride.

Frederick William and his son came home at the crisis of Sophia Dorothea's pregnancy, when she was in great pain and thought to be dying. A truce to family war was called at her bedside. Wilhelmina was embraced and forgiven; Frederick was told that if he behaved himself he would be forgiven also. The relief caused by his Fiekchen's recovery no doubt contributed to Frederick William's cordial reception of Sir Charles Hotham, but during the period of dickering that followed Frederick relapsed from favor.

The King had discovered more serious crimes to punish with fist and cane than Fritz's failure to say goodnight or allowing his hair to grow too long. From Reichenbach, Grumbkow, or Seckendorf—no matter which; the three were in close cooperation—Frederick William had learned of last year's secret letter to Queen Caroline. He knew also of Frederick's having borrowed money and how some of the money had been spent. An order had been placed in Leipzig for a traveling carriage. The King issued a decree forbidding loans to all members of the royal family without his permission. Since the use to which the carriage might be put was patent, Colonel von Rochow, the more trustworthy of Frederick's two guardians, was ordered to keep an even closer watch than usual. Rochow was to be particularly alert during the visit of the King, the Crown Prince and all top military men to the King of Poland's camp at Radewitz.

Augustus's Field of the Cloth of Gold extended for twelve miles along the River Elbe. An army of workers had leveled the terrain on which a city of tents had been set up, the most magnificent pavilion being that in which Augustus received his distinguished guests, surrounded by turbaned Negro pages, grooms in tiger skins and crimson velvet, guards in baggy-trousered Polish uniforms.

For a fortnight dust drifted up from the artificial plain as thirty thousand troops stamped back and forth and thundered at one another in sham battles, directed by Wilhelmina's suitor, the Duke of Weissenfels. Fireworks needled the night sky. One of the set pieces in which the God of War was shown embracing the Goddess of Peace spelt out the moral of this stupendous picnic—the safety to be found in military preparedness. On the final day, June twenty-sixth, all of the guests, high and low, dined in the open air, the kings and princes riding on horseback back and forth between the rows of tables. A monster cake was drawn in on a wagon and cut up by a carpenter with his saw; into it had gone six hundred eggs, two tons of milk and a ton of butter.

Augustus had announced that everyone was here to enjoy himself—but he could not speak for Frederick of Prussia. Frederick had to trail his father from dawn to dusk. He was humiliated before strangers and slashed at with the cane. "If I had been treated like this by my father," Frederick William snarled," I would have killed myself, but it makes no difference to you. You can put up with anything!"

On their way to Radewitz Frederick had taken the opportunity of speaking of a break for freedom to Hans Hermann von Katte, his friend of the bushy eyebrows and the sallow complexion. Though he deprecated the idea at first, Katte's resistance was perfunctory, and, to win him over, Frederick hardly needed to threaten to find someone else to help him.

But how to get away and where to go? Wherever Frederick went he had only to look over his shoulder to see Colonel von Rochow close behind him. Frederick thought of leading the Colonel to a secluded spot, tripping him up and tying him hand and foot. First, however, he must get horses, one for himself and one for Von Katte. Frederick tried to borrow the horses from a Saxon acquaintance, Count Hoym, saying they were wanted by two officers who would like to ride over quietly to visit the fair at Leipzig. Hoym guessed who one of the officers would surely be and invented an excuse for saying no.

Frederick had told Von Katte he would go to France, but only for a short time, only until the King had come to his senses. As the difficulties of slipping away from camp accumulated, a deferred, a more elaborate scheme took shape.

It was now known that Frederick William—and presumably his son—would make a tour of southern Germany in the interest of the Empire, a follow-up to the Radewitz demonstration. Frederick had also heard of the imminent departure for England of Mr. Guy Dickens, the secretary of the English Embassy who had come to Saxony with Sir Charles Hotham. In one of the rare moments he was free of Von Rochow, Frederick followed the Englishman to his tent and slipped in behind him.

"I have been wanting to speak to you for a long time," Frederick said.

Having discovered how dangerous letters could be, Frederick asked Dickens to report his plans verbally to the King and Queen of England. One of the southern principalities to be visited by Frederick William was Ansbach. There, Frederick thought, he could get help from his sister Eeka and her husband, the Margrave, to cross the Rhine and make his way to Paris, via Strassburg. In Paris Frederick would stay for several months before setting out for his real, his final destination, England. He had chosen the route through France to protect his mother and his sister; the King must not be allowed to think they had plotted his escape. Frederick feared particularly for Wilhelmina. He would try to get her to a place of safety before leaving Berlin, but if he failed, he wanted his uncle to protect her and also to see that he, Frederick, was well received in France.

For the first time no criticism was offered. Frederick was heard to the end. Guy Dickens promised to deliver the message, and Hotham, to whom it was retailed later, put it in writing. Hotham added a persuasive footnote of his own. There was talk at Radewitz—it was only gossip—of Frederick's being converted to Catholicism so that he might be married to the Archduchess Maria Theresa. A Catholic King of Prussia, Hotham pointed out, would diminish the Protestant bloc to which England looked for support on the Continent. He asked that Dickens should be sent back promptly to Berlin with an answer, for the tour of Southern Germany was set for the middle of July.

A week before that date all of the Prussian party, including Sir Charles, were back in Berlin; so also was Mr. Guy Dickens. Dickens had brought a light dispatch case from London, but he had much to say to Hotham and to Frederick, whom he met after nightfall in the embrasured doorway of one of the side entrances to the palace. While two disembodied voices whispered in the dark, Von Katte kept watch, with his back against the outer wall.

The report from England was discouraging. Frederick's uncle disapproved of his plan and asked him to give it up. Time was too short, he said, to make arrangements for a reception in France, and if Frederick went there unheralded there might be serious international repercussions. George was sorry for his nephew's unhappy state, but all he could do for him at present was offer to settle any debts Frederick had been able to conceal from his father.

There were many such. Katte, Frederick said, would bring Dickens an accounting. But he could not promise to do as his uncle wished. He would give up his plan and wait for better days only if the King should have a change of heart and decide to leave him at home during the southern expedition.

As usual there was a crippling uncertainty in Frederick's mind as to what his father intended. He did not know, and apparently Dickens did not tell him, of an interesting proposition which had been made that very afternoon by Sir Charles Hotham. Hotham had told the King that Wilhelmina's marriage could take place at once if Frederick's followed within the next few years. Given verbal assent, Hotham would go home at once to bring back a contract. No political strings were attached to the offer; there would be no demand for a break with the Empire.

On the morning of July tenth, only twelve hours after Frederick's conference with the secretary, Dickens and Sir Charles called at the palace for their answer. Hopeful of success, Hotham thought now was the moment to put an end to the career of General Von Grumbkow, who, after Reichenbach's recall, was England's enemy number one in Prussia. Hotham had brought with him a letter, the last to be passed between the General and the Ambassador. In it Grumbkow expressed the hope of their correspondence being destroyed before Reichenbach left London. This was a frank admission of what the British Foreign office had termed "a scene of villainy."

The contents of the letter was described before it was handed over, but as Frederick William took the sheet, his face, the face of an inflated cherub, turned red, sure sign of oncoming frenzy. These impudent and haughty foreigners were meddling in affairs that did not concern them!

"Messieurs, I have had enough of this kind of thing," Frederick William shouted. He dashed the letter to the floor and, before thudding out of the room, raised his foot as if he were going to kick Sir Charles. Frederick William had flown out. The dignity of Britain had been desecrated.

That afternoon at three o'clock there was a note from Hotham on the King's desk, asking for a passport and post horses; he wished to leave Berlin at once. A note from Dickens urged reconciliation.

The gesture was made; Hotham was invited to dine at the palace and declined. The Dutch and Danish ministers offered mediation. Sophia Dorothea did her frantic best through her friend, the English Ambassador. The most moving of all appeals was made by Frederick directly to Sir Charles: "Think, monsieur, that my happiness and that of my sister depend on your decision . . ." Hotham's reply was stuffy. "If only my own case were concerned, I would attempt the impossible . . . but as the affront I have received touches the King, my master, I cannot yield to Your Royal Highness's wishes . . . "

✦ ✦ ✦

Hotham was gone when Sophia Dorothea and her children came to Potsdam to say goodbye to Frederick William and his son before they started on their travels. Frederick William had told Sophia Dorothea her daughter would die an old maid. He would appoint Wilhelmina co-Abbess of Herford, one of the great religious communities dating from the Middle Ages that, in this post-Reformation era, provided a stipend for unmarried or widowed members of the princely caste.

Frederick and Wilhelmina had a few brief minutes alone. Wilhelmina said sadly she had not really wanted to marry the Prince of Wales, but life in England could not be worse than life here.

Frederick, who was sore in mind and sore in body, for he had been given the beating his father would have liked to give Sir Charles, was unsympathetic. He didn't see why Wilhelmina and her mother were so upset, he said. There were worse things than being an Abbess of Herford and having an income of one's own.

"I am sick and tired of plotting," he added. "I've done all I could for your marriage. Now you will have to get along as best you can. It's time I thought of my own interests."

He spoke so bitterly, so vehemently, that Wilhelmina was wounded and struck back. He was unjust, he was cruel, she cried. They stabbed at one another. Not since childhood had they quarreled, and to quarrel now when Frederick was going away, perhaps forever, was more than Wilhelmina could bear. She said in a broken voice, "If you have any feeling left for me, you will give up your idea of escape."

"I have thought it through," Frederick replied coldly, "and I have changed my mind. I will return."

There was only a moment for Wilhelmina to press her lips to Frederick's cheek, for their father was coming. They must not be seen whispering together. Frederick murmured in Wilhelmina's ear that he would come to her later in the evening.

For hours Wilhelmina waited in her bedroom. At midnight Frederick's valet, Grummersbach, brought a note saying Frederick could not come, but he loved his sister now and forever. Wilhelmina was unable to sleep. She and Madame von Sonsfeld talked until dawn. Though Frederick had said he would return, they felt less sure he would keep his promise than when he had gone to Dresden. There was one hopeful sign: Lieutenant von Katte, for whom Wilhelmina felt the same jealous dislike as for the page, Christopher von Keith, would not be going on the tour of southern Germany.

WHILE Wilhelmina and her governess were talking away the night of June fourteenth, 1730, Frederick and Hans Hermann von Katte were crouched in the shrubbery surrounding the Potsdam Palace. They were discussing the practical problems of escape. Frederick had not meant to deceive his sister; one of the reasons for their quarrel, perhaps, had been his indecision. Now his mind was made up. Though Von Katte had again shown a token resistance, he, too, had taken fire.

There was the question of money. Frederick in drawing up a financial statement for Guy Dickens had made a generous allowance for something over all debts incurred, but that source of revenue was contingent on his remaining in Prussia. The little Frederick had in hand was a sum given him by his father to pay the monthly hunting expenses at Wusterhausen. More would be needed. Frederick had pried some diamonds out of their settings in the military decorations presented to him at Dresden. He gave them to Von Katte, who was to raise three thousand thalers by their sale and by borrowing small amounts from bankers and from fellow officers.

It was decided that Von Katte should ask for leave to go recruiting. This was a form of holiday smiled upon by the high command. He would meet Frederick in Wesel on the Rhine, or in Holland, where he would take the name of Count Sparre and Frederick that of Count d'Alberville. They would continue to use these names in France. Since much would depend on improvisation, the conspirators needed a means of communication during Frederick's journey. Fortunately a cousin of Hans Herrmann, a cavalry captain, would also be recruiting in the region through which Frederick would travel and would play postman.

There were other details to be settled, one of them being a letter to King George of England Frederick had given to his friend and which he asked him now to destroy. Without mentioning the name of Doris Ritter, Frederick told Von Katte there was a girl in Potsdam whom he loved and whom he would have liked to take with him to France; she had refused to go with him and had tried to dissuade him.

For two hours the eager, whispered conversation continued. Then Von Katte set off on horseback for Berlin, and Frederick went to his room. It was hardly worthwhile to go to bed, for the short summer night would soon be over, and the train of carriages would leave at dawn.

On their way to Ansbach the travelers stopped at Meusselwitz to pick up Count von Seckendorf, who had an estate there and who would be Frederick William's chief collaborator in imperial propaganda throughout the tour. The Ansbach visit was important to Frederick William; he wished to inspect his daughter's ménage and to see how she and her husband were getting on together.

They were getting on very badly. The Margrave, a violent youth, resented the dictatorial ways of his father-in-law and felt he had been tricked into marriage. Though Eeka was conceded to be the beauty of a family well above the average for good looks, her husband found fault with her appearance and refused to sleep with her. He would not cooperate in producing the grandchildren Frederick William bluntly demanded.

Frederick, finding his brother-in-law hostile and Eeka too much of a stranger in her own house to be of service, did not press his demand for horses, or reveal his reason for wanting them. For him the chief event of a week spent at Ansbach was a letter from Von Katte with the bad news that his request for furlough had been refused. Frederick wrote back to meet him at the Hague, leave or no leave. He sent his collaborator a manifesto he had drawn up, stating the reasons for his flight; it would be published as soon as they were both safely in Holland. Frederick also wrote to Peter Christopher von Keith, who was at Wesel, on the Prussian side of the Rhine, giving him similar directions.

Von Katte's cousin, the cavalry officer, who had delivered the letter and promised to send the reply, seemed well disposed. Frederick asked him if he would be his companion on a little journey. The answer was a startled no. The Captain said it would be dangerous for a pair of men to travel alone in this part of the country; unlike Prussia, where crime was held to a minimum, there were band of robbers and gypsies hidden in the hills. He begged Frederick to give up the idea and, in taking his leave, kissed the hem of Frederick's coat, an unusual act of homage. It was not robbers and gypsies the Captain feared; he had guessed Frederick's intention and later warned Colonel von Rochow to keep an eye upon his "highborn subordinate."

Having failed to corrupt the relative of one of his friends, Frederick tried to corrupt a relative of the other. A younger brother of Peter Christopher von Keith was now one of the King's pages, a guileless youth, with none of the sharpness and audacity Frederick took for granted as a family characteristic. After leaving Ansbach, at a town near Augsburg, Frederick beckoned to the boy and asked him to see if somewhere along their way he could hire a pair of saddle horses.

"Where does Your Royal Highness want to go?" young Keith asked in all innocence.

"Where do you think?"

"I don't know."

"From the place I am going there is no return," Frederick said enigmatically. He added that anyone who decided to go with him would never regret it.

At Augsburg Frederick gave the page some money and told him to buy himself a plain blue coat. He himself bought some red cloth and had it made up by a tailor. There was time for this because several days were spent at Augsburg, the country round-about having a sentimental interest for Frederick William. It had been the scene of various battles with the French he had witnessed as a young man and he wanted to relive those happy days.

At Heilbronn the train of carriages quitted the valley of the Neckar it had been following and turned toward the Rhine. By this time Frederick had clearly in mind both the hour and place of his absconding; from the little town of Sinnsheim at two A.M. on August fifth he and young Keith would ride away to freedom.

But the evening of August fourth found the party short of its goal, at Steinfurth, a village so small that there was no inn and no hospitable castle in the neighborhood. There were, however, a number of big, substantial barns at the edge of the town. As twilight fell the travelers scattered to find themselves beds in the hay, a circumstance favorable to Frederick, since it gave an excuse to go to bed fully clothed. He told young Keith to get the horses—there must be plenty hereabout—and to bring them around at two o'clock in the morning.

At two o'clock Frederick rose and put on his new red coat. He went to the door of the barn. Keith was not there. For half an hour Frederick stood, looking out into the moonlight, listening with anguished ear for the sound of horses' hooves.

Grummersbach, the valet, appeared. He had wakened and found Frederick missing. Where was the Prince going, he asked anxiously? "To the King," Frederick said, though he must have realized how absurd the reply sounded at this small hour of the morning. Grummersbach vanished. He had gone to wake Von Rochow, for in a moment the Colonel came running, followed by the two other officers, Von Buddenbrock and Von Waldow, who rode with Von Rochow in Frederick's carriage. Then, most unwelcome of all to Frederick's sight, Count von Seckendorf joined the group at the door.

Without a word, Frederick turned back into the barn. He took off his red coat and felt about for that of his uniform. A moment after he had gone a figure materialized from the shadows, leading two saddled horses.

"Whose horses are those?" Von Rochow called out.

"They're for the pages," Keith replied.

"You go to the devil, you and your horses," Rochow roared. And Keith went, as if the devil was behind him instead of before.

On the evening of that same day, but many hours later, for the sun had risen, had traveled across the sky and was about to go down again, Mannheim was reached. The sixth of August was a Sunday. The King, as usual, went to church, followed by his retinue. After service young Keith trailed his master and, in a moment when Frederick William was alone, fell on his knees before him. The boy relieved himself of his terrible secret as though it were a vomit.

The King said nothing, but a few minutes later, on his way to dinner, he drew Von Rochow aside. "Fritz," he said in a fierce, low voice, "has tried to desert. I am amazed no one has thought to tell me! You Von Rochow, are responsible on your head, on your neck, and on your military rank, to deliver him to me, alive or dead, at Wesel. I haven't time to say more. Tell Von Buddenbrock and Von Waldow."

"He won't escape us, sire," Von Rochow murmured.

This was a chilling moment for the Colonel but for the King, no doubt, a moment of ferocious triumph. Frederick William had tried to goad his son into an act of open rebellion. Now the act had been performed, and Fritz could be dealt with. Fritz had tried to desert. Desertion was the crime most cruelly punished by the Prussian army code. In Frederick's case it might encompass treason, or even—the King's imagination had been working overtime—regicide.

At Mannheim, the capital of the Palatinate, there were a number of Frenchmen who had come to visit the Elector. Frederick William saw them as secret agents, with whom Frederick had made a rendezvous. "I am surprised to see you here," the King said ironically across the dinner table. "I thought you might be at Paris."

Frederick chose to treat this remark as if it were a joke, but he had caught the hidden meaning. Some witness of the Steinfurth fiasco had betrayed him; he had no suspicion it was Keith. On a scrap of paper Frederick wrote, "Things look bad. Do what you can to get us off." He slipped the note into the page's hand in passing.

The chances of getting off, however, were nil. Frederick could not move without the sound of footsteps following behind him. It was easier for the watchers to keep him in sight when, at Frankfurt, horsepower was abandoned and the party embarked on a river boat that would take them down the Rhine to Wesel. At all important river towns, Mannheim, Darmstadt, Frankfurt, Mainz, Bonn, Cologne, the Prussian visitors were entertained, and Frederick William and Seckendorf spoke for a united German front. However burdened he might be by private concerns, Frederick William would be faithful to the Emperor. His son, as Crown Prince, was treated with consideration, but realized he was as much a prisoner as though he wore a pair of handcuffs and was led about by a chain.

At Bonn Frederick, having heard his father whisper to Von Rochow to be vigilant, made a desperate appeal to Count von Seckendorf. He told the Austrian Ambassador he had meant to run away, but then had thought of the consequences to Wilhelmina, to his mother and to his friends, Von Katte and Von Keith. If the King would forgive them all, he, Frederick, would tell everything; otherwise, nothing would make him confess. "Lead me out of this labyrinth," Frederick begged, one of the phrases that meant so much to him and to Wilhelmina having slipped from his tongue.

Seckendorf agreed to speak to the King, but gave no assurance of amnesty.

On August twelfth the traveling boat anchored beneath the walls of Wesel. Its occupants stepped ashore on Prussian soil, and the fiction of Frederick's freedom was no longer necessary. As he crossed the courtyard of the fortress, two officers closed in from either side and told him he was under arrest. Frederick was led before his Commander-in-Chief.

It was soon being said by those who did not witness the meeting that when Frederick appeared his father rushed at him with drawn sword. The governor of the fortress sprang between them, crying, "You can run me through, but spare your son!" No mention of this melodramatic episode was included in the minutes kept of Frederick's interrogation, but its tone was sinister throughout. Frederick was warned by his father to tell the truth; if he didn't, there were ways of getting it out of him.

"Why did you try to do such a wicked thing as this?"

"Because Your Majesty has been so hostile. Over and over you have proved that you hated me."

Throughout the hearing the prisoner struck back when he could and kept his wits about him, swiftly sorting out what was hopeless to conceal from what might be left in shadow, or unsaid. Frederick insisted he had meant no harm to his father, or to the state; he insisted also it was he who had persuaded Von Katte and the brothers Keith.

The elder Keith, Peter Christopher, was out of harm's way, having followed instructions and crossed over into Holland just before the royal party arrived. Frederick William sent an officer post haste to The Hague, armed with a request for extradition, but Keith had already left for England. Frederick was pressed hard to admit this was also per agreement. He repeated, however, what he had said to Seckendorf: the idea of England as asylum had been given up because it might reflect on Wilhelmina or her mother, neither of whom had had any part in Frederick's schemes.

After the first examination, the questions were put by Colonel von Derschau of the Wesel garrison; Frederick William remained invisible. Was this a good sign? Frederick could not be sure, but he wrote his "dear Papa," asking for pardon and liberty. There was no reply.

Frederick found, as every prisoner finds with horror, that he was cut off from communication with the rest of the world. There were no answers to his questions. He did not even know where he was being taken when, on August fifteenth, 1730, he left Wesel with the three men with whom he had set out from Potsdam a month earlier, Von Rochow, Von Buddenbrock and Von Waldow.

Frederick William had thought first of sending Fritz to Spandau, but decided the more remote fortress of Küstrin in West Prussia would be the safer prison. The trio of officers had been given their instructions. They were to travel day and night. Large towns were to be avoided. Meals were to be eaten in the carriage, and when Frederick had to relieve himself, the stop should be in open country where there were no hedges, no thickets, no hiding place for a fugitive. If a rescuing party should attack the carriage and its escort—the idea of international conspiracy was still in the King's mind—Frederick should be shot rather than allowed to escape.

Frederick William had sent word to Berlin of what had happened—a letter to General von Grumbkow; a letter to Sophia Dorothea's chief lady-in-waiting, Madame von Kamecke, which read: "Fritz has attempted to desert. I have had to arrest him. I ask you to tell my wife so as not to terrify her, and to pity an unhappy father."

Strongly contrasted was a note to Sophia Dorothea herself: "I have arrested the scoundrel Fritz and will treat him with the severity his crime and cowardice deserve. I no longer consider him as my son. He has dishonored my family. Such as he should not be allowed to live."

The King had also sent an order for the arrest of Von Katte. He was afraid Katte might have been warned by Wilhelmina. Between his daughter and his son's friend, a mythical connection was building up in Frederick William's mind.

Chapter 12

On the evening of August twelfth, 1730, the day Frederick was arrested at Wesel, Sophia Dorothea had returned from one of her evening receptions at Mon Bijou and was seated in front of her dressing table when a loud crash was heard in an adjoining room where *objets d'art* were stored. The Queen thought a large vase of Chinese porcelain must have toppled over, but one of her ladies who flew to investigate found everything in perfect order. The door had hardly been closed when the noise broke out again. After a third manifestation in the storeroom, groans and a wailing noise sounded in the corridor between the Queen's bedchamber and the King's.

Sophia Dorothea, candelabra held high, went to investigate, her ladies, less intrepid than she, tiptoeing after. The sounds were heard again, but there seemed to be nothing to account for them. The corridor was empty, every door on either hand was locked. Though Wilhelmina was not present, she heard of the outbreak of poltergeist activity the following day and was told by her mother to mark down the date upon her calendar.

That afternoon there was a concert at Mon Bijou. Wilhelmina played accompaniments for the soloists on the clavecin. She had finished her part of the program and was just going into the cardroom when Von Katte, who never missed a musical event at the pleasure pavilion, barred her way. Katte was out of

[99]

favor not only with Wilhelmina, but with the Queen. They both had heard he was talking openly of Frederick's leaving the country and had boasted of his friendship with the Prince. He also boasted of owning a miniature of Wilhelmina, which he refused to give up when the Queen sent one of her ladies to confiscate it. Wilhelmina would have passed Von Katte now without a word if he had not said in a low, beseeching voice, "Let me speak to you for a moment—for your brother's sake."

What the young man had to say concerned himself rather than Frederick. Katte was in despair, he vowed, because of Wilhelmina's anger. He had not encouraged Frederick to run away; he had urged patience and restraint. This was true to a certain extent, but Wilhelmina was too prejudiced against any interloper between her brother and herself to be convinced. Nor did she believe Katte's assertion that Frederick would never go off without him. "I swear it on my head," Katte exclaimed.

"I can see your head wobbling about on your shoulders," Wilhelmina said severely. "If you don't look out, I may see it rolling at your feet."

Katte seemed to enjoy Wilhelmina's scolding. When she took him to task for keeping her likeness, he said he had painted the miniature himself from an original Frederick had lent him. It had only been shown to a few intimate friends as an example of his skill. At present he felt quite easy in his mind concerning "his dear prince," for even if Frederick should be caught in an attempt to escape, no harm could come to him. "After all, he is heir to the throne. No one would want to offend him."

Wilhelmina was irritated. To hear Von Katte talk, one would think King Frederick William no longer reigned in Prussia! "You are playing a dangerous game," she warned. "I only hope I'm a false prophet."

Katte said flippantly that if he lost his head it would be in a good cause, but he was sure his prince would never let him suffer.

There the conversation ended. Wilhelmina found it more disturbing than the ghostly thumps and groans reported by the

Queen. Disturbing also was the behavior of General von Grumbkow, who, like Katte, forced himself upon Wilhelmina and tried to talk to her of Frederick. During the heyday of Sir Charles Hotham in Berlin Grumbkow had had a hangdog look; now he was debonair. Weighing every word he spoke with distrust, Wilhelmina wondered what Grumbkow was trying to convey when he said mysteriously she would soon see what a good friend he was to her and to Frederick.

On August sixteenth there was a ball at Mon Bijou, a deferred celebration of the King's birthday. Sophia Dorothea's dining room was decorated with lanterns. The supper table had been converted into a miniature flower garden; beside each plate stood an appropriate favor. Wilhelmina was reminded of childhood birthday parties and could hardly wait for supper to be over so that the dancing could begin. It was six years now since she had danced; she had been quarantined at the time of Eeka's wedding; earlier, her father's attack of pietism had dampened gaiety.

Wilhelmina forgot time was passing as she rediscovered how well and how joyously she moved to music. "For heaven's sake, let me dance my fill!" she cried impatiently when one of the Queen's ladies came to tell her how late it was. "I may not have another chance for a very long while."

A half-hour later there was a second interruption. "Haven't you eyes in your head?" the lady chided. "Look at the Queen."

Wilhelmina looked and saw her mother pale. Sophia Dorothea was talking breathlessly with Madame von Sonsfeld and Madame von Kamecke in a far corner of the room.

"Is it my brother?"

There was no answer. Before the music could begin again, Sophia Dorothea wished her guests a gracious goodnight. During the short drive back to the palace she was so forbiddingly silent that no one in the carriage spoke.

As soon as Wilhelmina was alone with Madame von Sonsfeld, she clamored for an explanation. At first the governess would say nothing, but when Wilhelmina cried out hysterically that Frederick was dead, Sonsine relented. She told of the letter Madame von Kamecke had received from the King.

After a brief and sleepless night Wilhelmina was called to her mother's room to read the second and more terrible letter. She also heard of Von Katte's arrest. Frederick's friend had been warned by the Danish Minister, who had heard of the catastrophe at Wesel from Grumbkow; Grumbkow, apparently, was the first in Berlin to get word from the King. Instead of throwing himself upon a horse and galloping away, Hans Hermann had lingered to burn his papers and to contrive a special saddle in which he could hide money and what documents he decided to take with him. He was still at his lodgings when his superior officer, who was in no hurry to carry out the King's orders, came to find him and to put a seal on everything in Katte's room.

With horror, Wilhelmina and her mother realized that all the very private, the very seditious, letters they had written to Frederick over the years might have been left with Katte for safekeeping. For Frederick's sake, and for their own, they must find out if the letters were there and, if so, how this mass of damaging evidence could be destroyed.

Sophia Dorothea's first idea was to work upon the sympathies of Marshal Natzmer, Katte's superior, a kindly man. She would use as intermediary her chaplain, Parson Rhinebeck, but when the Chaplain was summoned to the palace he sent word he was too ill to leave his bed, too ill with fright, presumably. Equally terrified, equally anxious to avoid responsibility, was Countess Fink, one of the Queen's ladies, who early the following morning came to Wilhelmina's room.

The night before the Countess had gone home to find a large sealed box, addressed to the Queen, which had been left at her house by two men wearing masks. An unsigned note declared the box to be filled with Frederick's correspondence. The lady did not dare deliver it and did not dare keep it. She could not bear to hand it over to the King! What should she do?

After consultation with the Queen, after long, anxious discussion, it was decided to send for the box openly; to smuggle it into the palace would be too difficult and too incriminating. Sophia Dorothea wanted to burn the letters at once and to tell her husband she had thought them unimportant. Wilhelmina had a more subtle scheme. The letters should be destroyed, but new and utterly innocent ones should be written to take their place. This would mean much hard work, for time was short. It must be done with the greatest secrecy.

Sophia Dorothea gave her entire household a day's holiday. There was one woman Wilhelmina was particularly glad to be rid of, Frau Ramen, a lady's maid, her mother's latest confidante and under suspicion of being a paid informer to the King. Left alone with Frederick's writing case, the conspirators found it too heavy to lift. They had to call in a man servant, a trusty fellow who had been with the Queen for many years.

For a long time Wilhelmina tried unsuccessfully to pry off the seals without breaking them. She asked the valet to see what he could do.

"Why I have a seal like this in my pocket," the man cried. "I found it in the garden of Mon Bijou." Katte's seal—no doubt of that! A moment later the wax had been splintered, the cords had been slashed, and the lock of the writing case was forced.

No wonder the box was heavy! It contained some fifteen hundred letters, the bulk of them being letters that had traveled surreptitiously to Frederick, telling of Sophia Dorothea's intrigues with England and of the harsh and satirical judgments passed upon Frederick William by his wife and daughter. Some of Wilhelmina's letters also had messages written in lemon juice, criticizing the Queen's behavior and her blind faith in Frau Ramen. These sheets of paper had been heated and the messages were now visible; Wilhelmina was embarrassed by the thought of her mother's seeing them. Fortunately Sophia Dorothea was called out of the room for a moment, and before she came back the mass of paper had been fed to the fire.

There was still left in the box a large number of letters from various people to be examined, also scraps of paper on which Frederick had written notes on his historical and philosophic reading. There was a pocketbook containing a thousand thalers, some odd bits of jewelry and precious stones, and a chit from Frederick to Von Katte, written in May, when they were both at the camp at Radewitz and hoped to go off to England via Leipzig.

This most dangerous proof of complicity went up in smoke. Wilhelmina and Sophia Dorothea trimmed their pens. During the next three days and nights they wrote, between them, seven hundred letters. They were careful to use paper that had the proper watermark for the year in which the originals had been written. They were careful also to follow the chronology of events and to be innocuous to the point of boredom—no needle thrusts of wit, no entertaining sarcasm. When they put their compositions into the case, it still looked suspiciously empty. Wilhelmina would have continued to write doggedly, but Sophia Dorothea was becoming so nervous that she vetoed further effort. The box was filled with odds and ends of paper, padlocked, corded and sealed exactly as before.

A few days later some of the King's servants arrived in Berlin ahead of their master. They could tell the anxious mother and sister nothing of Frederick except his having been at Wesel when they left.

On August twenty-ninth Frederick William arrived in Berlin.

✦ ✦ ✦

Sophia Dorothea was alone in the King's room when the fearsome figure of her husband appeared, tramping down the corridor where, on the evening of Frederick's arrest, premonitory groans and shrieks had sounded. As soon as he caught sight of his wife Frederick William shouted, "Your miserable son is dead!"

"What—you've killed him!" Sophia Dorothea shrieked. "You had the barbarity—"

"Yes, and now I want the letters."

"Oh God, my son—oh God, my son," Sophia Dorothea moaned as she stumbled toward her room, where Wilhelmina, her brother and sisters and several of the Queen's ladies were gathered. Through the open door they had heard everything. Sophia Dorothea picked up the casket, which was now light enough for her to carry, and disappeared. When she returned all tried to comfort her. Frau Ramen declared there was definite proof of Frederick's being still alive.

Suddenly the King was among them. There was the moment's silence of the herd that has just caught sight of its predator. As if hypnotized, Wilhelmina and the other children moved forward to kiss their father's hand, but at sight of his eldest daughter, Frederick William's face turned dusky red, his eyes rolled, foam appeared at the corners of his mouth. "Wretched scum," he shrieked. "You dare show yourself! You're going to keep company with your criminal brother!"

Wilhelmina was snatched at so roughly that her long hair fell down upon her shoulders. Wrapping it about his fist, Frederick William dragged her about, striking her savage blows in the face. As she fell, Madame von Sonsfeld caught her. After Wilhelmina was down the King would have trampled on her if the others had not thrown themselves between. The victim was dragged to a chair by the open window. Sophia Dorothea, all courage and presence of mind gone, ran back and forth in the room, screaming and beating the air with her hands.

Above his wife's cries, Frederick William shouted that Fritz was still alive, but soon would be dead. Wilhelmina would be shut up between four high walls for the rest of her life. She was guilty of aiding Frederick in the crime of *lèse majesté* and of having been the mistress of Von Katte, by whom she had had several children.

"That's not so," Madame von Sonsfeld protested stoutly. "Whoever told Your Majesty that was telling a lie!"

But Frederick William did not hear her. Nor did he hear Wilhelmina's feebly voiced offer to marry the Duke of Weissenfels if Frederick's life was spared. At this moment Von Katte was being led across the courtyard by four guards. A porter followed, carrying Frederick's box of letters. A servant came to say the prisoner had arrived.

"Now I'll have the evidence to convict that devil of a Fritz and that riffraff of a Wilhelmina," Frederick William roared.

Frau Ramen ran after the King and, plucking at his sleeve, begged him to kill the Prince, if he would, but spare the Queen. A far more valiant figure stood between Frederick William and the door. Madame von Kamecke, the senior lady-in-waiting, was short of stature. Dumpy, but indomitable, she drew herself up to a full five feet and spoke like a prophetess of ancient Israel.

"Your Majesty has always prided himself on being a just and God-fearing prince," the little lady declared. "God has showered you with blessings, and now you should tremble at the thought of sinning aganist His word. Two great kings have been punished for shedding their sons' blood, Philip II [of Spain] and Peter the Great [of Russia]. Both of them died without male issue; their kingdoms have been devastated by wars. They themselves have become the horror of all mankind. Control yourself, sire. A first outbreak might be forgiven, but unless you make an effort to get the better of your anger, you will suffer for it!"

Frederick William had allowed Madame von Kamecke to speak without interruption. He stood looking at her for a moment in silence. In his ordinary tone of voice he said, "You're very bold to talk to me like that, but I am not angry with you. You mean well. You are sincere, and I like you all the better for it. Go calm my wife." He left the room.

Wilhelmina, whose face was swollen and bleeding, was lifted out of her chair. She was trembling so violently that she couldn't walk without support. While Von Katte was being examined she was hidden away in the part of the palace where her father was least likely to find her.

Later Wilhelmina heard how Von Katte was assaulted by the King, and how Grumbkow had had to interfere before the investigation could begin; the return to sanity accomplished by Madame von Kamecke's tongue lashing had only been temporary. One bit of Katte's evidence counted against Wilhelmina. He said—and said truly—that once he had given the Princess a letter from her brother. This was enough to condemn her as a conspirator in the King's eyes. He ordered Wilhelmina to be guarded in her room until she could be questioned and sent to a less comfortable prison.

Sophia Dorothea bid her daughter a long, a passionate, farewell. Her last words, whispered in Wilhelmina's ear, cautioned her to keep secret the affair of the forged letters and to say no to every question. Wilhelmina was carried in a sedan chair across the courtyard of the palace, where a large crowd had collected. Since the Queen's rooms were on the ground floor and the windows stood open, much of what had happened within could be seen and heard. It was now common knowledge that the King had cruelly beaten his daughter and threatened to kill his son.

FOR SEVERAL WEEKS Wilhelmina kept to her bed. Her head ached. Her bruises were long in healing. She still trembled uncontrollably when she tried to walk or to lift her arms higher than the level of her shoulders. Madame von Sonsfeld and Nurse Mermann were her only companions, though twice Wilhelmina was visited by her mother's maid, Frau Ramen, who told her Frederick would be brought to Berlin on his way to Spandau; he and Wilhelmina would be questioned at the same time. The idea of an inquisition was terrifying, but all the following day Wilhelmina reclined in her chair by the window, hoping she might at least catch a glimpse of her brother as he was being led across the courtyard. There was no sign of him there, and no indication of his being anywhere else in the city. Shortly after, Wilhelmina was told of Frederick's being many miles away at Küstrin.

On September thirteenth the King left for Wusterhausen, and that same evening Sophia Dorothea came to see her daughter. She gave what consolation and what news she could. That Wilhelmina might escape the ordeal of prison and a rigid examination seemed likely now. She would be interested, the Queen thought, to hear of her father's having proposed a marriage between his daughter Sophia and the Hereditary Prince of Bayreuth, who was about to complete his education by a visit to France and Holland.

"Now I don't need to fear for you in that quarter," the Queen said. "It will be a good enough match for Sophie, but it would have been most unsuitable for you."

Later Sophia Dorothea announced with a satisfied air that the young prince had died of a fever in Paris. Wilhelmina thought this a pity. Much good had been told her of Bayreuth; he might have made her sister happy. "I am sorry to hear it," she said.

"And I am charmed," Sophia Dorothea exclaimed. "It's one worry the less for me."

From all of this it was plain that the Queen's fighting spirit had returned and that her intentions were unaltered.

After her mother had gone to join the King at Wusterhausen the days passed quietly for Wilhelmina. She became used to never leaving her room. An inner corridor leading to it was unguarded, so that she could be visited by her sisters as well as by some of the Queen's ladies who had been left behind in Berlin. Wilhelmina read, she wrote, she amused herself by composing music. Had it not been for the uncertainties of the future and her fears for Frederick she might have been languidly happy.

A way to communicate with Küstrin soon was found. Madame von Sonsfeld had a brother there, a major. Wilhelmina wrote guardedly to Frederick, and before the end of September she had heard from him. "I am alive, I am well, and I am bearing up as best I can," he told her. Her little letter had been kissed a thousand times. If he had some paint he would daub a picture of himself and send it to her—but what a mad idea! How could anyone paint a picture of all he felt, his love for her, his admiration?

Frederick was glad Wilhelmina was in Berlin and not at Potsdam or Wusterhausen. He himself found his prison more endurable than those hateful places. But she had said so little, she had been so reticent! He wanted to know more. Were there no lemon trees in Berlin to provide juice for secret messages?

Frederick's tone in this and later communications was playful, and, though he complained of "a father's hatred being the worst misfortune," his playfulness implied a hopeful outlook. Wilhelmina was not so optimistic. She lay awake at night to fret over news that came in late October. A court martial was to judge Frederick's case. He would be declared a heretic, he prophesied; the verdict would reflect the "will of the Master." But what of that? Nothing mattered as long as Wilhelmina knew her brother to be innocent. There were enough good people left in this corrupted world to keep them in touch with one another.

> My dearest sister, as long as I know you're happy I will be happy also in my prison. *Chi ha tempo, ha vita* [time is on our side]. That thought should console us. I only wish from the bottom of my heart we needed no intermediary and that those happy days were here again when your *principe* and my *principessa* made sweet music.

This letter, the last of a series, did not travel the accustomed route, but was handed in at Frau Mermann's door by a stranger. The poor woman lived in fear that she and her husband might suffer for their close connection with the Princess. A few days earlier a sergeant of police had come to them with a package that he said was from Lieutenant von Katte. They refused to accept it at first, but when they learned the parcel contained a picture, the miniature Katte had painted of Wilhelmina, they bravely changed their minds. If the miniature should fall into the King's hands, it would give substance to his insane notion of a liaison between his daughter and Frederick's accomplice.

Wilhelmina waited in great suspense to hear the decision of the military court. She was told that Frederick would be imprisoned for a year, but that Von Katte had received a life sentence. It seemed a harsh verdict—but *chi ha tempo, ha vita.* Weeks went by before Wilhelmina learned by chance, and with horror, of having been deceived. Katte was dead. And Frederick? In the interval no word had come to Wilhelmina from Küstrin.

✦ ✦ ✦

Should Frederick die? All during September, all during the last days of summer into autumn, the idea flashed in and out of Frederick William's mind. He was blinded by it in his moments of madness. The hints of bloody vengeance he dropped at the Tabagie sobered his semidrunken friends; foreign ministers who were present, wrote home shocked reports of his mutterings to their governments.

"May God protect good men from having unnatural children," Frederick William wrote to his friend, the Prince of Anhalt-Dessau. "It is a great sorrow. But before God and humankind, I have a clear conscience. I tried everything [with Fritz]. Scoldings, punishments, kindness and forgiveness—nothing helped. I have a hundred witnesses . . . "

Out of the mouths of the hundred witnesses had come reports of Frederick's extravagances, chief manifestation being his library of three thousand books, hidden away in a house near the palace. The books, as well as Frederick's saddle horses, musical instruments and his wardrobe of Paris clothes, must be sold. The books were packed in barrels and sent off thriftily to Amsterdam, where they would fetch a higher price than in Berlin. For Jacques Duhan, who had built up the collection and who, as Frederick's "spiritual father," had taught him the love of reading, there was prison at Memel. A fine was imposed on the banking house that had supplied the Prince with money.

One day early in September, two grim-faced individuals, a man and a woman, appeared at the ivy-covered cottage of Cantor Ritter in Potsdam. The duets with Doris, the little presents Frederick had given her, were now on record for the archives of state. The terrified girl learned that her visitors were the regimental doctor and a midwife, who had come to give her a physical examination. She was found to be a virgin. Later Herr Hofrat Leute appeared, a malevolent hobgoblin in spectacles and a wig, who read out an order that Doris Ritter, a woman of lewd morals, should be imprisoned for life, but first should be publicly whipped before the City Hall, her father's house, and at all four corners of the town. Doris fainted, and fainted again after the first beating. Her executioners, more merciful than her judge, carried her off, unconscious, to the spinning house, the woman's section of the Spandau Prison.

But of this Frederick knew nothing. During his first days at Küstrin no one would speak to him. His door was unlocked three times a day for food and water to be carried in and the empty dishes and the soil bucket to be carried out. There was no candle in his cell and nothing to read except the Bible.

On the fifteenth of September the silence was broken. Frederick was given a final, a grilling, examination. One hundred and eighty-five questions had been prepared, to be answered in writing, the first three being: "Who is your father? Who is your overlord? Who is your Commander-in-Chief?" Some of what followed was so irregular, so outrageous from a legal point of view, that the examiner, an expert in military law, only consented to put the questions on special command of the King.

In conclusion, Frederick was asked what sort of punishment he deserved for having destroyed his honor and plotted desertion. "I don't think I have acted dishonorably," Frederick wrote, "though I am sorry for what I have done."

"Do you deserve to be King?"

"I cannot be my own judge."

"Having compromised your honor, would you abdicate to save your life?"

"I don't value my life as highly as that."

Frederick could see that his father was counting on fatigue forcing him to abdicate his rights of succession. He would not be caught so easily. Nor did he believe now that his father meant to kill him. His spirits rose.

Frederick William, on the other hand, who was sleeping badly, who suffered from nightmares and who would leap from bed, screaming someone was after him with a knife, had received cautionary letters. George of England, Augustus of Poland, the Stadholder of Holland, and the Empress Anne of Russia, niece of the man whom Madame von Kamecke had spoken of as "a horror to all mankind," recommended leniency. The Emperor himself put in a reminder that Frederick could not be disinherited or put to death without his case being carefully reviewed by the Imperial Diet.

[112]

A court martial seemed to the King to be the best way out of his indecision. On October twenty-fifth, 1730, the council convened at Köpenick. It was composed of three major generals, three colonels, three lieutenant colonels, three majors, and three captains, who would vote by rank, but not as individuals. In case of a tie, the deciding vote would be cast by the presiding officer, General von der Schulenberg. Before the court was laid all the evidence concerning Frederick and lieutenants Von Keith, Von Katte, Von Spaen and Von Ingersleben.

After two days of hearings, the court retired to deliberate. It was unanimous in voting that Keith should be summoned by beat of drum, and, if he failed to appear—Keith was now in England—he should be hung in effigy. The minor malefactors, Von Spaen and Von Ingersleben, the one having ordered the traveling carriage at Leipzig, the other having introduced Frederick to Doris Ritter, were given short prison terms. When it came to Katte's case the vote was evenly divided between life imprisonment and death. General von der Schulenberg voted for imprisonment. For Frederick, the court refused to assign any sort of penalty; as prince, he was recommended to the King's mercy.

Frederick William felt he had been cheated. He ordered the court to meet again on October thirty-first to reconsider its findings, but failed to get a new verdict. These men, the King complained to Seckendorf, were time-servers and were "adoring the rising sun." As so often before, Frederick William saw himself dead and Fritz, unchastened, doing exactly as he wished, reversing all his father's policies, and, as climax, setting Von Katte free, loading him with honors. There was only one way to banish the horrid vision and to break Frederick's spirit: Katte must die.

To the Council of War the King condescended to explain that, though Von Katte had not actually deserted, he had abetted the much more serious crime of lèse majesté. The order for execution was signed on November second. An appeal for mercy had already come from the young man's father. Frederick William's reply was, "Your son is a scoundrel, and so is mine. What can we poor fathers do?" There was no reply at all to a moving petition from Von Katte's maternal grandfather, General Field Marshal von Wartensleben. The only concession to the family record of long, devoted service to the state was changing the penalty from death by hanging to death by decapitation.

The condemned man heard his sentence with unshaken courage. Von Katte was sustained by the sense of drama Wilhelmina had noted in him as well as by a stalwart religious faith. He was sure of God's mercy; he was sure he was about to die innocent and in a good cause. Eloquent letters of farewell were written to his family. On November third Von Katte started on the two day journey to Küstrin, where the execution would take place within sight of a certain prison window.

Frederick was completely unprepared. The restraints upon him had been relaxed and, as his letters to Wilhelmina showed, his mood was buoyant. When, early on the morning of November sixth, he was roused, given a plain brown suit to put on and taken to a room on the ground floor, he was merely puzzled. The news of what he was about to witness came like the slash of a knife. For two hours Frederick ran back and forth in his cell, beating against its walls, rattling at the door, shouting through the wicket for word to be sent at once to the King. He, Frederick, would do anything, he would abdicate, he would change places with Von Katte.

Frederick was still hysterical when the commandant of the fortress, the chaplain, and two husky guards entered the cell. Drums were throbbing in the square. There was the sound of marching feet. Frederick rushed to the window and pressed his face against the bars. The procession was passing so near that he could almost touch a shoulder had he been able to lean out. The prisoner was in the center of the column.

"Katte, dear Katte, forgive me! For the love of God, forgive me!" Frederick shouted.

The prisoner turned his head toward the window. "There is nothing to forgive . . . I die happy."

As Katte mounted the platform where the masked execu-

[114]

tioner was waiting for him, Frederick drew back. The two guards stepped forward and seized him each by an arm. He struggled helplessly. His body was forced against the bars. His head was held in position so he could not fail to see. Katte had refused the bandage for his eyes. He knelt down. Before the axe rose and fell Frederick had fainted.

Until two o'clock in the afternoon the body of Katte was left lying where it had fallen. The stained clothing blackened as the blood dried, but it could still be seen that the corpse was wearing a brown suit identical with the one Frederick had put on that morning.

Chapter 14

Two months after Von Katte's death, in January of 1731, Frederick William for the first time spoke of his eldest daughter. How was Wilhelmina? What was she doing? Sophia Dorothea's hopes revived. She had allied herself—it was an alliance of bitter necessity—with General von Grumbkow. The ever receptive General had been given four thousand British crowns on the off chance of his being able to bring about a renewed offer of marriage from England. As a result of his activities, Parson Rhinebeck, the Queen's chaplain, called on Mr. Guy Dickens, who had taken Sir Charles Hotham's place as ambassador extraordinary. As he entered the embassy the Parson said, "Thanks be to God, all is now calm and quiet and we may hope to see happier days." Dickens, who was strongly pro-Frederick and pro-Wilhelmina, wrote a warm dispatch to England on the subject of how easily happy days could be brought to Prussia.

Wilhelmina herself perceived something was afoot when she was visited by Eversmann, the palace chamberlain. This detested individual spoke threateningly of Weissenfels and Schwedt and of the immediate marriage of Wilhelmina's sister Sophia to the Prince of Bayreuth, who, it seemed, had not died of a fever at Paris, but was expected home at any moment. Wilhelmina would have paid little attention to Eversmann if she had not been warned by her mother to stand firm if pressure, pressure of any kind, was exerted in the wrong direction. Wilhelmina had been exhorted not to be a milksop and not to be afraid of everything. She had also been reminded of her mother's curse if she yielded to her father.

But Wilhelmina, without having taken counsel of anyone, not even of her dear Madame von Sonsfeld, had decided to yield. She recognized her own limitations. She had neither her mother's persistence, her mother's fortitude, nor her mother's physical stamina. Moreover, as price of her submission, Wilhelmina was determined to ask for a full pardon for Frederick. She had begun to hear from him again and knew he was released from prison, though still at Küstrin and still in semibondage.

When the moment for action came, however, Wilhelmina was shaken to the depths. It was not easy to cast off the allegiance of a lifetime. On May eleventh, 1731, four representatives of the King appeared in her room. Two of them, General von Grumbkow and General von Borcke, had been members of the delegation that waited on Sophia Dorothea a little more than a year earlier. Grumbkow was again the spokesman. He told Wilhelmina that the English negotiations had broken down. She, instead of her sister, was offered the Prince of Bayreuth, who was a relative and whom her mother had once been willing to accept. "Since you don't know him, madame," Grumbkow said with unconscious irony, "you can't have any great aversion for him." In addition, there would be a handsome dowry and freedom for Frederick. If Wilhelmina refused, she and Madame von Sonsfeld would go to prison.

"I'll say yes if my mother will consent," was Wilhelmina's answer.

Impossible. The King would take no ifs; Grumbkow was blandly positive. General von Borcke's eyes filled with tears. He begged Wilhelmina not to force him and his colleagues to be harsh.

The four messengers retired to the recess of a window to consult, as though they were a team of medical experts, while Wilhelmina, the suffering patient, paced back and forth from wall to wall of the room. She could see no way of escape from the knife. One of the delegates, Herr von Thulmeyer, who was of the Queen's party, came to her and said in a low voice he would appease Sophia Dorothea by telling her this was only a ruse of the King to prick England on.

Wilhelmina could not believe a ruse would work at this late date, or that her mother could be pacified so easily, but she told her visitors she would submit, even though this would bring more troubles tumbling down upon her. At Grumbkow's dictation, with tears rolling down her cheeks, Wilhelmina wrote out a formal statement of her decision to be delivered to both Frederick William and Sophia Dorothea. "I don't care about England, my only worry is the Queen," she cried despairingly.

"Never fear. We will bring her round," Herr von Thulmeyer said.

Long after he and his fellows had left the room Wilhelmina continued to weep. There was no feeling of accomplishment to sustain her, no one to applaud what she had done. Even Madame von Sonsfeld, who found her ex-pupil dampening the brocade of an armchair with her tears, was disapproving.

The following evening Eversmann came with a note from the King: "I am very glad, my dear Wilhelmina, that you are going to do what your father wants. God will bless you, and I will never forsake you. I will take care of you for the rest of your life."

From the Queen, to whom Wilhelmina had written abjectly and at great length, bringing forward every argument, every excuse, there came a terrible outpouring: "You have stabbed me to the heart. You have caused me the greatest sorrow of my entire life. I had placed all my hopes in you—but how little did I know you! . . . I no longer look on you as a daughter . . . You need not count on me in the future, for I will never forgive you."

The meetings with her parents were of a piece with their written communications. Wilhelmina was tenderly kissed by her father, who, the last time he had seen her, had struck her in the face. Her mother raged. Only Frederick, promptly informed, dealt with her gently.

Frederick was afraid his *carissima sorella* had sacrificed herself in vain, for though a solemn oath had been taken to set him free, the oath had been sworn by that slippery rascal, Grumbkow. Frederick would have liked Wilhelmina to be guided by her own heart, rather than by the interests of the many who expected to profit by her marriage, one of those interested parties being himself.

In a latter letter—they came often now, though still *sub rosa*—Frederick unveiled a surprise: he had turned poet. Though books, the kind of books he prized were still denied him, he had by heart the rules laid down in Boileau's *Art of Poetry*. According to this universally accepted authority, verse should show balance, lucidity, good sense and wit; it should pay eternal homage to the ancients, an homage that came easily to Frederick, who had never been forced to study his classics in the schoolroom. To become a poet overnight would be impossible; Frederick was well aware of that, but at least a pastime had been found for many dull and empty hours. Frederick's first poem was enclosed, an "Ode Addressed to My Sister." In it Wilhelmina was represented as Iris, the female counterpart of Mercury, bringing messages to mortal men from the gods, her rainbow path the road to inspiration.

Reverting to the subject of marriage, and to sober, unadorned prose, Frederick said he had heard the Prince of Bayreuth was a pleasant youth. He would try to like him, but only for Wilhelmina's sake. He himself loved his sister better than any husband, any brother, any member of her family, could. He had hoped she might dazzle all of Europe with her talents, and only England could have given her sufficient scope. In quiet Bayreuth, however, Wilhelmina might be happier than at the English court, and it was reassuring to think they might meet more frequently than if they had to ask permission from an arrogant, interfering British Parliament.

By the time this letter was received negotiations had been

opened with Bayreuth, and Wilhelmina's fate had been settled. Only a few days after she was restored to the prickly bosom of her family, guests began to arrive for the spring review at Potsdam, among them being the Duke and Duchess of Brunswick-Bevern and their son, a prospective husband for Charlotte. Having reached the age of fourteen, Lotte was the next in line for betrothal.

The King had gone to bed early on the evening of May twenty-seventh so as to be up at four o'clock for the final spit and polish of his troops. Sophia Dorothea was entertaining the company with a game of cards when a carriage was heard in the courtyard below, drawing up at the entrance reserved for royalty. The Queen stiffened with horror and surprise when she learned who the latecomer was—the Prince of Bayreuth. That detestable young man, she thought, was still at a safe distance, in France or Holland. He need not be seen this evening, but there would be no avoiding him on the morrow.

On the morrow, Wilhelmina, who had spent a sleepless night, was taken so ill on the parade ground she had to be removed from her mother's carriage and sent back to the palace. She did not meet her future husband, therefore, until later in the day.

Frederick of Brandenburg-Bayreuth, whose graceful bow was acknowledged by a profound curtsey, was tall and well made. He was not handsome, but he had a frank and friendly look Wilhelmina found more attractive than a high bridged nose, expressive eyes, or any other feature of rococo manly beauty. Except for a slight tendency to stammer, the Prince seemed unembarrassed and responsive—not that Wilhelmina dared to speak to him—not with her mother's cold, ferocious eye upon her!

Barely twenty, two years younger than Wilhelmina, Bayreuth seemed able to cope with any situation. Two days later, a date was set for the exchange of rings. Sophia Dorothea had been so threatened by her husband that as long as he was in the room she hid her feelings. When the King had left, her manner changed. The Prince, instead of ignoring her snubs, said he knew the reason for them; she had wanted a crown for her daughter. Though he himself would never have dared propose the match, and though he would feel honored to be united with such a distinguished princess as Wilhelmina, he did not want to force himself upon the family. If Wilhelmina or her mother wished to break the engagement, they should do so now before it was too late. This direct attack took the Queen by surprise. All she could find to say was that the King had spoken, and she and her daughter would obey.

Cannon thundered throughout the ceremony of betrothal. Wilhelmina's knees trembled so violently she had to lean on her mother for support. Frederick William was also glum. That morning Mr. Guy Dickens had called to show him a letter, just received from Lord Chesterfield, the British minister at The Hague, offering the long disputed, long withheld, single marriage. Frederick William had declined, but now, as always when a definite step in international relations had been taken, his mind was filled with queasy afterthoughts.

As for Sophia Dorothea, she had decided on a double course of action: she would put off the wedding as long as possible, and she would get rid of the Prince of Bayreuth by making him the most uncomfortable man in Prussia. It was fairly easy to persuade Frederick William it would take six months to ready the trousseau and etceteras, but the Queen was not always successful in her harassment of Bayreuth. She tried, for example, to embarrass him by describing Wilhelmina's elaborate education and comparing it with his own. Did *he* know all there was to know of history, geography, Italian, English, painting and music?

"Yes," the young man said with a smile, "and I know my creed and catechism, too."

Wilhelmina admired her fiancé's good humor and his self-control. She could only observe him from a distance, however, for her mother saw to it that they were never alone and scolded her for immodesty if she so much as smiled at the man with whom she might spend the rest of her life. Everyone noticed how cold and wooden the Princess was. The gossip even reached Frederick at Küstrin; in one of his letters he suggested a little less reserve, a little less frigidity.

But the chances for improvement were minimal, and Bayreuth's constancy was put to a severe test. The Prince was a good shot, a good rider, and could hold his liquor well, but he had had no military training whatsoever. Frederick William offered insistently the command of a regiment. It was accepted with great reluctance. Bayreuth had come here to be married and not to spend months in a garrison town learning an unwanted trade!

The evening before he was to leave Berlin, Wilhelmina was walking alone in the garden of Mon Bijou when her fiancé came hurrying after her. He had to tell her, he said, how unhappy he was to see that she disliked him. Or was there some other reason for her sadness? If she hated him, he would withdraw from the marriage contract and would brave the wrath of the King and of his father, the Margrave.

Wilhelmina stood motionless, tongue-tied. The moment called for eloquence. She should reward the Prince's consideration for her feelings by saying something gracious—but what could she say? The high-flown vocabulary of gallantry was unfamiliar to her except on the printed pages of a book. At last Wilhelmina managed to squeeze out a few stiff words, renewing the pledge she had been forced to give in public. This was as close as she could come to a declaration of love.

Though Bayreuth then declared he would have been doleful for the rest of his life if she rejected him, Wilhelmina had to wait for several weeks to be sure of his real, his personal, feelings. While he was away she went with the family for a final, purgatorial stay at Wusterhausen. Soon after he returned from his regiment in late October a flutter of interest in an alliance came from England to the King in roundabout fashion, the Margrave of Hesse acting as negotiator.

"Now your stupid marriage will be broken," Sophia Dorothea said, "and your good-for-nothing Prince will go home."

The Queen was amazed, as well as infuriated, by her daughter's reply. She had given in earlier, Wilhelmina said, to save her brother, but, having met the Prince, she was more than willing to keep her word, for she could find no fault in him.

This was not absolutely true. Wilhelmina had found a fault, a not very serious fault; at this time she could hardly consider it a threat to future happiness. The Prince had made himself so agreeable to all the family, except the Queen, that Charlotte, a mischief making adolescent if there ever was one, found him much more attractive than the heavy, serious Prince of Brunswick-Bevern, to whom she had just been pledged. Why not swap suitors, Lotte suggested? Before Wilhelmina could protest, her engagement ring had been snatched from her hand and her sister's had been substituted for it. It took time, teasing, and eventually the interference of the Queen to get the right token back upon the right finger. Wilhelmina was all the more annoyed because she had noticed how readily her fiancé responded to Lotte's flirtatious advances.

When the Prince heard, however, that an English envoy was closeted with the King, he seemed very much depressed. For a whole day he could hardly speak to anyone. An entirely different, a smiling, young man came down to dinner and whispered in Wilhelmina's ear that all was well; her father had again said no. For the first time Wilhelmina felt she would find a friend, perhaps a lover, in her future husband.

✦ ✦ ✦

November twentieth, 1731, at six o'clock in the evening—the day and the hour for the wedding had been set. Frederick William wanted the English relatives to hear how well he married his eldest daughter; his preparations were more elaborate than they had been for Eeka's wedding. A large train of artillery was ordered to Berlin to fire the bridal salutes; regimental bands were brought from distant provinces.

The dressing of the bride began early in the afternoon and continued hour after hour. Sophia Dorothea, who was officially in charge, was still playing for time and still was looking for a miracle to halt the ceremony. She was too sorrowful to pay attention to what she was doing. No sooner was Wilhelmina's hair pinned up on one side of her head than it fell down on the other. All the artificial curl was brushed away, but, as it turned out, this made little difference. Wilhelmina was to wear the royal crown of Prussia, and, since the circlet was found to be much too big for her head, a tight fitting velvet cap was inserted as a cushion, completely concealing the coiffeur. Wilhelmina thought she had looked like a little boy with her hair falling across her forehead, but now she looked like a madwoman!

The wedding gown of silver tissue was so stiff with Spanish lace and had such a lengthy train that Wilhelmina could hardly move about. Closely observed, she stumbled and dragged her way through the series of state apartments which had been decorated at the time of the visit of Augustus the Strong in 1728. In the final room the bridegroom was waiting for her, wearing a white embroidered coat, and soon the guns were set to thundering throughout the city.

Weary, head aching from its weight of gold and precious stones, Wilhelmina presided at a banquet to which thirty-four royalty sat down. Later she and her husband led the torch dance, an ancient German folkway combining the emotions of war and mating. Torches flared before and behind as the company paraded to the roar of trumpets and the thumping of drums.

Nothing was to be done by halves. After the bridal bed had been inspected, the bride was undressed by the female guests and the groom by the males. Wilhelmina was blindfolded and, lifting the crown from her head, held it out while all the unmarried girls in the room circled about her. The winner of the trophy was eight-year-old Amelia, the youngest of the Hohenzollern sisters. Even after the newlyweds were in bed together they had to listen to the singing of a prothalamion and the preaching of a jocose sermon on matrimony by Frederick William.

For a week the Prince and Princess of Bayreuth were the hero and heroine of every court function. Wilhelmina enjoyed herself whenever there was dancing. On November twenty-third a ball was given for seven hundred couples at the palace. Wilhelmina was halted in the middle of a minuet by General von Grumbkow, who exclaimed goodhumoredly, "Mon Dieu, madame, you must have been bitten by the tarantula! Don't you see that some strangers have just arrived?"

Wilhelmina looked and saw a group of persons at the farther end of the room, among them a young man in a plain gray suit whom she did not recognize.

Grumbkow was beaming. "Go kiss the Crown Prince," he said, "for there he is!"

"But which one is he?" Wilhelmina cried.

Grumbkow pointed to the stranger in gray, and Wilhelmina ran to throw herself into Frederick's arms. She wept, she laughed, she dragged her brother by the hand to where the King was standing and fell upon her knees.

"Are you satisfied with me now?" Frederick William asked.

For answer, Wilhelmina clung to Frederick and kissed him again and again. But it was true she had not known him. He had put on weight and stature. The willowy youth, with the haunting eyes, had gone; the young man who had taken his place was less beautiful, Wilhelmina thought. How deep did the difference run? Had Frederick really changed for the worse?

✛ PART 2 ✛

[Chapter 15]

THE changes Wilhelmina had noted with dismay in her brother after their reunion in 1731 were changes of growth, an acceleration of the maturing process. While Wilhelmina would never fully recover from the effects of the ordeal through which they both had passed, Frederick had been toughened by it. More important still, he had learned to accept the role of king-to-be from which he had tried so hard to escape.

Every detail of the tragedy at Küstrin had been arranged in advance by Frederick William. He had written to Pastor Müller, the chaplain of the Küstrin regiment, ordering him to be present at Von Katte's execution and to go to Frederick's room as soon as Katte's head had fallen. He and all others in the cell should kneel down and pray with the prisoner for repentance. From certain of Frederick's replies at his hearings, Frederick William suspected his son of a belief in the Calvinist doctrine of predestinaton. In his discourse Müller should press home the point that it is wicked to believe some are brought into this world to do good and others evil. He could quote scriptural passages combatting the odious dogma, but it would be better to phrase the argument himself and to make it potent. Frederick had a subtle mind; his conversion would not be easy.

Müller did precisely what he had been told to do, but the

scene the King had imagined could not take place. Frederick had not yet recovered from his fainting attack when Müller arrived. The Parson returned later in the day, at two o'clock, just as Katte's corpse was being lifted into its coffin and carried away. Frederick had been staring at it for hours and was in no condition to speak to anyone. He could neither eat nor sleep. During the night he began to hallucinate. Those who came to his door to listen heard him moaning and talking to someone, someone who was not there. In the morning Frederick said to General Lepell, the governor of Küstrin, "The King thought he had taken Katte from me, but he couldn't. He's here. I can see him standing before me now!"

The visits of the Chaplain—for Müller came and came again —seemed proof to Frederick that he himself was being groomed for death. It would hardly be worthwhile to sweep away the bloody sand in the square before another execution took place. All the arguments brought forward against predestination were familiar and acceptable; Frederick could believe in God's forgiveness, but not in his father's.

But he must believe, Müller insisted. He brought Frederick the final testament of Von Katte, in which the dead man urged his princely friend to submit to the King. A few days later Müller produced an authentic offer: if Frederick would take a solemn oath of obedience, he would be allowed to leave the fortress, though not the town. He would be given work to do in the local office of administration. Frederick had to see the King's letter before he could believe that Müller was speaking true, that life would go on, that there was a future.

The taking of the oath was a mere matter of routine. On November seventeenth, 1730, five generals, two colonels and Councillor von Thulmeyer came from Wusterhausen, bringing with them a list of the culprit's sins. The King, on reading over the document, had objected to the final paragraph, in which Frederick, after admitting his transgressions, was to swear on his honor to obey. "This is a rubbishy oath," Frederick William commented. "He has got to submit—the rogue—or else give up his rights to the crown and the electorship."

Frederick put his name at the bottom of the revised paragraph without demur, and the whole company then marched to the garrison church for a service of prayer and thanksgiving.

The following Monday Frederick went to work at the Küstrin Office of War and Domain Administration. This body had been in existence for only seven years and was part of the masterly scheme for efficiency in government devised by Frederick William. More than a quarter of the land in this particular district was held by the crown, the leases being granted to the highest bidders. The matters dealt with by the board were those of practical farming, of ploughing and manuring, of sowing and reaping, of the breeding of cattle, the grinding of grain and the brewing of beer. Complaints were received and reports and recommendations were sent on to higher authority.

Frederick's part in all of this was minuscule. He sat by himself at a small table in the rear of the room, listening to the debates, sketching surreptitious caricatures of members of the board, and making himself useful now and again as copyist. When documents were to be signed, his signature came last and without a distinguishing title.

No one in the office, however, failed to realize that here was an unusual underling. Frederick was closely observed, not as a clerk, but as the future ruler of Prussia. The director of the bureau, Herr Hille, passed on his findings to two interested parties, the King and General von Grumbkow. After a month he could report the Prince was "as cheerful as a chaffinch." Frederick would never be afraid of hard work—but how ignorant he was! "His Royal Highness has the poetics of Aristotle at his fingertips, but whether his ancestors won [the city of] Magdebourg at a game of cards or in some other way he doesn't know."

The Prince's quickness of perception and his wit were noted, also his politeness to everyone, particularly to those of inferior rank—a pleasing trait, perhaps, but also a shortcoming. To Hille, a middle-class servant of the Prussian state, Frederick's elaborate courtesy seemed alien and more appropriate to a French marquis than to a German heir apparent. When King, he would tend to favor foreigners.

Frederick, though later he came to give Hille his due for efficiency, thought the Director shrewish, false, pedantic and horribly untidy in his dress. He was in no mood to make allowances, for, though he realized the value of the worm's eye view he was getting of the Prussian economy, his life outside the office was cruelly tedious and exasperating. Again Frederick's father had drawn up one of those schedules in which he so delighted, detailing how every moment of the day should be spent, from reveille—at five in summer, six in winter—to early supper and the bedtime prayer. Frederick could waste no time and could never be alone. One of the three men with whom he kept frugal house—Counsellor von Wolden, Count von Natzmer, and Lieutenant von Rohwedel—must sleep in his room at night and be with him wherever he went. Only to them could he speak, and only in German. No music, no French books, no guests for dinner. Even the topics for conversation were outlined. Politics and philosophy should not be mentioned at the Prince's table; even such drily speculative subjects as geometry and military tactics were taboo.

Boredom was inevitable, and boredom was the one thing Frederick could not abide. He liked Von Wolden, distrusted Rohwedel, and found he and Von Natzmer had the most in common. Natzmer was an amateur musician and helped Frederick in writing a solo for the flute. In spite of regulations, the two sat up late one night in February, talking of Prussia's destiny in Europe.

Frederick put his views in writing the following day. He saw his country as a force for peace. Because of her geographical position, Prussia was too exposed to risk an aggressive war. She should try to knit together her scattered provinces by annexing neighboring territory, but this should be done by negotiation, not by violence. Frederick concluded with the hope that Prussia would remain the refuge for all who were persecuted: the Protestant, the widow, the orphan and the poor.

There was nothing in this analysis to offend Frederick William, but it was a misdemeanor for the office boy at Küstrin to think of himself as a politician or a strategist. Fritz was allowed to write to his father once a month, but without hope of his letters being answered. What he needed, quite literally, was a friend at court, and the friend who had already presented himself was General von Grumbkow, who soon would be so active in arranging Wilhelmina's engagement to the Prince of Bayreuth. Given the uncertain state of Frederick William's health —the King had again been ill in February—Grumbkow felt he should lose no time in propitiating Frederick. He had managed to be present on various significant occasions, at one of Frederick's hearings and at Frederick's taking of the oath in November. At this time Grumbkow had a long talk with the prisoner and was given Katte's testament, stained with Frederick's tears. The gift was a relinquishment, not a symbol of trust. Frederick realized the reason for Grumbkow's friendliness and his offers of help. In accepting them he would pit his wits against those of one of the cleverest men in Prussia.

Open correspondence was impossible, but Frederick and the General were able to communicate through Hille and Von Wolden, who were in constant touch both with the King and his chief adviser. In April, along with a report of Frederick's having been ailing and of tempers wearing thin at Küstrin, Grumbkow received from Hille a royal marriage scheme Frederick had conceived. It was in line with the idea of Prussia as mediator between rival power blocs. Frederick proposed that he should marry one of the Emperor's daughters, either Maria Theresa or her younger sister, Maria Anna, and that Wilhelmina should marry the Prince of Wales. Grumbkow, who was just about to call officially on Wilhelmina and tell her she could not possibly dislike a husband she had never seen, scoffed at the idea. He pointed out its obvious drawbacks: the difference in religion, the impossibility of getting the King to accept any suggestion coming from Frederick. Nevertheless Grumbkow passed on the information to Seckendorf, knowing that through him it would reach Vienna.

A few weeks later the General came again to Küstrin and, without saying he had brought up the subject himself, told Frederick his father wanted him to marry. He mentioned the names of three princesses who might be suitable, all of them Protestant, the Princess of Gotha, the Princess of Eisenach, and Elizabeth Christina of Brunswick-Bevern, who was a niece of the Empress. Frederick said he did not want to marry, but would do almost anything to be free of his present tether.

The time was approaching, Grumbkow thought, when father and son should meet. Frederick agreed, but dreaded the encounter. The King had written him once in reply to a letter of thanks for some religious books, but the tone of the communication was not encouraging. There were many underlinings, many references to Frederick's "false heart," his "pride of intellect," and "the damnable and godless doctrine of predestination."

It was Frederick William's wanting to make sure Fritz had been purged of heresy that brought them face to face. August fifteenth, the King's birthday, was chosen as a suitable date. Frederick and his guardians were summoned to government house. They went with forebodings which were fully realized.

The King spoke at first with restraint, but soon with headlong passion. "I was harsh with you at the Saxon camp," he said, "hoping you would mend your ways . . . I could have forgiven youthful follies, but not dishonorable deeds. Now I am determined to put an end to your stubbornness. Listen to this, my fine fellow, if you were sixty or seventy years old, I would still force you to submit."

Frederick, crouched at his father's feet, was told what would have happened if he had gone to England. His mother would have been suspected of connivance, his sister would have been put for life into a place "where she could see neither sun nor moon." And this was not all. The Prussian army would have marched into Hanover, burning and laying waste. Blood would have been spilt; lives would have been sacrificed.

Having mounted his high horse, Frederick William rode it hard. All the seemingly trivial, but basic, grievances were rehearsed. Frederick had been unhappy at Wusterhausen. Did he like Küstrin any better? He had called his uniform a shroud. Did he prefer the threadbare suit he had been wearing since last November?

Frederick remained prostrate throughout and only spoke when forced to speak. He may have flinched, but he did not fail to answer the most cruel question of all: "Did you lead Katte astray, or he you?"

"I led him astray."

"I'm glad to hear you speak the truth at last," Frederick William cried.

To demonstrate repentance, Frederick kissed his father's feet, not once, but twice. He followed the King to his carriage and would have bowed to the earth again if Frederick William had not lifted him up, embraced and kissed him upon the cheek before at least a hundred persons who had gathered outside the building.

To Director Hille, one of the many onlookers who shed tears —for here was high drama—Frederick said, "I never thought my father had any feeling for me whatsoever; now I am almost certain that he has."

This was a simple statement of fact, and one of which Frederick took immediate advantage. Three days after the reconciliation, he wrote, asking to be reinstated in the army. He had asked too soon. It would be better, his father replied, to send an orchestra, some actors and actresses, some French ballet dancers, fops and hussies, to Küstrin, for that was the kind of company Frederick preferred to a regiment of grenadiers.

Horses and a wagon, however, were provided, and a new outfit of clothes, so that Frederick, still chaperoned, could visit the farms and rural industries with which he had become so familiar on paper. With exercise and wider range, Frederick's health improved and he began to put on the weight Wilhelmina was to find so unbecoming. Twice and sometimes three or four times a week letters went to Wusterhausen or Potsdam, describing what Frederick had seen and what he thought ought to be done to improve the husbandry of the crown lands. Here the soil needed a long-term program of enrichment, there the farm buildings had rotted and were about to fall down. As in the letters he wrote in childhood, Frederick added flattery, pledges of affection, and items he was sure his father would appreciate: a tall man had been seen, a present of fat pork was on its way, in a certain forest there was said to be a stag with antlers of twenty-eight prongs. One who looked over Frederick's shoulder while he wrote would have thought the attention of this dutiful and loving son never strayed far from the humdrum duties of the day.

Quite a different picture of Frederick's inner life was given to Grumbkow. In the hearing of Hille and Wolden, Grumbkow's eyes and ears, Frederick mused upon the future. When king, he would attend to business, but would leave details to subordinates, he said. At his court there would be theater, dancing and much music—but never music at mealtimes, for then he would forget to eat. As generalissimo, he would wear a uniform, but over it a richly embroidered overcoat. And if his father should force him to marry a woman he did not like he would put her aside as soon as he was master.

This last statement was repeated over and over, for marriage was a matter of immediate importance. Frederick had a conversation on the subject with General von der Schulenberg, who had presided over the court martial last October and voted against Katte's execution. Von der Schulenberg had just come from Vienna. Frederick wanted to know what matrimonial plans were hatching in the Austrian capital. Was there a chance of his being given either of the Emperor's daughters, or perhaps the Duchess of Mecklenburg, who was rich and beautiful and a niece of the Czarina Anne of Russia?

Certainly not, said Schulenberg. In either case Frederick

would have to give up his religion and perhaps his kingship. Would he be willing to do that?

"No, that would be foolish," Frederick replied. But, he added, it would be foolish to expect him to be faithful to a woman he disliked, and it would be only fair to give the lady the privileges he enjoyed. They each could go their separate ways.

Schulenberg was shocked. He chided the Prince on the score of morality and health.

Oh, the doctors could cure you of the clap, Frederick said airily. He was young and wanted to enjoy himself. "You were young once yourself . . . And"—his tone was teasing—"who knows what you may have been up to lately in Vienna!"

"I have never been debauched," Schulenberg said huffily. "While I was in Vienna I never so much as touched a woman."

To Grumbkow the General wrote that Frederick liked to make fun of people. That was a great defect in a prince. Princes were all alike, and Frederick was no better than the rest.

✦ ✦ ✦

But while he was gaining the reputation of a libertine in certain quarters Frederick was carrying on a delicate and soulful flirtation with a woman for whom he felt the greatest respect and admiration. In one of the earliest letters written to his father, Frederick mentioned having inspected Tamsel, the estate of a Colonel von Wreech, with whom he went duck shooting. He said nothing about staying to dinner and meeting the Colonel's wife, for his new charter of liberties did not include association with women.

Like La Orczelska, Louisa Eleanora von Wreech was older than Frederick—twenty-three years to his nineteen. Tamsel was the rich inheritance she had brought to her marriage. The manor house had been built by her grandfather von Schöning, a famous general, who had returned from a campaign against the Turks, bringing with him Greek craftsmen to decorate his home. There was fine carving and paneling throughout the house, a picture gallery, spacious rooms, a spacious outlook.

Even if Frederick had not been hungry for a little luxury and female society he would have found his hostess charming. Eleanora was fond of poetry, and for the past six months poetry, so called, had been gushing from Frederick's pen, the average output of an hour's scribble being one hundred lines. Frederick warned his "dear cousin"—he was enchanted to find the lady a distant blood relation—that soon some grasshoppers would be coming her way, four-footed grasshoppers, who had been shooed off Mount Parnassus because they were of such inferior quality. He sent her an ode and an epistle he had been working on for several months in which some of the irritation he felt with his Küstrin associates found satiric vent.

To the ode, Eleanora replied in verse. Frederick's effusion had been loverlike, and she delicately suggested a more tempered friendship by saying her husband and all her household had helped her with her lines. Frederick came back with a little narrative: one day when he was walking by the banks of the Oder River he met Urania, the Muse of Poetry, who told him how his talented cousin had just been elected tenth member of the sacred band and how in future she would help him with his poetizing.

It was impossible for Frederick to come to Tamsel as often as he wished, though he was like a dog, he said, who is always getting into church and has to be put out. In November Frau von Wreech and her husband were going to Berlin for Wilhelmina's wedding, but Frederick had no thought of being invited there himself. He had sent a sorrowful ode to his sister, and to the fair cousin, a bitterly comic description of what the ultimate return of the prodigal would be like: a mock triumphal march —he riding on a donkey, with a club in his hand, a straw hat on the back of his head; his followers bumping along in a dung cart; the procession headed by a flock of sheep, of mooing cows and squealing pigs.

When, at the last moment, he was summoned, Frederick went unwillingly. His subdued manner at the ball, which Wilhelmina took for coldness, was due to embarrassment at finding himself in his dull gray suit among so many well dressed people and also to fear of fresh humiliation from his father. To this was added, no doubt, annoyance at seeing General von Grumbkow in his self-appointed role of master of ceremonies. Grumbkow had given Frederick a set of suggestions as to how he should behave if he wanted the King's favor, one of them being to show less affection for Wilhelmina than he felt.

The brother and sister had a chance to talk the day after their reunion, and some of the old rapture of exchanging confidences was rediscovered. When Wilhelmina's husband entered, Frederick's manner became politely formal. Wilhelmina was hurt because Frederick left so soon and because he had made so little effort to become better acquainted with his brother-in-law.

I COULD see plainly you doubted of my love, but I swear to you
it has not diminished," Frederick wrote after his return to
Küstrin.

Having judged Wilhelmina's husband to be a likeable but
commonplace young man, Frederick chose to look upon his sister's marriage as a sacrifice. She had been so noble, he exclaimed,
he so foolish! She had led him "out of the labyrinth." Now it
seemed once more as if their fates were similar, since they both
were headed for obscurity. That, however, could be a blessing,
for "peace of mind is better than riches or renown."

This philosophic truism may or may not have been a comfort
to Wilhelmina, who had just discovered how poor she was.
Trusting to her father's promise to care for her, Wilhelmina had
only recently inquired into the financial aspects of her marriage
and had found them closely tied to a business transaction between the Hohenzollerns of Bayreuth and the Hohenzollerns of
Brandenburg-Prussia a generation earlier.

In the time of Frederick I, Wilhelmina's grandfather, the
Margrave of Bayreuth had no son. His heir was his cousin, a poor
man with many children, who was willing to hand over his rights
of succession to the King of Prussia in exchange for a pension, a
modest home in the town of Weferlingen near Bamberg and the
education of his two sons. The elder of these sons, George Fred-

erick Charles, was now Wilhelmina's father-in-law—and the Margrave of Bayreuth. He had bought back his inheritance by agreeing to pay an indemnity to Prussia in annual installments. Since his predecessor had left debts and an empty exchequer, George Frederick Charles had had to borrow heavily and at heavy interest to satisfy his creditors and to keep up his indemnity payments.

Frederick William therefore gave the Margrave an interest free loan of two hundred and fifty thousand thalers, while Wilhelmina's marriage portion was pared down to less than half that amount. The cost of her father's gift of wedding silver had been deducted, as well as the cost of her husband's regiment. From what remained the income would be small. Wilhelmina, Sophia Dorothea was quick to point out, would have less money in her pocket than the head lady's maid of a Princess of Wales. Reminders of poverty, the Queen's continued persecution of her new son-in-law, and a sharp little quarrel between the latter and one of the wedding guests, Eeka's insufferable young husband, the Margrave of Ansbach, made Wilhelmina anxious to leave for her new home.

A few days after Christmas she fainted in church and thought it just a symptom of her nervous and debilitated state, but the doctors found her to be pregnant. This was good news for Frederick William, who could hardly wait to be a grandfather, but it was a blow to Sophia Dorothea. She had urged Wilhelmina not to have intercourse with her husband, since it would be easier to arrange a divorce if the marriage had not been consummated.

On January eleventh, 1732, husband and wife set out for Bayreuth. With them went Baron von Voight, the Prince's right-hand man, the companion of his travels. Wilhelmina's household included Madame von Sonsfeld, Madame von Sonsfeld's younger sister, Flora, and a niece of the two ladies, Dorothea von der Marwitz, a motherless girl of fourteen. It was necessary to get the King's permission for Dorothea to be one of the party. She and her two sisters were heiresses to the large fortune of their father, General von der Marwitz, and Frederick William did not want them to marry outside of Prussia. Wilhelmina had to promise not to find a fiancé for her youthful protegée in Bayreuth.

Ten strenuous, abnormally frigid days were spent upon roads, bad enough in summer, now deep with snow. On the second day out the carriage in which Wilhelmina was riding turned over. She was buried under an avalanche of luggage, atop of which two loaded pistols had been placed. Madame von Sonsfeld kept screaming, "Oh Lord Jesus have mercy on us," until she heard Wilhelmina laughing and calling out she was unhurt. The Prince, who had jumped out through the window, pulled his wife from under the debris and held her in his arms until the coach could be righted. Everyone expected a miscarriage and wanted Wilhelmina to rest in bed for several days, but she was eager to push on. Her longest journey hitherto had been to Wusterhausen, and in the last two days she had seen enough of the world to want to see more.

Mountains appeared after Leipzig had been passed. The Thuringian hills seemed mighty peaks to a girl who was lowland born and lowland bred. Wilhelmina was frightened by the steepness of the roads and preferred to get out and walk to being whacked about as the carriages jolted down from boulder to boulder.

At Hof the travelers crossed into Bayreuth. This part of the principality had once belonged to Austria, and its inhabitants were restive under margravial rule. Baron von Voight, a native son, urged Wilhelmina to make a good impression. She bowed until her back ached, but could hardly keep a straight face while all the notable and self-important citizens of the province passed before her. They had dug out of attic chests the moth-eaten finery, the flea-infested wigs of their fathers and grandfathers. At dinner these figures of fun were speechless until Wilhelmina introduced the subject of farming, and then she thought her guests would never stop talking. There were thirty of them about the board, and thirty were drunk before the meal was over.

The following day was Sunday; one could not travel on the Sabbath. Wilhelmina sat out a two hour sermon dealing with biblical marriages from Adam and Eve to Noah's flood. The men guffawed when the discourse became realistic, the ladies tittered and blushed, or tried to blush, while Wilhelmina, nose uplifted, became more and more sure she had come to live in Barbaria.

Nor was she delighted by her first view of Bayreuth proper, in spite of its picturesque situation, on a high plateau, surrounded by darkly wooded hills. The town had been almost completely destroyed during the Wars of Religion a hundred years ago. Most of the houses lining its streets, though fairly new, were unpretentious.

When Wilhelmina saw the margravial residence she was reminded of a building of which she had unpleasant memories, the Potsdam palace. Its outstanding feature was an octagonal tower, enclosing a ramp, up which horse and rider or horse and cart could climb. The interior of this onetime fortress was dilapidated. Wilhelmina was led down a corridor, thickly hung with cobwebs, to her bedroom suite, which might once have been splendid, for the ceilings of the rooms were carved and one could see here and there the traces of paint and gilding. The walls were covered with antique tapestry, so faded and so full of holes that the figures looked like ghosts which came to life as a draft blew through the chinks behind.

Wilhelmina's conductor on this first tour of inspection was her father-in-law, whom she had already met at the time of her wedding. George Frederick Charles was only forty-three years old and might once have been handsome, but he was now broken in health, cadaverous and bandy legged. His life had not been easy: a shabby childhood at Weferlingen, an unhappy marriage—he was now, thank God, a widower—years of travel and litigation to obtain his birthright, years thereafter of scrimping to maintain it. Drink had been, and was, his solace. The King of Prussia might overindulge at dinner, but the Margrave of Bayreuth was fuddled all day long.

Since he stood much in awe of his son's wife, and since he had heard how well read she was, George Frederick Charles would talk of nothing but books. The only two he had read apparently were Fénélon's *Telemachus*, the romance which had so captivated Frederick as a boy, and a once fashionable, but now outdated, *History of Rome*. Wilhelmina found the conversation wearisome and longed to sit down. She had just made the acquaintance of two sisters-in-law, Charlotte, who was very beautiful but who seemed to be mentally retarded, and Wilhelmina, far less handsome and far less ingratiating than her simpleminded sister. There were two other members of the family to be encountered later, William, a younger brother of the Prince, who was with his regiment in Italy, and the Margrave's younger brother, Prince Albert of Culmbach, who was also in the Emperor's service.

After the newcomer to Bayreuth had been granted a few days in which to recuperate, a series of entertainments was given in her honor. Wilhelminia was too easily tired and too squeamish to appreciate what was done for her. The sight of food was nauseating, and she was in no condition to learn to like the unfamiliar cuisine of Bayreuth, in which onions, raisins and vinegar seemed to be the chief ingredients. Though she had been so anxious to leave Prussia, Wilhelmina was suffering from homesickness as well as the unpleasant side effects of pregnancy. She herself realized that in Prussia she had absorbed a scale of values by which everything here seemed second-rate. The austerity of her father's court had been based on voluntary saving and not on necessity.

Wilhelmina also failed to find the peace in obscurity Frederick had predicted. Though cabals were not as violent in Bayreuth as in Berlin, here hearts could burn and tempers sputter. Just because she was a newcomer, Wilhelmina was called upon to arbitrate family disagreements and to get favors from her father-in-law, whose mood was as unpredictable as that of most alcoholics. Wilhelmina had come to love her husband dearly, but saw less of him now than during their honeymoon. Much of the Prince's time was spent in hunting and he was a devil-may-care rider. After one nearly fatal accident, when the Prince's horse had collided with a tree and split its skull, Wilhelmina quaked each time she heard the hunting horn.

In the afternoons Wilhelmina took to retiring to her bed, ostensibly to rest, but actually to shed a few tears behind the curtains. Letters from home were snatched at eagerly, and none more so than the letters that came, still secretly, from Küstrin. There Frederick was passing through a crisis in which his feelings for his sister were involved and in which her name was constantly invoked as patron saint.

✦ ✦ ✦

"I will take a wife only at the hands of my sister of Bayreuth," Frederick had written to General von Grumbkow.

Ever since his trip to Berlin Frederick had been carrying on a deceptively cheerful correspondence with the General, sending him snatches of humorous verse and piquant bulletins of life as it was lived in the "Küstrin monastery." Frederick knew he had a good audience, for the General was literate and had a hearty appetite for satire unless the satire was directed at himself. Beneath the frosting of Frederick's wit, however, lay the heavy, ill-flavored substance of his anxiety. What was in store for him? What would Vienna decide and, via Seckendorf and Grumbkow, suggest as a self-conceived idea to Frederick William?

Marriage was never mentioned in the letters passing back and forth between father and son, but through his intermediaries Frederick learned that the field of choice was narrowing down to no choice at all, a single candidate, the Princess of Brunswick-Bevern. Frederick had heard she was dull. "I don't want a stupid wife," he lamented. "Unless I can carry on a reasonable conversation with her, she is not for me."

In January Frederick fell ill, his delicate digestive apparatus being thrown off balance by mental turmoil. His weight declined to the low level it had reached in prison. Promise from his father of a house, a set of silver, horses and a carriage was so ominously domestic that for two nights the patient was unable to sleep.

Then there came a knocking on his bedroom door at dawn, and Frederick was roused to read a letter from his father, brought by special messenger, a letter which had been written on February fifth, 1732: "My dear son; You must know by now how much I love my children when they are obedient. I have thought of nothing else than your well-being and seeing you again in the army and married to a suitable wife."

Frederick William declared, somewhat naively, that he himself had reviewed all the princesses of Europe and had decided on Elizabeth Christina, the elder of the two daughters of the Duke and Duchess of Brunswick-Bevern. The girl was well brought up and modest, neither beautiful nor ugly; pious, too, "one of those creatures who fear God—and that is all important!" Although the wedding would not take place until next winter, a house had been bought for Frederick in Berlin, and in April he would be given his regiment. When he had a son he would be allowed to travel to foreign countries. As a final irony, Frederick was told to state his point of view.

There could be only a single point of view; Frederick was well aware of that. He replied immediately and submissively, on the same day pouring out to Grumbkow his sense of injury, his rage. Frederick's pride in himself as an individual had been stung by the reference to his producing an heir. Was that his only significance? He had hoped to serve the King with his sword and not by a certain intimate portion of his anatomy! As for the Princess, he pitied her from the depth of his heart, for she was going to be very, very sad.

In the letters, scribbled at frantic speed during the next few weeks, Frederick was now pathetic, now ferocious. He referred to his intended fiancée as "the corpus delicti," or "the abominable object of my desires." It was useless for Grumbkow to respond with a description of how the King had shed tears of joy on receiving Frederick's letter of consent, and how he, Grumbkow, had seen the Princess, who was already in Berlin with her parents. Elizabeth Christina, it seemed, was not at all bad looking and only a little shy and colorless.

But lack of color was the quality to which Frederick reacted most violently—that, and dismal piety. "I would rather be a cuckold or henpecked," he wrote, "than tied to a fool, who would drive me mad by her stupidities. . . . Better the biggest whore in Berlin than a religious fanatic." He would have the Princess spend some time with her grandmother, the Duchess of Brunswick, who was accounted worldly wise. He would have her get by heart Molière's *School for Wives* and *School for Husbands*. "For love of the wounds of Christ," Grumbkow was exhorted, "see to it that I am not forced to marry a woman I could never love . . . My only hope is in God, in you, and in my own firmness."

The date for Frederick's coming to Berlin to meet his "Dulcinea"—yet another hateful epithet—was twice deferred. Frederick continued to wheedle and threaten Grumbkow. At last he went too far, revealing incidentally that the demon of predestination had not been exorcised. He had been unhappy all his life, Frederick wrote. That perhaps was his fate, but there was one way out: he could always put a pistol to his head.

Grumbkow's reply was vigorous and tart. "I have just received your *beautiful* letter. Can I believe my eyes and ears! Your Royal Highness gives in meekly to the King and raves on to me like a madman. You would like me to meddle in affairs that could cost me my head. No, thank you kindly, monseigneur! My shirt is closer to my body than my vest . . . and I am not obliged to ruin myself and my poor family for love of one who is not my master. I am a God fearing man and don't want to attach myself to a prince who is planning suicide."

Frederick apologized, for he could not dispense with Grumbkow's services. But now it was the General's turn to lose some sleep. He told Von Wolden and Hille he was afraid Frederick would not be able to control himself when he came to Berlin. There would be a dangerous explosion—and for all he cared Frederick could marry the Lady Venus herself!

But there was no explosion. Grumbkow had underestimated Frederick's ability to make the best of a cruel situation. At one point in their correspondence Frederick had suggested his being allowed a visit of several weeks in Bayreuth, for he loved Wilhelmina "better than life itself." This reward for obedience was not forthcoming, but, on arrival in Berlin, Frederick was told he could write to his sister as often as he chose. Every few days thereafter a letter traveled southward by ordinary post.

Frederick, who was still trying to dispel the shadow that had fallen between him and his sister, wanted to make his attitude toward his marriage clear. His description of "the Person"—he could not bring himself to pen the name of his fiancée—was harsh, though he had to admit he exaggerated his distaste for Grumbkow's benefit. As their father had said, Elizabeth Christina was neither beautiful nor ugly. She had some good points —a pink and white complexion, softly curling blond hair—but her eyes were set too deep, her teeth were crooked and discolored, and her laugh was shrill. She walked like a peasant and danced like a duck. Though not entirely witless, the Person had been so badly educated she was unsure of herself and rarely spoke. "And so you can see, dear sister, whether or not she suits me." Only when the unfortunate girl had gone home to Brunswick would Frederick admit that Elizabeth Christina might have a kind heart.

Kind heart or no, Frederick could never, never love her. He loved only Wilhelmina and, on second thought, his mother. He thought of Wilhelmina all day long on March tenth, the day of his betrothal. It was as though he made his vows to her, and only because of her was Berlin bearable. Each time a door opened Frederick thought Wilhelmina might be coming in, and each time his heart sank as he realized his deception. Frederick begged Wilhelmina to send him some little thing she had worn for a week or two, a scarf, for instance, so he might wear it close to his heart, a talisman.

Chapter 17

WILHELMINA had been told by her father she should come home to bear her child. Frederick, who dreaded her ordeal, tried to make her feel she would be welcome in Berlin. He had spoken of her often to their mother. Though Sophia Dorothea still thought of Wilhelmina as a turncoat, she had been much disturbed by the discouraging reports of her daughter's pregnancy.

Wilhelmina was suffering from insomnia and violent attacks of asthma, her face turning blue as she struggled to suck the air into her lungs. In May, however, she and her husband set out for Prussia. They got as far as Himmelskron, the country house, a remodeled convent, where the Margrave spent most of his time. There a covey of doctors considered Wilhelmina's case and decided she would die if she went any farther. They discussed, in Latin, whether or not she should be bled and which vein should be opened. "I am in the hands of murderers," Wilhelmina wrote to Frederick. "They make my ears ache with their gibberish—but what can you do but laugh?"

It would be no laughing matter, however, if the opinion of Wilhelmina's father should run contra to medical advice. She humbly offered to risk her life to do as Frederick William wished and was relieved to hear she could stay where she was. The King was going on a journey to Prague for a conference with the Emperor. On his way home he would stop in Bayreuth; he was due to arrive there during the first week in August.

By midsummer Wilhelmina was at the Hermitage, an estate only a few miles from the capital which had been the plaything of the extravagant predecessor of George Frederick Charles. Wilhelmina had fallen in love with the place. There were walks through the woods, there was a cluster of hermit cells and a subterranean grotto, equipped with a fountain to drench the unwary visitor. Wilhelmina was so delighted with a nearby cottage her father-in-law had given her for a birthday present that she named it Mon Plaisir. The house, however, was so small it took a good deal of contriving to find accommodations for the King, for his staff, and for Eeka and her husband, who were summoned hastily from Ansbach for the visit.

Frederick William was in a benignant state of mind. He was pleased by the simplicity of Wilhelmina's establishment and was touched by her efforts to make him comfortable. "It seems as if I were at home," he said. "I find stools and tables and bathtubs just where I want them. I don't see how you managed to do so much on short notice."

The King was shocked, however, to see how badly Wilhelmina looked and how thin she had grown. Walking about to show him her property brought on an asthmatic attack. It seemed as if the baby, not due for several weeks, might be born at once, but it was not until her father and all other visitors had gone that Wilhelmina returned to Bayreuth, where, on August thirtieth, 1732, she gave birth to a daughter, who was christened Elizabeth Frederica Sophia. Wilhelmina had been in labor for forty-eight hours and came close to dying of exhaustion.

For a fortnight Frederick, who had been waiting anxiously for news of the birth, "suffered all that man could suffer." He had asked to be the child's godfather and hoped before long to see its mother, for Wilhelmina intended to come to Prussia as soon as she was able to travel; her husband had been recalled to his regiment, and she could not bear to be separated from him.

Frederick was told of an amazing violinist Wilhelmina had

discovered in Bayreuth whom she wanted to bring with her to delight his ears, but he advised her to leave her prodigy at home. It would make a better impression on their father to bring the baby and only a few attendants. If she wanted to get money— this was a secondary, but pressing, reason for her journey—she would have to play the part of penny-pinching *Hausfrau*.

This was undoubtedly true, but Wilhelmina, who thought she had been pinching pennies, but who actually had been more generous to the violinist and others than she realized, did not even have enough for traveling expenses. When she asked the Margrave to contribute he petulantly refused until commanded by Frederick William. Wilhelmina, also commanded by her father, had first to make a trip to Ansbach to patch up the latest quarrel between Eeka and her husband, and it was not until November that she set out for Berlin, with only enough in her purse to pay for post horses part of the way; the rest would have to be borrowed from members of the party. The baby, too young to travel so late in the season, was left in the care of Flora von Sonsfeld, Sonsine's sister, to save the cost of engaging a governess.

Wilhelmina was overjoyed to find her husband waiting for her in Berlin, but the greetings from the rest of the family were cool—or at least so they seemed to one who was painfully aware of being a poor relation. Though the King said he was glad to see his daughter and took an interest in the health of little Frederica, he refused, even more categorically than the Margrave, to be generous. The Queen's attitude fluctuated between veiled and open hostility. Her welcoming words to Wilhelmina were, "Why have you come?"

Frederick, though absent, had promised help. Frederick was with his newly acquired regiment at Ruppin, to the north of Berlin, living in a house next to one owned by Colonel von Wreech. He saw Eleanora only occasionally. She had tactfully put an end to their intimacy after his engagement was announced by inviting him for a last visit to Tamsel and by suggesting a valedictory exchange of pictures. Frederick's miniature was sent with the hope she would think of him sometimes and say, "He was a nice boy, but he bored me by loving me a little bit too much." Eleanora's full-scale portrait was handed over to Wilhelmina for safekeeping and was much admired in Bayreuth.

A rumor, nevertheless, was going about that Frederick was responsible for Frau von Wreech's latest pregnancy. The gossips who set the story in motion, Grumbkow and Seckendorf, were convinced their young friend had a taste for expensive women, and thought this might be a way of getting a hold upon him. They let him know Vienna would be glad to pay his debts. Frederick saw no reason why he should not accept the offer, for housekeeping on his father's allowance was almost impossible. For fear of the King's knowing what was going on, the money was being handed over little by little. Once a month a confidential servant of Grumbkow called at Frederick's house with a remittance, which in the correspondence between the two men was mentioned as "a book," while the receipt was termed "a song." Frederick had also made use of his powerful adversaries to get his teacher, Jacques Duhan, out of prison and installed as librarian to the Dowager Duchess of Brunswick. Doris Ritter, the other victim of Frederick's downfall, had been released after a year in the Spandau spinning house and had been dowered for a marriage arranged by her father.

Before Wilhelmina's arrival Frederick brought her financial difficulties to the attention of Grumbkow and Seckendorf. "If I knew how to make gold, I would pass on the secret to my poor sister of Bayreuth," Frederick wrote. "She certainly has need of it." Since at that time the Margrave's stinginess seemed the predominant factor, Frederick wished Wilhelmina's father-in-law "would remove himself from this earthly scene. If he was sure of plenty of brandy being distilled in heaven, he'd find full consolation there."

Early in December Frederick sent Wilhelmina some money via Herr Quantz, his secretly engaged flute teacher. It was little enough, he said; it would be better if she were a regular recipient of Austrian bounty. Unknown to Frederick William, an interview was arranged with Seckendorf. While echoing Frederick's hope that the Margrave of Bayreuth would drink himself to death before so very long, Seckendorf told Wilhelmina how grateful the Empress would be for her help in preparing Frederick for matrimony. He was being pushed in the opposite direction by his other female relatives. The Queen, as Wilhelmina herself could testify, spoke of Elizabeth Christina as a simpleton in Frederick's hearing, and sister Charlotte made the most spiteful comments on the fiancée's physical defects.

At Wolfenbuttel, the seat of the Brunswick-Beverns, everything possible was being done to better the situation. A governess had been appointed to sharpen the Princess's wits and smarten her appearance. A dancing master had been sent from Dresden to correct her ducklike motions on the ballroom floor. To Frederick, who complained periodically that he was not a donkey to be cudgeled into love and that he wished the Sultan of Morocco would run off with his Dulcinea, Grumbkow sent a letter from one of his married daughters who had seen Elizabeth Christina during the summer and found her much improved.

Meanwhile a curious alteration had taken place in the royal marriage market. Augustus the Strong of Saxony-Poland was dying. For years his massive physique had been gnawed by the diabetes that had necessitated the amputation of several toes. Augustus had designated his son, the fat prince whose elaborate wardrobe Frederick had envied at the Dresden carnival, to be elected as his successor in Poland, the Emperor's blessing thereto having been obtained by a somewhat tardy recognition of the Pragmatic Sanction. There was a strong rival candidate, however, in Stanislaus Leszczinski, a native Pole, ex-king and father-in-law to Louis XV of France. The great powers were astir, a new pattern of alignment was forming. In order to uphold the Saxon claim against the French, Austria would need the help of both England and Prussia.

In November Grumbkow was flabbergasted by a letter he received from Seckendorf, who was in Denmark and had just talked with Degenfeld-Schonburg, the Prussian ambassador.

Degenfeld proposed that Frederick should marry Anne, his English cousin, and that Elizabeth Christina should marry the Prince of Wales. An alternate plan, hatched by the English ambassador in Vienna, paired the brother of Elizabeth Christina with Anne of England and Lotte with Anne's brother. Grumbkow was to suggest these changes to Frederick William, along with an assurance of backing in the still unsettled Jülich-Berg affair.

"You don't know him," Grumbkow wrote to Seckendorf of the man they flattered so adroitly to his face. "He's not as stupid as you think! He hates the English and particularly that wishy-washy Prince of Wales. You break the news to him. I won't!"

Though the King remained officially unenlightened, he heard gossip of what was afoot and expressed his opinion of it with customary *brio* at sessions of the Tobacco Parliament. Sophia Dorothea was again uplifted until she broached the subject with Frederick when he came to Berlin for Christmas. Frederick's opinion of the Guelfs now coincided with that of his father. Complaints of her son's anti-British attitude and of the ruin of all her hopes for her two eldest children were poured into Wilhelmina's patient ear. When Frederick came to the throne, his mother said, with a catch in her voice, she would leave Berlin; she would never want to be a burden to him!

Though once more a confidante, Wilhelmina was still unsure of her mother's forgiveness. After a year of comparative freedom, she found it trying to adjust herself to her parents' whims and wishes. Her father, whose conscience had once so troubled him on the score of theater-going, now had a Master of the Revels, an acrobatic strong man, who had collected a troupe of players and was allowed to give Italian comedies, translated into German, before the court. All were forced to attend. These performances, in which Hans Wurst, the traditional Teutonic clown, played a prominent part, seemed idiotic and endless to Wilhelmina. She sympathized with her sisters' governess, whose snores could sometimes be heard above the slapstick doings on the stage.

More serious trouble arose when in January Wilhelmina's husband fell ill with a consumptive cough. Frederick William sent all the doctors in Berlin, *en masse*, to examine the patient, but made the young man's life a burden by finding fault with everything he did, in particular with the performance of his military duties. Even a good-natured man can be pushed too hard. One night at a stag dinner, Bayreuth, less drunk than the rest of the company, described hotly and loudly what he would do if the King were not his father-in-law. Wilhelmina was the unhappy go-between in this quarrel.

"The way the King treats her and the Prince is pitiable," Frederick complained to Grumbkow. The least his benefactors could do for these unfortunates was to give them some small financial independence. Not long thereafter a readjustment was made in the disposal of Seckendorf's secret funds, some of the money that had been going to Frederick being deflected to his sister.

✦ ✦ ✦

But the time had come for the value of imperial bribes to be tested. On the first of February, 1733, Augustus died at Warsaw, and electioneering for a new king of Poland was brought into the open. Frederick was to be married in June at Salzdahlum, the Hanoverian seat of the Brunswick-Beverns. Only father and mother went with the reluctant bridegroom, though both Seckendorf and Grumbkow were of the party. Twenty-four hours before the wedding Seckendorf appeared in the King's bedroom so early in the morning that the King was still in bed. To a bemused Frederick William Seckendorf presented his plan for no wedding on the morrow and a whole new slate of betrothals, the climax being Frederick's eventual marriage to Anne of England.

Frederick William was too astonished to be angry. His rejection of the entire scheme began with, "If I didn't know you for an honest man, I would think I was dreaming." He assumed Frederick and his mother to be responsible and had to be convinced that Frederick was willing, if not eager, to keep his word.

"The ceremony is over, thank God . . . I am yours entirely," Frederick wrote to Wilhelmina on June twelfth. To demonstrate to the world in general his indifference to his bride, Frederick allowed himself to be seen fully dressed and sauntering about the courtyard of the castle less than an hour after he had been conducted to the bridal chamber by the wedding guests.

A few days later the Crown Prince and Crown Princess of Prussia made their entry into Berlin. Wilhelmina was introduced to her sister-in-law. She knew there was no reason for her to be jealous of this awkward, inhibited girl; her appraisal was dispassionate. Elizabeth Christina looked younger than her eighteen years. Her face was that of a child of twelve, a pretty child, if one could overlook the unattractive mouth, the inexpressive pale blue eyes. Frederick's introduction did not help his wife to conquer her embarrassment. "Here is a sister I adore," he said fervently and added that Wilhelmina should be consulted and her advice taken rather than that of the King and Queen.

Wilhelmina kissed the bride and, seeing the heat had damaged Elizabeth Christina's make-up, helped her to prink and repowder. Frederick swore beneath his breath when nothing was said in return for these services. "The least you can do is thank my sister," he exclaimed. But this was his only outburst; in general, he managed to be studiously polite.

As soon as the festivities were over the groom went back to his bachelor hall at Ruppin, while Elizabeth Christina and the rest of the company remained in Berlin. Fetes for Frederick and his bride merged into fetes for Charlotte and Charles of Brunswick-Bevern, who were married the day before Wilhelmina's twenty-fourth birthday, on July second, 1733. All during the succession of balls, reviews and theatrical performances Wilhelmina felt so ill she could scarcely drag herself about. At court functions she found herself paired with the Duchess of Brunswick, Elizabeth Christina's worldly grandmother, and was so annoyed when the old lady insisted on taking precedence that she once got into a carriage first and seated herself firmly on the right. These matters of protocol, always important to Wilhelmina, had acquired a double significance. She felt demoted, pushed aside; she had lost the title of Crown Princess of Prussia that had linked her name to Frederick's.

It was time now to go home. Wilhelmina and her husband were sure they were needed there, for the Bayreuth news had not been reassuring. Wilhelmina's psychotic sister-in-law Charlotte had been much depressed and had tried to throw herself out of a window; the baby, in spite of maternal protest, had been moved to Himmelskron during the dangerous period of teething; little Frederica's tippling grandfather had almost broken his neck by falling downstairs.

Permission to leave, however, was withheld. Having reviewed the Bayreuth regiment and found it in good condition, the King was beginning to value his daughter's husband. He wanted them both to stay on indefinitely and offered a salary and the services of an expert accountant to investigate the finances of Bayreuth. It took the combined efforts of Grumbkow, Seckendorf and Frederick, now a married man and high in favor, to get the young couple free on August twenty-eighth.

Wilhelmina did not see her brother again before she left. She and her mother wept at parting. It had been an ordeal for Sophia Dorothea to see another of her daughters, Charlotte, married to a man who was not the Prince of Wales. In Wilhelmina, the Queen had found a useful and familiar vent for her emotional vapors.

Frederick William, on the other hand, was sulky when he said goodbye. His daughter was to remember this with sorrow, and later her recollections of the entire visit were stark. Little had been gained. Wilhelmina had had glimpses of Frederick from time to time; her father had given her a grudging tithe of what he owed her as dower, and she had received her modest share of Austrian largesse. Yet none of these benefits, except perhaps the first, could compensate for the hurt to her feelings and her pride. Her health, she felt, had suffered.

To Frederick, Wilhelmina wrote, revealing the tragic sense of the past which had begun to weigh so heavily upon her. She would never return to Prussia, she vowed, until her brother was king of Prussia. She was now an alien, an exile. "Nothing could persuade me to set foot in that labyrinth again. I was so unhappy there it almost killed me! Though I have so many reasons to hate my native land, it is still dear to me because you are there."

Chapter 18

WHILE Wilhelmina and her husband were traveling
home to Bayreuth in the late summer of 1733 Stanislaus Leszczinski, the French-backed candidate for
the Polish throne, was making his way across Central Europe disguised as a coachman. On September eleventh Stanislaus arrived
in Warsaw and the following day was elected king of Poland
for the second time. As a puppet of Charles XII of Sweden,
Stanislaus's first experience of kingship had lasted only from
1704 to 1709. His second reign was even shorter. Ten days after
the election Stanislaus was on the run for Danzig, pursued by a
Russian army. The Polish Diet quickly changed its intimidated
mind, and a majority of votes was cast for Augustus of Saxony,
the imperial and Russian candidate. On October twelfth a
French army crossed the Rhine.

Now there would be another war fought not so much on Polish as on German soil. An attack on Austrian possessions in Italy
had already been launched. Without being summoned, Frederick went to Berlin to ask his father if he could go with the ten
thousand troops pledged by treaty to the Emperor. He wanted
to see how he would behave in battle, but his sympathies were
not involved. Frederick had no love for the son of Augustus the
Strong, and he felt he had been a victim of imperial policy all his
life. He told Wilhelmina he had been watching the European

turmoil with detached interest from his "mouse hole" at Ruppin.

Already the result of the disputed Polish election had been felt in Bayreuth. Wilhelmina came home to a warm welcome from her father-in-law and to find her baby daughter had grown to be "the finest child in all the world." Little Frederica was so endearing that her father got up early every morning to have her to himself for the first two hours of the day. He was soon off, however, for a visit to the imperial forces gathering at Heilbronn under the command of Frederick's father-in-law, the Duke of Brunswick-Bevern.

Wilhelmina was relieved when her husband returned at the end of three weeks, for he was spoiling for action, and she was afraid he would be as reckless in war as on the hunting field. Soon it seemed as if he might be forced to stay at home. Word came from Italy in November of the death of Prince William, the younger of the Margrave's two sons. There was now a single male heir in Bayreuth, and his life ought not to be risked for such an ephemeral object as the crown of Poland.

The question immediately arose, however, of the Prince's military status. He had inherited from his brother the command of an imperial regiment, recruited in Bayreuth by the late Margrave. George Frederick Charles wanted his son to resign his commission in the Prussian army to head this and a second regiment which was being formed for home service. This move, plus the arrest of a Prussian recruiting officer for poaching within the human game preserve of Bayreuth, roused the wrath of Frederick William. For once George Frederick Charles refused to back down. Wilhelmina, who had been in miserable health ever since her return from Berlin, was at the center of the storm. Her husband's future was at stake, she felt. He had married her for love, and now she was ruining his career!

"May I tell you something?" Frederick wrote. "You are much too sensitive and take things too much to heart. . . . Let me scold you a little, dearest sister. The worst is behind you, and all your other troubles can be solved."

The next trouble seemed so monstrous that Wilhelmina did not dare to put it on paper and could only hint, but Frederick was quick to guess the secret she had learned from Dorothea von der Marwitz, the young girl she had brought with her from Prussia, the niece of Sonsine and Flora von Sonsfeld. During the long absence of Wilhelmina and her husband, Flora, who had been left in charge of little Frederica and who was dumpy, good-humored, fat and fortyish, had become the darling of the Margrave's heart. He had offered her marriage, a title and a large financial settlement. Debt-ridden Bayreuth was threatened with disaster; a blow had been struck at Wilhelmina's pride. Worst of all were the repercussions one could predict with certainty in Prussia. When it was pointed out to Flora by Wilhelmina and Sonsine that Frederick William would take revenge for his daughter's reduction to second rank on the entire Sonsfeld clan, the good-natured little lady shed a few tears for lost grandeur and wrote a letter to the Margrave, telling him she could never be his wife.

A solution had been found to a problem Frederick had never been able to take too seriously. At about the same time he was told by his father he could go in the spring for a visit to the imperial army. Frederick could not be sure, however, of the promise being kept, for, as always, the royal mind was changed from day to day, and almost hour to hour.

Frederick William had never liked the idea of a united Saxony-Poland as his neighbor on the east. He had also been seriously snubbed. According to the secret treaty, signed at Berlin in 1728 between Prussia and Austria, the two nations would be on an equal footing in war, but no request for advice and leadership had come to Frederick William. All that was wanted from him was his quota of troops. The over-all commander would be Prince Eugene, the aging victor of countless battles. "Tell me," Frederick William wrote plaintively to the Prince of Anhalt-Dessau, "would you have thought we'd ever live to see this day —a war with the French, and Prussia left out in the cold?"

Frederick was in Berlin again in March. He envied Wilhelmina her absence from Castle Bewitched, he said. Added to the King's indecision and evil temper, induced by the most recent attack of gout, Lotte was there for a visit and, as usual, had managed to set everyone to quarreling. An added annoyance was the engagement of sister Sophie, just fifteen, to the Margrave of Brandenburg-Schwedt, the bête noire of Wilhelmina's girlhood, and twice the age of his intended victim. Wilhelmina could sympathize with Frederick's harassment and was sure he found comfort and support in Elizabeth Christina. Frederick's wife was seldom mentioned in the letters exchanged by brother and sister, but never without a dutiful tribute to her loyalty.

There was tension on either hand, for Frederick planned to stop in Bayreuth on his way to the Rhine. Wilhelmina danced for joy at thought of his coming and told everyone they should bow in passing to his picture, which hung above her harpsichord in the music room. She continued, however, to fear her husband's going against his father's wishes and was distressed when a letter came from Frederick William, saying he, Frederick, and all the royal cousins would be leaving for the front in six weeks' time. Was a son-in-law of Prussia to stay home, planting cabbages in Bayreuth, when all of the princes of the Empire were on the march? George Frederick Charles's permission was begged once more, but he continued to stand firm, upheld by an expression of sentiment in the Bayreuth Council. The war was unpopular in a land so close to the fighting area, a city so scarred by ancient battle.

In May the French were only eight miles from the Bayreuth border. There were stories of atrocities: children's faces slashed, women nailed to their beds, parsons slaughtered at their prayers. Ansbach was also threatened, and there Eeka and her husband were packing for flight. Wilhelmina considered where she would go in case of need; not to Prussia—of that she was sure. She waited anxiously the arrival of her Prussian defenders. Prince Eugene, apparently, was waiting also. He had abandoned Heilbronn; he had allowed the French to invest Phillipsburg.

At last the Prussian troops were on their way. On June thirtieth, 1734, Frederick left Berlin in advance of his still gouty father, the most minute instructions having been given to his two guardians, General von Kleist and General von der Schulenberg. As an observer, Frederick was to make careful notes of everything he saw, and was to gather information on such useful subjects as the durability of shoe leather on the march. He was to consort only with "virtuous princes," which would greatly restrict his social contacts. He was forbidden to play cards, or to have anything to do with women.

And he was not to visit Bayreuth until his return journey. Wilhelmina heard from Frederick on July second at Hof, the town where she had first become acquainted with her new land and its inhabitants. Frederick would obey the letter of his instructions, but would meet her somewhere outside the limits of Bayreuth proper.

At dawn of a hot July day Wilhelmina and her husband set out for the mountain town of Berneck. A mistake had been made in the rendezvous, and it was not until twenty-four hours later that the travelers met. Wilhelmina had been shaken about on precipitous roads, had survived a thunderstorm that seemed to crush the landscape flat, and had had no sleep. Frederick was horrified to see how exhausted and feeble she looked. They had a brief, tantalizing hour together, during which Frederick promised to wheedle the Margrave into letting his son join the army. When Wilhelmina protested, Frederick reassured her. He foresaw little fighting.

This prediction was confirmed. The military magic of the great Eugene had shriveled. His memory was failing; he did not always recognize old friends. Without any serious counterattack being made, Phillipsburg was taken. There were skirmishes in which Frederick's hand remained as steady on the bridle rein as though the hum of bullets was the hum of insects. All was well until Frederick William arrived. "We have a virtuoso here in camp who is driving us all crazy," Frederick wrote with fury.

"Pray with me that he leaves, or else you will have to build a madhouse and save a cell in it for me and for a lot of others who are about to lose their wits."

Even if he had not come to Phillipsburg in poor health, Frederick William would have been made sick by the confusion and inefficiency he saw there. Was this the force to which he had lent his hand for so many years? He himself could criticize Austrian defects, but when Frederick did so, he was accused of Francophilism and of filial disrespect. There was truth in the charge. Frederick William wrote to Sophia Dorothea that "Fritz seems to be ashamed of my being his father." Wilhelmina was informed by her brother that "Our fat man is off on the eighth [of August]. He has been ill and complains of pain in his chest, but he is taking good care, I notice, to avoid the way of all flesh!"

The King was to go down the Rhine to Wesel, and from there a short way into Holland. Possessed of Phillipsburg, the French were on the move, and so were the Prussian troops. So also was Wilhelmina's husband, who had received the word he had waited for so long. In camp he was proving to be an eager pupil and a popular recruit. Wilhelmina, however, was very uneasy until she heard her father had actually started for Wesel. She saw him as a menace to both her loves, for he might push them into a position of danger. Soon her feelings underwent a rapid change.

✦ ✦ ✦

It was Wilhelmina who heard first of Frederick William's having been stricken while on a visit to the Dutch ambassador, Van Ginkel; he had turned black in the face, it was said, and went to sleep standing up. "After the way he has treated us I don't know why we should care what happens to him," Wilhelmina wrote. But the voice of nature, as she called it, the metaphysical bond between parent and child, had spoken; she could not bear to think of the father she had once loved ill, in a strange place, and with none of his family to care for him.

The next word from the invalid came via Frederick, who was at Heidelberg and had made no move to hurry to his father's side. "The news from the King is very bad," Frederick reported on September ninth. "They say he will not live long. Well, I have decided in advance to be consoled for whatever happens, for as long as he is alive I can be sure of being miserable." Frederick told Wilhelmina not to grieve. She was touched because she had not seen her father for two years. "If you saw him again, I think you would let him go in peace and would feel no regret."

Frederick William, who was being taken by slow stages to Berlin, was suffering from pleurisy, shortness of breath and dropsy. His legs were swollen to the knee, his torso to the navel. Frederick's visit to Bayreuth on his way home might have to be shortened, but would not be omitted altogether. He impulsively begged his sister to come to Prussia, as soon as he was king, for he could not live without her. She could command everything in his house as though she were his queen.

For four days in early October Frederick was Wilhelmina's guest, flushed with the expectation of freedom and power close at hand. The two could not openly rejoice, and a private conversation they had concerning the future took an unfortunate turn. Frederick said he would make sure Wilhelmina received all the dower her father had promised her and had not yet paid, but he advised economy and retrenchment in Bayreuth. The old Margrave could not live forever. After he was gone Wilhelmina and her husband should give up the pretense of a court, with its expensive retinue of gentlemen of the bedchamber and ladies-in-waiting. They should live like ordinary folk and save to pay their debts. They could also save by coming often to visit King Frederick II at Berlin.

At this point Wilhelmina began to cry. It always depressed her to talk of money. Frederick had touched a sensitive spot, her littleness, her poverty. His realistic advice seemed to her insensitive.

"But why are you crying?" Frederick asked. Wilhelmina was

too easily upset. She mustn't give in to melancholy. Taking his sister by the hand, Frederick drew her into the next room, where the others were waiting for them. All the time she was playing an accompaniment to Frederick's flute the tears kept running down Wilhelmina's cheeks, and she was grateful to her devoted attendant, Dorothea von der Marwitz, for standing beside her to screen her from the rest of the company.

During the remainder of the visit there were no more tears. Frederick was gay. He teased Wilhelmina's ladies, who adored him and dubbed him Prince Charming. On the night of his departure the "dear brother's" health was drunk so deep at dinner that Madame von Sonsfeld had to keep to her room the following day.

A very different Frederick stood beside his father's bed in Potsdam and looked down at the hideously inflated body, the cherubic face gone yellow, flecked with blue. Frederick William could only breathe sitting up and was very patient, very resigned to the will of God. "I never knew I loved him so much," Frederick wrote. "My heart aches to see my poor father suffer."

Wilhelmina would have sped to Potsdam, but Frederick's next letter told her not to come. The invalid might last for several months. He was a little better now, and his temper was very bad.

Another reason for delay was that the Margrave was ailing. George Frederick Charles had suffered a slight stroke, and, though he, too, rallied, it seemed as if this would be his final illness. Unlike his relative of Prussia, George Frederick Charles had no desire to die; he clutched at life and would not let it go. There was a recrudescence of the flirtation with Flora von Sonsfeld. Wilhelmina, anxiously alert, wondered if Flora's resolution to resist would hold out during the long hours of hand-holding and whispered conversation with the invalid. Forgetful of economy, the Margrave had begun to build a new wing on the Bayreuth residence and a menagerie at Himmelskron.

In Prussia it was accepted that the King was doomed; for the present, however, life would go on as usual. Frederick William had ordered two hundred of his grenadiers to tramp through his bedroom; Sophie's marriage to the Margrave of Schwedt was performed at his bedside.

It was possible now for Frederick to go back to Ruppin for a few days at a time. Wherever he went the buzz of speculation concerning his future followed him. What would be his domestic and his foreign policy? Who would be his favorites? Would he carry out his threat, expressed to Grumbkow, of discarding his wife?

There were wiseacres who professed to be in Frederick's confidence, but they spoke without authority. Frederick remained closemouthed. He would be twenty-three his next birthday, yet Lotte had written she looked upon him as her second father, and Sophia Dorothea was training the little princes—August William, aged twelve; Henry, aged eight; and Ferdinand, aged four—to be very respectful to their elder brother. In November Frederick received a letter from Prince Eugene, offering to be his political mentor and gently reminding him of the benefits, financial and miscellaneous, bestowed upon him in the past. At the same time he had a quiet talk with the Marquis de la Chétardie, the French ambassador, to whom he offered the hope of assistance in putting Stanislaus Leszczinski back upon his slippery throne in Poland.

Frederick's calm concealed a busy mind, a pulse staccato with excitement. He found relief in writing to Wilhelmina twice a week and in opening his heart to her more fully than to any other. Though she wept on receiving a dictated letter from her father, showing how weak he was, she was convinced that all was for the best. Her brother would soon be free; a happy day was about to dawn for her country. As for her own prospects, Wilhelmina experienced, though in lesser degree, the same vacillation of mood concerning the illness of her father-in-law as she felt for her father. Now she was impatient, now she was tearful as she watched the Margrave's slow decline.

When the new year of 1735 came in, a modified carnival was celebrated in Bayreuth. Wilhelmina and her ladies were rehearsing a play, Racine's tragedy of *Iphigenia*, but whether the news from Berlin was tragic or grimly comic it would be hard to say. Frederick had written to announce a miracle. The abscesses which had formed on the King's legs had opened and drained profusely; he was much improved.

> He can walk, and is better than I am. . . . I dined with him yesterday . . . he ate and drank for four . . . in two weeks he will be able to ride. . . . To recover from three deadly illnesses all at once is superhuman. The good God must have had His reasons for granting this new lease on life. Now I must retire again into the background.

But there would be a relapse! Wilhelmina, the comforter, was sure of that. There was the old belief in a common destiny for hope to rest upon. Wilhelmina's invalid was very low again, so why not Frederick William?

When later Wilhelmina complained of the tyranny of the moribund, Frederick coined a bitter maxim, worthy of La Rochefoucauld: "The old Margrave is doing everything to make you feel no sorrow when he dies. I think that is the way of many fathers. They know their children are soft hearted and while they are alive do everything to drive them to despair."

On May seventeenth, after months of expectation and an agony that lasted for nine harrowing hours, George Frederick Charles expired. Wilhelmina had never witnessed death and was prostrated, but Frederick sent his crisp congratulations. "Since you are half of me," he wrote, "I am half happy."

Chapter 19

A FTER the death of George Frederick Charles only three of
his family remained in Bayreuth, Wilhelmina, her husband, who was now the Margrave, and their four-year-old
daughter, Frederica. Wilhelmina's two sisters-in-law had married, one to the Duke of Ostfriesland, and the other, Charlotte,
to the Duke of Saxe-Weimar. Poor Charlotte, as beautiful as an
angel, but mentally disturbed, would seem nowadays a bad matrimonial risk, but the science of eugenics had not been born in
1735. Saxe-Weimar seemed heaven-sent when he appeared as
suitor, for he was so odd himself that it was thought he would
never notice Charlotte's peculiarities. The betrothal was one
day, the wedding was the next, and the eccentric pair went off to
live more happily and harmoniously than many, or even most, of
their princely kind.

Wilhelmina, therefore, on becoming Margravine, had no one
to consider but herself. She had a brief misunderstanding with
her husband, who had immediately reappointed all the members
of his father's council. These men showed signs of wanting to
stand between husband and wife in financial matters, but Wilhelmina's fears of losing her husband's confidence and access to
his purse were quickly set to rest. The new Margrave was the
most amiable of men; he wanted to please everybody. Having
been allowed no part in government hitherto, he needed the

help of experts. Having failed to take to heart the advice of his brother-in-law, Frederick, he had no intention of saving to pay his debts.

The council, no doubt, looked down their noses and hoisted their eyebrows when, on Wilhelmina's twenty-sixth birthday, July third, 1735, she was given the Hermitage, the entire estate of which her little pleasure cottage, Mon Plaisir, was part. Embellishments would be expensive, but Wilhelmina set to work on plans with the help of architects and landscape gardeners. She enlarged her household by sending for the two sisters of Dorothea von der Marwitz, Albertine and Caroline, to come from Prussia. New gentlemen of the bedchamber were also appointed.

At this time Wilhelmina's health took a turn for the better. She had been prescribed asses' milk and exercise, did a great deal of dancing, and went hunting with her husband. Frederick was shocked when he learned of this, for he abhorred all forms of animal slaughter. That Wilhelmina learned to ride horseback seemed scandalous to the conservatives of Bayreuth; they had never seen a woman on a horse except riding pillion behind her husband.

With the return of summer, war between France and Austria was resumed, but without enthusiasm on either hand. The Czarina Anne had sent troops to the western front, and Wilhelmina and her husband went to a Benedictine monastery in the Upper Palatinate to see the Russians, as if they were side-show monsters. She reported them to be undersized, their equipment primitive. Their commander was a Scotchman, one James Keith, who later was to become an intimate friend of Frederick.

Frederick himself had asked permission for a second tour of inspection with the army. When rebuffed, he made use of Elizabeth Christina as advocate, but without success. Frederick William was now afraid Fritz would become an out-and-out imperialist, and instead of letting him go to Bayreuth and the Rhine, sent him to East Prussia, where a failure of crops had been reported. He might as well have been banished to Siberia, Frederick wrote. During the six weeks he was out of touch with his sister the only sight he saw worthy of Wilhelmina's attention was a dignified elderly gentleman at Königsberg, Stanislaus Leszczinski. The French candidate for the Polish crown, having been driven from Danzig, was now the guest of Prussia, a symbol of the deepening rift between Frederick William and the Empire.

To his father, Frederick made a report of great poverty and want in the province he had just visited. He recommended that grain from the royal granaries should be distributed to prevent a famine. His duty as inspector and errand-boy done, Frederick could hardly wait to get back to seclusion and a new and consoling enthusiasm.

Two years earlier the King had paid a visit to Ruppin for the express purpose of giving his son a present. Frederick William had been able to buy cheap a neglected manor house, twelve miles from Berlin, six from the garrison town, its walls lapped by the waters of a lake, in its rear a backdrop of rising ground. With the gift of Rheinsberg came fifty thousand thalers to restore the building and grounds. The work, carefully overseen from Ruppin, had been going on slowly. Underbrush had been cleared, trees trimmed. A terrace and an entirely new façade to the Gothic mansion had been built. Over the entrance to his new home Frederick had had carved *Frederico tranquilitatem colenti*. This would be a place where peace of mind was cultivated.

For the decoration of interior walls, Frederick had chosen pale, restful tones of rose and gray and green. He had engaged Antoine Pesne, the artist who had painted the picture of Wilhelmina and himself as children, to fresco the ceiling of the music room. The subject chosen was the rising sun, Apollo bringing light through dark clouds. Perhaps it was just as well this work was not begun when Frederick moved in in August of 1736, for his father came to visit a few weeks later. That there was a music room and a library received no unfavorable comment. Frederick William was chiefly concerned with the relations between the master and the mistress of the house. He drew

Frederick aside to renew his offer of a trip to Italy as soon as a child had been born.

The King was not the only one to bring up the subject of procreation at this particular moment. Grumbkow, angling, no doubt, for information, congratulated Frederick on the Crown Princess's being pregnant and received the noncommital answer that, since the stags were also in rut at this season, it might be so. By a friend to whom he spoke less guardedly than to the General, Frederick was advised to produce an heir immediately. He had three younger brothers, and before long the oldest of them, August William would be marriageable. There would be cabals as to the succession. Frederick said he knew this to be a danger, but it was an unfortunate fact that he did not love his wife.

"However," he added, "I would be the meanest man in the world to say I didn't like her. She has a sweet disposition, she is as docile as one could find, and she will go to any lengths to please me. What is more, she cannot complain of my not having slept with her. I don't know why there has been no child."

Frederick intended to collect a group of congenial men to be his housemates at Rheinsberg, but a society without women, he said, would be barbarous and insipid. Elizabeth Christina brought with her a troupe of such attractive young ladies-in-waiting that there was constant speculation as to which of them would be Frederick's mistress. Would it be the Baroness Morien, who was nicknamed "the Whirlwind," or "Furette," the equally vivacious and charming Mademoiselle von Tettau?

Elizabeth Christina herself seemed to be willing to accept any eventuality. To her brother Charles, Lotte's husband, went a sincerely rapturous account of Frederick's virtues. He was the greatest man as well as the greatest prince now living—learned, witty, just and charitable. "He doesn't want to harm anyone, is generous, temperate, has no weakness for wine or other excesses. . . . In short, I would say he was the Phoenix of our Age, and that I am gloriously privileged to be the wife of such a great prince. . . . When one knows him one cannot help but love him."

The days at Rheinsberg were long and busy. From early morning until one o'clock Frederick remained in his library overlooking the lake. Dinner at one-thirty, with twenty or more at table, was leisurely, followed by coffee which was taken in the parlor of each of the ladies-in-waiting in turn. From four to seven, all went their separate ways; then music, with supper at ten, sometimes followed by a dance, Frederick leading off in a pale green satin coat; or there might be amateur theatricals. Ball, or play, or further enthralling conversation, no one thought of going to bed until two o'clock in the morning.

In spite of lack of sleep—Frederick had experimented with doing without it altogether—Elizabeth Christina was perfectly well and spent hours of every day in study. She was taking lessons in French composition from Vizyierre de la Croze, Wilhelmina's old instructor. With Frederick's secretary and librarian, Monsieur Jordan, she was reading two of her husband's favorite authors, Cicero and Marcus Aurelius. To this was added practice in painting and music—all in all, a brave attempt on the part of a badly educated girl to make herself worthy of the one whom she called "the dear master."

After a twelvemonth, most of which was spent at Rheinsberg, Frederick said they could put upon his tomb: "He lived—for a year." He, too, had entered on a period of self-improvement. It was true he had once possessed a hidden library of three thousand books, but he had never had time to more than dip into the more learned volumes. He set himself now to read carefully, systematically, with pen in hand and with the intense application he was able to give to everything he did. Extracts and comments were noted; after a work was finished a review and critique was drawn up.

Having passed through many dark experiences, Frederick's chief interest was in philosophy, from which he wanted answers to the questions asked since time began and to which religious dogma had hitherto given the replies. What is the meaning of human life? Is there a God, and, if so, why is there so much sin and sorrow in the world? The outlook of Frederick's boyhood teachers, Duhan and De la Croze, was that of the mathematical French philosopher, Descartes, whose thought had dominated the preceding century and who had ushered in the Age of Reason. With his famous opening premise, *Cogito, ergo sum* (I think, therefore I am), Descartes undertook to prove the existence of God as though it were a problem in geometry. Frederick found that Wilhelmina had written to De la Croze, asking how this could be done, for she, too, without realizing it, perhaps, was a Cartesian. Frederick had to apologize for the old man's answer; De la Croze had begun to lose his intellectual grip and was fit only to correct Elizabeth Christina's compositions.

Frederick doubted the immortality of the soul, but was convinced there was a God; Wilhelmina was afraid his intuitive certainty would fail to impress an unbeliever. She read what books she could, she said; she discussed religion with an atheist and with everyone who would talk to her on the subject, but there was, alas, no one in Bayreuth who could speak with authority. With apologies for her lack of knowledge, Wilhelmina undertook proof of divine creation, using Descartes's theory of matter being made up of revolving atoms of various shapes and sizes, deducing therefrom that someone, or something, must have set these particles in motion.

Frederick praised her analysis and said she reasoned like a man, but Descartes's ideas were now old hat. His atomic theory was much too vague; he could make no satisfactory connection between spirit (thought) and substance (the brain). A new star had swung within the reach of Frederick's telescope. There were two men with whom he talked philosophy, an old friend, Count Suhm, the Saxon ambassador, and Count Manteuffel, who had been in the service of Augustus the Strong, but was now living the life of a scholar at Berlin. Both had recommended to Frederick the writings of Christian von Wolff. Wolff was a professor of philosophy whom Frederick William had banished from the

University of Halle in 1723 because of his deterministic teachings. He was now at the University of Marburg, and, since he wrote in German—a new and revolutionary departure—Frederick found his books hard to read. He persuaded Suhm to make a French translation of the treatise that appealed to him most, *Some Reasoned Thoughts on God, the World, and the Soul of Man.* Suhm's work was promised to Wilhelmina in manuscript, though she protested it would probably be above her head. When it reached her, she was repelled by Wolff's mechanical theories of human nature and human events. She could not believe that the fate of the individual was determined in advance by character alone, or that a good god could have created evil. She preferred to remain with Descartes, who promised her free will.

The correspondence that for a time had been so spiritedly erudite turned to other subjects than philosophy: to music, to gardening, to the architectural developments at Rheinsberg and the Hermitage. Though Frederick boasted of his sister's intellectual prowess to his friends and told her he was like a newly married man who is always bringing his wife's name into the conversation, he realized how much broader his horizon was than hers. Wilhelmina's husband was not interested in abstract thought; Bayreuth was off the travel route of scholars. She herself was well aware of this and would have sent for Frederick's old teacher, Jacques Duhan, if it had not seemed best for Duhan to stay quietly where he was in Brunswick out of range of Frederick William's eye. Wilhelmina continued to envy Frederick the clever men who sat down to dinner with him day by day, or whom he invited to visit him, for he wrote to many living authors of the books he most admired. Wilhelmina was dazzled when she learned of her brother's having entered into correspondence with the most celebrated writer, the most dynamic mind, in Europe.

✦ ✦ ✦

Among the books that had once been Frederick's and which were sold by his father at Amsterdam in 1730, was a volume of the collected works of François Marie Arouet de Voltaire. There were also two copies of the *Henriade*, Voltaire's epic poem celebrating the brave and tolerant Henry of Navarre, the fourth of the name to rule in France. It was as a poet and a dramatist that the great man had first made his mark, but Frederick had recognized the talents of a superb storyteller when he read *The History of Charles XII*, which was lent him by General von Grumbkow. Like many youthful enthusiasts, Frederick took it for granted that man and author were identical.

"Although I do not have the pleasure of knowing you personally," Frederick wrote on August eighth, 1736, "I know you through your works. They are treasures of the mind . . . so exquisitely fashioned that their beauties seem new at each rereading. I have discovered in them the character of their gifted author."

Voltaire, Frederick declared, was the first poet to have popularized philosophy by presenting it in rhyme; he was, therefore, taking the liberty of enclosing an account of the banishment of Christian von Wolff from Prussia and Wolff's subsequent defense of himself and his opinions. Suhm's translation of Wolff's treatise would follow. In return, Frederick would be grateful for any works of Voltaire which, for one reason or another, had not yet been published; they would, of course, be screened from public view. "Even if I am not so fortunate as to possess you," Frederick concluded—by "possess," he implied a visit—"I hope some day to see the one I have admired so long."

The hero to whom this worshipful letter was addressed was forty-two years old. Though Voltaire's face had not yet taken on the look of an amused, but highly efficient, nutcracker, its trademark to posterity, its likeness was seen in every printshop from London to Saint Petersburg, and wherever books were sold. Voltaire's youthful, witty trifles had convulsed high society, but he had gained an even wider audience by being twice imprisoned in the Bastille for his attacks on the French establishment, in particular on the establishment of organized religion. His own outlook had broadened during a three-year exile in England, during which he was patronized by Queen Caroline and met all the greatest English scientists and writers.

Years ago Voltaire had begun to speculate with the proceeds of his most successful stage play, *Oedipus*, which ran continuously for forty-five nights at the Théâtre Français. He was now a man of substance and was spending freely to make more comfortable a country house at Cirey in Champagne, conveniently close to the eastern borders of France. This house did not belong to Voltaire, but to the husband of the lady with whom he lived, the Marquise du Châtelet.

The Marquise was an unusual woman in her own right, but she was none the less fortunate for having found Voltaire for a press agent. The two were first drawn to one another by a common interest in the writings of Newton and Locke, with whom Voltaire had become acquainted in England. While he wrote in one wing of the chateau, she carried on her mathematical studies and scientific experiments in another. They were sometimes interrupted by visitors from Paris, but seldom by the Marquis du Châtelet, who had long ago come to the amiable conclusion that he and his wife were happier apart.

Even Voltaire's most intimate friends could not know what he would do or say in a given situation; his reaction to Frederick's letter, however—surprised delight—might have been guessed. Voltaire, the son of a notary, had always consorted with influential folk. He had political ambitions, the yearning of a theorist to express his ideas in action. Since his life had been a continual struggle against intolerance and against the many violent enemies he had managed to make during his career, he was looking for a safer refuge than Cirey. Voltaire's reply to the Crown Prince of Prussia's bid for friendship was lusciously flattering.

When Frederick had asked to see unpublished manuscripts he was hinting at permission to read a poem which Voltaire had been secretly polishing—and talking about to all the world—for years. The heroine of *La Pucelle* was Joan of Arc; its handling of her legend was rumored to be so irreverent, so earthy, that it would be sure to get its author into trouble. *La Pucelle* was not sent to Rheinsberg, but other verses went back and forth as the correspondence ripened. Voltaire praised Frederick's stuttering verse and thanked him—with equal insincerity—for the gift of Wolff's philosophy. Though he himself had written a treatise on metaphysics, Frederick's new friend was constitutionally unfitted to deal with intangibles. He gracefully sidestepped giving his opinion of Wolff by saying that men and women are like mice who nest and scurry back and forth in the wainscoting of a great house without knowing why the house was built, or who was its architect.

Voltaire also sidestepped the suggestion of a visit. Friendship, he said, bound him to Cirey. He referred so constantly to Madame du Châtelet, whom he called by her given name of Émilie, as though she were a reigning sovereign, that Frederick realized how important it was to propitiate the lady. He included a message, or an elaborate compliment, in every letter.

Émilie, Voltaire said, was yearning for a portrait of the only prince she could really respect or admire. In the spring of 1737 one of the liveliest of the Rheinsberg group, Count Keyserlingk, nicknamed Césarion, was sent off to Cirey with Frederick's picture and with instructions to bring back an essay on Newton, on which Madame du Châtelet and Voltaire had collaborated; the opening chapters of a new historical work of the master, *The Century of Louis XIV*; and, of course, and if possible, *La Pucelle*.

Earlier in the year Voltaire had been in Holland, waiting for a small tempest concerning one of his recent publications to blow over. Much to Frederick's regret, an item appeared in a Dutch newspaper, saying Voltaire was coming to Prussia. Frederick did not want his father to know of his association with one who was considered an atheist and a subversive. A Nürnberg paper picked up the paragraph and Wilhelmina read it. She wrote Frederick that she could not believe Voltaire was as attractive in the flesh as in his books. Envy caused her to see the famous Frenchman as a fop.

[Chapter 20]

WILHELMINA's health had again declined. Her symptoms—headache, indigestion, insomnia, pains in the chest and stomach, with occasional bouts of fever —might have puzzled a physician with every modern aid to diagnosis up his sleeve; they completely baffled the doctors available in eighteenth century Bayreuth. The Margrave took his wife to spend the month of June, 1737, at Ems, where Wilhelmina took the waters in company with pigs, geese and a dozen other invalids. She was bored, she wrote, with talk of baths and enemas. She would just be thinking about something more to her taste when a miserable doctor would seize her by the arm and say, "Come, Highness, it's time to take a walk."

The waters, whether taken externally or internally, were supposed to be a cure for sterility, but Wilhelmina failed to become pregnant, though she realized how important it was to have another and, above all, a male child. Ill health had become a habit with her, something of which one spoke lightly and turned to humorous account. Wilhelmina noticed, however, that she could only forget her bodily ills when absorbed in some intellectual or aesthetic pursuit. There were four thousand books in her study, she boasted to Frederick; she was reading madly, and, with the hope of a legacy from a rich relative, had begun to build a grotto and lay out a labyrinth at the Hermitage.

Between the Hermitage and Rheinsberg there was constant musical traffic; original compositions for flute or harpsichord, as well as performers, were exchanged. Wilhelmina had learned to play the violin well enough to enjoy chamber music with Dorothea von der Marwitz and two of her professional musicians. She now intended to import singers from Italy so that opera could be given in her redecorated palace theater. This was something Frederick would like to do in his own house, if he was not so certain his father would object. Though he maintained a small, but excellent, orchestra, Frederick had dared to send for only one singer, a *castrato* from Naples.

What with buying paintings by the most elegant contemporary artists, Watteau and Lancret, what with sending Césarion to Cirey, his architect, Knobblesdorf, to Italy, and two other friends to France and Spain to garner political information, Frederick was living far beyond his budget. He was forever borrowing and had even accepted a small loan from Wilhelmina. A new source of revenue was found when Count Suhm, the translator of Wolff's metaphysics, went to Russia as envoy of Saxony. Frederick pursued his friend there with questions about the country and its history, not only for himself, but for Voltaire, who was meditating a biography of Peter the Great. Could the financial wind be raised in Russia, Frederick asked? It could, Suhm replied cautiously, and in cipher. Through the Duke of Courland, lover of the Czarina Anne, gifts came from "a certain lady," whom Frederick was advised to thank in German, since her sympathies were strongly Teutonic.

Frederick was keeping an unblinking eye upon the European situation. Somewhat more than two years earlier a peace treaty, which had only just been signed, put an end to hostilities between France and Austria. Augustus of Saxony was allowed to retain the Polish crown, while Stanislaus Leszczinski was consoled by the gift of Lorraine, which after his death would become part of France. Austria was further weakened by having to give up Milan and most of Lombardy to the French, and Naples and Sicily to Spain. With all of this in mind, Frederick wrote in the spring of 1738 what he hoped would be a political pamphlet to be published anonymously with the help of Voltaire in England.

Considerations on the Present State of Politics in Europe was addressed to the English public and to the princes of the Empire. Make no mistake about it, Frederick warned, France was determined to dominate the entire continent, and Austria was no longer fit to lead and to protect the Germanies. She had allied herself with Russia; she had provoked a senseless war without the consent of those who would have to fight it. The results of Austria's defeat would be only too plain when the present Emperor died. There was a moral to Frederick's tale of disaster: he saw as the greatest danger to Europe the greedy pride of princes who considered only their personal grandeur and not the welfare of their people.

The duties of a prince as servant of the state and as a responsible human being was the subject of another writing project Frederick had in mind even before his political essay went to Voltaire. Frederick had been reading *The Century of Louis XIV*, which Césarion had brought back from Cirey. He was enchanted by the work as a whole, but criticized a passing reference to Machiavelli as one of the noblest of Renaissance Italians. Machiavelli's book, *The Prince*, Frederick maintained, had standardized a pattern for international trickery, well illustrated by the doings of Cardinal Fleury, the French prime minister, during the recent war. Without mentioning the Cardinal's name, Frederick would undertake to prove his point and would send chapters of his work as he finished them to his literary adviser.

But not all of Frederick's time could be devoted to writing. During that same spring of 1738 he was drilling troops at Ruppin. There was drilling all over Prussia, Frederick William having announced to the Great Powers that he would fight for Jülich and Berg, if, as promised by Austria and France, these precious morsels of the Rhineland fell to the House of Sulzbach.

"A fine reward for my ten thousand men!" Frederick William

roared. Grievance had piled upon grievance. Seckendorf, the friend, the leal companion of the Tabagie for many years, had been recalled to Austria for military duty and was now in prison, a scapegoat for the disasters of an Austrian campaign against the Turks. Vienna had refused to pay for troops quartered on Prussian soil. Vienna had withheld twenty tall Bohemians from the Potsdam Guard and had failed to send an announcement to Berlin of the wedding of the Archduchess Maria Theresa to her kinsman, Francis, late of Lorraine, and now of Tuscany. Tears brimmed in the eyes of Frederick William as he counted off his woes. Once when Frederick was present his father pointed to him and cried, "There's the one who will avenge me!"

There was a recurrence of the King's former maladies toward the end of the year. Frederick's response to the ups and downs of his father's condition was ambivalent. Now he said, with cynical ferocity, that the old man had the constitution of a bear and would outlive him; now he was willing to give his good right hand for another twenty years of Rheinsberg. The present episode was severe. As Frederick William's body bloated, his vindictiveness swelled. Frederick came to spend Christmas as usual in Berlin and couldn't get away. For six weeks he was the butt of his father's wrath and of sarcasms, all the more painful to the victim because they were so crude. "It's inhuman," Frederick raged to Wilhelmina, "to take one's anger out on people who can't retaliate!"

He himself was seized with such violent stomach cramps that he thought his end was near, and the news of Wilhelmina's continuing ill health caused a familiar reflection: "If we have to leave this world, it should be together. . . . It wouldn't be the first time such a thing has happened. Friends have been known to die on the same day, or to kill themselves when one hears of the other's death."

Nevertheless Frederick was determined Wilhelmina should have better medical care and arranged for a new court physician, Daniel de Superville, a French Huguenot, who had been pro-

COURTESY OF THE ADMINISTRATION OF THE CITY'S CASTLES AND GARDENS.
CHARLOTTENBURG CASTLE, BERLIN

Frederick and Wilhelmina as children, painted by Antoine Pesne

COURTESY OF THE ADMINISTRATION OF THE CITY'S CASTLES AND GARDENS. CHARLOTTENBURG CASTLE, BERLIN

Frederick William I—also a Pesne portrait

COURTESY OF THE ADMINISTRATION OF THE CITY'S CASTLES AND GARDENS.
CHARLOTTENBURG CASTLE, BERLIN

Sophia Dorothea. By Pesne

COURTESY OF THE ADMINISTRATION OF THE CITY'S CASTLES AND GARDENS, BERLIN.
OWNED BY PRINCE LOUIS FERDINAND OF PRUSSIA

Frederick as Crown Prince. By Pesne

Frederick's wife, Elizabeth Christina. By Pesne

COURTESY OF THE ADMINISTRATION OF THE CITY'S CASTLES AND GARDENS, BERLIN.
MONBIJOU CASTLE

FROM *Frederick the Great* BY G. B. VO

Above: Von Grumbkow

Left: Voltaire

ENGRAVING FROM THE PORTRAIT BY
MAURICE Q. DE LA TOUR

Frederick, after the Battle of Kolin in 1757. Painting by J. Schrader

THE BETTMANN ARCHIVE

EWING GALLOWAY

COURTESY OF THE GERMAN INFORMATION CENTER

Above: Sans Souci Castle, in Potsdam

Left: The Teahouse at Sans Souci

FROM *Frederick the Great* BY G. B. VOLZ

The Temple of Friendship

The Hermitage

RADIO TIMES HULTON PICTURE LIBRARY, LONDON

COURTESY OF THE ADMINISTRATION OF THE CITY'S CASTLES AND GARDENS, BERLIN.
BRESLAU CASTLE

Wilhelmina in later life. By Pesne

FROM *Allgemeine Historische Porträtwerk* BY W. VON SEIDLITZ

Augustus the Strong

COURTESY OF THE ADMINISTRATION OF THE CITY'S CASTLES AND GARDENS.
CHARLOTTENBURG CASTLE, BERLIN

Anhalt-Dessau. By Pesne

THE BETTMANN ARCHIVE

THE BETTMANN ARCHIVE

Above: A flute concert at Sans Souci with Frederick playing the flute. Painting by A. von Menzel

Left: Frederick and his friends at Sans Souci. Voltaire is on Frederick's right. Painting by A. von Menzel

COURTESY OF THE ADMINISTRATION OF THE CITY'S CASTLES AND GARDENS, BERLIN.
OWNED BY PRINCE ERNEST AUGUST OF HANOVER

Frederick the Great, in 1763. Portrait by Johann Ziesenis

fessor of anatomy at Stettin, to visit Bayreuth. Wilhelmina's opinion of doctors was low; she was amazed by Superville. Here was no loutish, "Latin spitting," medicine man. Superville was a cosmopolitan and very well read, just the sort of far-ranging conversationist for whom the frustrated intellectual of Bayreuth had been searching. Though Superville had to return to Prussia for a time, he came back in the spring after the King was better and his heart had been softened by the gift of a "long fellow" from Bayreuth.

The doctor was soon an intimate adviser on almost every problem. Judging Wilhelmina's case to be consumptive, he recommended flight from the cold, damp Franconian winter to Montpellier in southern France. From this world famous health resort, Superville, Wilhelmina and the Margrave might travel farther still to Italy. The extension of their journey would not be mentioned in presenting the scheme to Frederick William, whose consent was still necessary to all important undertakings. Stress would be laid on economy, for the expenses of the trip would be paid by the state and would be less than the upkeep of the home establishment.

In July the Margrave and eight tall Bayreuthers went to Berlin for a surprise visit, which so pleased the King that no objection was made to the Montpellier expedition. Departure was set for August twentieth.

The day was warm. The party had hardly gone a mile from Bayreuth when the Margrave was taken ill with fever and vomiting. A stop was made at Erlangen. Though others of the party, Superville included, had the same symptoms, this was no ordinary case of food poisoning. Several weeks, a month, went by before the invalids were well enough to travel, and then, instead of going on toward France, they went back to Bayreuth.

Wilhelmina had made a disturbing discovery. Her female companions for the journey were Dorothea von der Marwitz and one of Dorothea's two sisters, Albertine. Caroline, the youngest of the family, was left behind with Madame von Sonsfeld, who was now too old to travel. Wilhelmina loved all three of these nieces of her much loved governess, but her feeling for Dorothea was particularly tender; if not maternal, it was big sisterly.

During the past eight years music had been made and innumerable books had been read together, Wilhelmina taking pleasure in the thought that she was playing the same part in Dorothea's education as Sonsine had played in hers. Though Dorothea was now twenty-two and should have been married long ago, Wilhelmina had kept the promise made to her father and had not tried to find a husband for her friend in Bayreuth. Dorothea was gay and pretty, Dorothea was an heiress, this being the reason for Frederick William's ban on her and her sister's marrying outside of Prussia. Four years earlier a suitor had presented himself, a Count Burghauss, an officer in the Bayreuth imperial regiment. It had not been difficult for Wilhelmina to discourage the match because Dorothea's heart was not involved. She was quite willing, she said, to remain single so long as she could stay with her dear Margravine.

This pledge had been repeated so often and in so many flattering forms that Wilhelmina believed it implicitly. But was there perhaps another reason for Dorothea's devotion? The idea had never occurred before the enforced stay at Erlangen. While the Margrave was convalescent and was still in bed he would send for Dorothea and Albertine to come to his room the first thing in the morning, and there they would stay throughout the day. The invalid liked to laugh and joke with both the sisters, but it was plain that Dorothea was his favorite.

Looking back, Wilhelmina realized an intimacy had existed for a very long time, a year at least, to which she had shut her eyes because both the offending parties were so dear, so necessary to her happiness. The chance of keeping her husband and her best friend apart would be better, she thought, in Bayreuth than on the road to Montpellier and Naples. It was impossible, however, for Wilhelmina to hide her feelings from either Dorothea or her husband. They protested innocence. Dorothea in particular seemed shocked and crushed by the mere suggestion of disloyalty; she promised to be very circumspect in future.

Hoping for the best, Wilhelmina wrote to Frederick, who was urging her on to France, that it was too late in the season to travel. She was going back to Bayreuth, she added bitterly, "where everyone hates me because I have no son." By everyone Wilhelmina may have meant her husband, who did not hate her, but who had turned to a younger, a healthier woman. Pride forbade her to say more. Frederick, on the other hand, thought his sister had weakly given up her plans because gossip of her extravagance had reached the ears of the King.

✦ ✦ ✦

Frederick had also been on the road, but traveling in the opposite direction. For the first time since the disastrous journey ending in imprisonment, father and son had made a tour together, of the eastern provinces. From Lithuania Frederick wrote Voltaire on account of how this region, depopulated by the plague, had been brought back to life and prosperity by Frederick William. The praise was all the more sincere because Frederick knew his father would never see it.

The attitude of the King had softened, due, no doubt, to the sudden death in March of General von Grumbkow. Frederick marked the passing of this ancient enemy and mistrusted associate in an epitaph in which the dead man's talents and his venality were mentioned in the same couplet.

To his wife Frederick wrote frequently and even affectionately throughout his tour, thanking her for shirts she had sent him, asking her to do his errands: he wanted to send soup to his old governess, Madame de Roucoulle, who had been ill; he wanted a suitable birthday present for his father—"something to do with hunting." Elizabeth Christina bought a dog. Her heart must have beat faster as she read in every letter how much her husband missed his home and how much he looked forward to embracing her.

Even while on the road Frederick was able to work on his refutation of Machiavelli. The manuscript was completed in November and sent to Voltaire to pull to pieces if he wished and to publish if he saw fit. Voltaire, though critical, favored publication. He had thought Frederick's earlier political essay could only be brought out anonymously, and even then its author might be recognized. The *Antimachiavel*, however, should appear with Frederick's royal name attached. Who knows but it might become a primer for all future heads of state? Voltaire offered to write a preface in return for the foreword Frederick was preparing for a new edition of the *Henriade*. It almost seemed as if the Crown Prince of Prussia and the uncrowned King of European Letters were collaborating on an equal footing.

Frederick had been afraid the wear and tear of travel might have a bad effect on his father. There would be more gout, more pains in the chest and a return to the wicked ways of the preceding winter. His fears were realized in January. Frederick, who had gone back to Rheinsberg after Christmas, was recalled to Berlin and, though he told Elizabeth Christina he did not want his father to die—"so help me God"—he also counseled patience, for the end might be long delayed.

The King's illness followed the same dreary course as others, a little better one day, a great deal worse the next, for the movement was ever downward. The sufferer was restless; he had himself rolled about in his wheel chair; he had a table laid across his bed and carpenter's tools brought so that he could pass the long hours of sleeplessness in making wooden boxes. In the small hours of the night the banging of a hammer could be heard in the street that skirted the palace.

Wilhelmina heard that sound in Bayreuth and wanted to come to Berlin, but Frederick told her not to hurry. He had returned to Rheinsberg to recuperate from the insults, the abuse, as well as the constant drain upon his sympathies. "I can't conceive," he wrote morosely, "why you should want to come here under present circumstances, though the King is very bad—I grant you that. Do as you think best, but if you're sad and sorry later, don't blame me. . . . You haven't been here in eight years and have probably forgotten the hundred thousand little things that would come back to plague you after two days in Berlin. 'Blessed are the absent,' say I, according to the Scripture."

A few weeks later Wilhelmina was told her father was on his feet again and was going to Potsdam. "Goodbye, Berlin," Frederick William had said on leaving his unloved capital, "in Potsdam will I die."

There was no talk of dying, however, when the patient was surrounded by his beloved grenadiers, whom he hugged and kissed. He had been "blowing the last squeak on his whistle," Frederick William said, but now, among his own dear children he would be well. Soon he would be able to ride, and they would all go off to fight the Poles, who were "only dirty dog shit." With all the cattle and treasure they would bring home, everyone would be rich.

The soldiers cheered this program. A favorite marching song, "*Flou, Flou, Flou,*" was sung, and Frederick William went to bed to sleep for four unbroken hours. When he woke he said he would abdicate and go to live at Wusterhausen. He had a good son, whom he could trust. Five years ago he could not have said as much, but Fritz was a reformed character now; he had promised faithfully to preserve the army.

When the inevitable relapse followed, the King was told by his chaplain, Parson Roloff, that he should forgive his enemies. He had only one enemy, Frederick William replied, his brother-in-law, George of England. After he, Frederick William, was dead, Sophia Dorothea should write to her brother to say he was forgiven.

But why not now, the Parson asked?

"Too soon," the King said firmly, "only after I am gone."

Frederick had been receiving daily bulletins. Toward the end of May he told Wilhelmina he was going "back to the galleys." As he approached the Potsdam palace Frederick saw his father being pushed about the grounds in his wheel chair on his way to inspect a new blacksmith shop. The King spread wide his arms. Frederick ran forward; he was embraced; he was called "my dear little Fritz"; he was told he had been always loved, even if at times he had been roughly handled. Father and son wept. The tears, the benignant mood persisted. Frederick's eyes were often wet during the next few days while being briefed on details of kingship never before revealed.

In the King's bedchamber stood his open coffin. He had given careful instructions for the laying out of his corpse and for his funeral, which was to be both thrifty and spectacular from a military point of view. Too weak for carpentry, the dying man asked that chorals should be sung, his favorite being one that spoke soothingly of death, "Why Should I Grieve." "Naked I came into this world, and naked will I go," the voices warned in plangent harmony.

"No, no, I will wear my uniform," Frederick William murmured.

He gave his old friend, Anhalt-Dessau, and his adjutant their choice of his saddle horses. A flicker of the old Adam appeared when, looking through the window, Frederick William saw the grooms had put on saddles that did not match the saddle cloths. He told the adjutant to go down and beat the rascals for their stupidity.

✦ ✦ ✦

Meanwhile Frederick's intellectual and artistic friends had removed themselves from Rheinsberg and, in order to be nearer to Potsdam, had crowded into the small house at Ruppin. They were waiting impatiently for the good word. To them, Frederick William was a monster and a barrier to their advancement; the sooner he was out of this world the better. Card games helped to pass the time. When a servant came in with a black-bordered letter for Elizabeth Christina, play was suspended, and she, the only one in the room who managed to be calm, laughed and asked what was the matter.

All were in bed when, at two o'clock on the morning of June first, 1740, a messenger arrived to say the King had died the preceding afternoon.

But was this really true? Couldn't there be, as so often before, a revival? Not a chance in a thousand, someone said. Monsieur Jordan, one of their coterie, had been ordered to perform an autopsy, and after he got through with his work the old fellow wouldn't come to life again!

Elizabeth Christina was awakened with the words, "Your Majesty." She was soon off for Potsdam, where Frederick gave her a ceremonial kiss upon the cheek and led her forward, saying to the assembled company, "This is your Queen."

A letter from Frederick was on its way to Bayreuth. It read, "By God's will, our dear father died yesterday. . . . I can only make up to you your present loss by my sincere friendship and my dearest love."

FREDERICK was addressed as "sire" in Wilhelmina's first letter after his accession, and she signed herself "Your Majesty's most humble and obedient servant." The title of brother—"*your* brother"—Frederick replied, was more glorious than that of a "Most Christian" or "Most Catholic Majesty," or a "Defender of the Faith"; her friendship was worth more to him than the groveling of slaves. He warned her not to expect long letters for the present, for he would be busy.

During the first three weeks of Frederick's reign he decreed complete religious toleration throughout all of Prussia, abolished the use of torture in criminal cases, and removed from the statute book the law that an unmarried mother, convicted of infanticide, should be sewn up in a sack of her own making and thrown into the river. It was announced that only political comment would be censored in the newspapers; a periodical for politics and literature was founded to which the King himself might contribute from time to time. A department for finance and industry was set up, as well as a series of public granaries to control and reduce the price of bread. The Academy of Science was revived. Invitations went out to scholars, one of them being the exiled philosopher, Christian Wolff, to meet in the autumn and form a more extended academy which would include literature and the arts. The architect of Rheinsberg, Knobblesdorf, was set to work on plans for an opera house to be built in Berlin.

These and other public acts, which caused Wilhelmina to shed tears of joy, took up only a small part of Frederick's time. He had, by innumerable personal contacts, to destroy the image of himself as dilettante and to establish the fact that he was master. On the afternoon of his father's death, while his eyes were still red from weeping, Frederick was approached by the Prince of Anhalt-Dessau, who, abjectly kneeling, pledged devotion and asked to be retained in all his offices and authority. Frederick assured the old man he would not be ousted. "But, as for authority," he said, "I don't know what you mean. I am the only one to exercise authority in this country."

Frederick would not be vindictive where merit was concerned and would retain as foreign minister Henry von Podewils, a son-in-law of General von Grumbkow, but he also wanted to make it clear that his friends would not be cosseted. Relatives of Von Katte were advanced in rank: Jacques Duhan was affectionately recalled from Brunswick, and Peter Christopher von Keith, Frederick's one time conspirator in escape, was summoned from England. All of these were given position and employment, but their rewards were moderate. The notion that Frederick would be spendthrift tottered when the functionary who was to buy black cloth for Frederick William's funeral was warned not to demand a rake-off from the dealers if he wanted his accounts to be endorsed. That the army would be maintained was certified by the creation of sixteen new divisions, though the giant regiment was disbanded as an expensive luxury. It was last seen by the Berlin public as it followed Frederick William to his grave.

In July Frederick went to Prussia to be recognized as king, but without, as he would have it "the superstitious and frivolous mummery of a coronation." A surprise visit to Bayreuth followed. Frederick had brought with him August William, whom Wilhelmina had not seen for eight years. He was now eighteen, tall, awkward, handsome and shy. A more articulate guest was Francesco Algarotti, an Italian, a friend of Voltaire, and the author of a book on optics who was slated to become a stalwart in the new Academy of Science and Letters. Frederick had brought jeweled gifts for everyone, including Eeka and her husband, whom he had invited to come from Ansbach. He scolded the sulky young Margrave, gave Wilhelmina and her husband some good advice on economizing, and, after only two days' stay, was gone in the direction of the Rhine.

Frederick said he wanted to inspect some French troops at Strassburg, but Wilhelmina heard from him next at Wesel, inviting her and her husband to come to Berlin in October at his expense. He had been so vague about the reasons for his journey that she wondered what they actually were. Would an agreement be signed with France? Would some sort of arrangement be made with the still living possessor of Jülich and Berg?

For some years now Prussia had been disputing with the Prince-Bishop of Liége the possession of Herstal, a small, unimportant township, in which stood a castle where Pepin, the father of Charlemagne, had lived. Herstal had refused to take the oath of fealty to Frederick. After receiving advice from his ministers against military action, since both France and Austria backed Liége, Frederick issued a brusque ultimatum to the Prince-Bishop. On September eleventh, the day the ultimatum ran out, Prussian troops crossed a river, took possession of a Liége town, and placarded it with a manifesto, giving the reasons for the invasion and levying a tax for its cost. Frederick thought apparently that this brisk and bloodless coup would hardly interest Wilhelmina. He was sure she would find much more enlivening his first face-to-face encounter with Voltaire.

Voltaire had greeted Frederick's accession with an ode that began:

> The best day of my life has dawned,
> For it the world was waiting; you alone felt fear.

In the final stanza Frederick was greeted as "the image of a living god," and "the Solomon of the North." Frederick sent a rhymed reply, which concluded:

Farewell to music and my verse,
Farewell delights, farewell Voltaire.

His duty as king now was paramount. Nevertheless Frederick made a rendezvous with the poet for late summer, somewhere on the Rhine, for he was already contemplating his action in Herstal.

Voltaire had suggested that the Queen of Sheba, alias Madame du Châtelet, was looking forward to meeting the Solomon of the North. Though Frederick had exchanged letters with the divine Émilie, had sent her gifts, and had read her scientific treatises, he preferred to keep her at a distance and to have Voltaire entirely to himself. When he heard at Wesel that the pair were at Brussels, ready to descend upon him if he would not come to them in disguise, he pleaded illness. He was fit, he said, only to receive a male visitor.

Frederick's excuse was not feigned. Like so many other inhabitants of the marshy country in which Rheinsberg was located, he was suffering from malaria, and when Voltaire came across the border to a manor house at Moyland near Cleves he found the King in bed, shaking and wizened with fever.

It was a pity, Frederick reported later, that he was in such bad shape, for, with a person like Voltaire, one should be in better health than usual. "He possesses the eloquence of Cicero, the gentleness of Pliny, and the wisdom of Agrippa. . . . His mind works incessantly. He declaimed *Mahomet*, the tragedy on which he has been working . . . and I could only admire in silence. The Châtelet woman is lucky to have him, for someone with a good memory and nothing more could make a book of his brilliant asides."

Voltaire was also charmed. He commented on how easy it was to forget Frederick's rank and his army of one hundred thousand men. "I don't know yet if there have been greater kings, but no more amiable person has ever lived. It is a miracle of nature that this son of a crowned ogre, educated by fools, and in a wilderness, should have developed all the finesse, all the natural graces that are the accomplishments of a few in Paris, and have made it famous."

Frederick had not yet shaken off his chills and fever when, a month later, Wilhelmina, her husband, and her eight-year-old daughter, Frederica, arrived in Berlin. Wilhelmina was alarmed when her brother did not come down to the foot of the grand staircase to greet her with the rest of the family. He had sent word he would see her the following day.

Wilhelmina went from the palace to Mon Bijou, where her mother was now living, and that evening there was a family dinner party to reacquaint the eldest of the brood with those of her brothers and sisters who were still at home. In addition to August William, already met at Bayreuth, there was twenty-year-old Ulrica; Amelia, not yet seventeen; Henry, fourteen; and Ferdinand, aged ten. All were in black; the court was still in mourning—and mournful was the mood of Sophia Dorothea. After thirty years of waging one losing battle after another, she had hoped that freedom would bring her the complete confidence of the reigning sovereign, but Frederick had politely and stubbornly refused to consult his mother on any but the most trivial domestic problems. As in the past, voices of discontent chirped throughout the pretty, painted rooms of Mon Bijou, the royal stinginess, the royal secretiveness being the chief causes of complaint.

Wilhelmina might have passed on some of what she heard to Frederick if August William and Elizabeth Christian had not advised to the contrary. Only a glimpse was had of Frederick before he went to Rheinsberg, whither his guests were to follow as soon as he could arrange to make them comfortable.

Frederick was taking quinine and, though still haggard and feverish, managed to do the honors of his country house, as well as an enormous amount of business he kept strictly to himself. Every evening there was a concert at which the King played flute concertos with his orchestra, Pesne's painted Apollo bursting through the cloudy ceiling of the music room.

In spite of the little she was able to see of her brother, in spite of the unhappy feeling of his having changed, a feeling which had recurred each time they met during the past ten years, Wilhelmina enjoyed the weeks she spent at Rheinsberg. She saw the people of whom she had heard so much and found them equal to her expectations. Algarotti she already knew, also Knoblesdorf, the architect, who had stopped off in Bayreuth on his way to Italy. A new acquaintance was Pierre Louis Moreau de Maupertuis, a French mathematician and astronomer, who had led an expedition to Lapland to measure a degree of the meridian. Frederick's favorites seemed to be Count Keyserlingk, his dear Césarion, a bouncing little man, a chatterbox crammed with enthusiasm for the arts; and Charles Étienne Jordan, ex-pastor of a Huguenot community in East Prussia, who had come to Frederick as secretary and who had just been made director of all the hospitals and orphan asylums in Berlin. A pupil of Wilhelmina's teacher of history, Vizyierre de la Croze, Jordan was almost as learned as his teacher, but had the gift of wearing his scholarship with grace and passing it on to others without arousing their antagonism. Another important member of the Rheinsberg community, Michael Fredersdorf, was far from learned; in fact his education had gone no further than a village school. Because he could play the flute, Frederick had employed Fredersdorf at Küstrin, first as a lackey and then as a valet; his present function was guardian of the privy purse. A tall, handsome man, Fredersdorf had instinctive good manners and an impressively dignified air.

Though the women of the household were less to Wilhelmina's taste, this was chiefly because she was afraid the romping maids-of-honor might have a bad effect on Dorothea and Albertine von der Marwitz, whom she had brought with her from Bayreuth and on whom she kept an anxious eye. Wilhelmina must have seen how much her sister-in-law had improved. Elizabeth Christina had the good sense to say little while the rest of the company was showing off its combined and individual cleverness.

The cleverness of all was put to the test by the presence in their midst of a super-talent for table, talk a super-personality, Voltaire. Merely to meet him would have made Wilhelmina's visit high adventure. She saw all the Voltairean virtues Frederick had seen on first encounter and, in addition, a charm reserved for her sex alone. Few women could resist the touching physical frailty, the impudence, and the quite honest admiration of this shriveled little man with the piercing eyes and sunken cheeks. Since Voltaire had come to Prussia without Madame du Châtelet, he was able to give the ladies of Rheinsberg all the attention he could spare from an interesting project of his own.

At their meeting in Cleves Frederick had suggested a visit, and while Voltaire was waiting at Brussels for a date to be set, he sent a verbal message to the French minister, Cardinal Fleury, saying he was going to Berlin and would take with him "a heart that was thoroughly French." This delicately phrased suggestion of passing on confidential information of a political nature was followed by a copy of the *Antimachiavel*, which had just been published, but without Frederick's name attached. Many thought the book to be another of Voltaire's irreligious and immoral works. Little did Cardinal Fleury realize he himself had sat for the portrait of Machiavelli. He had little time to read, he replied, but would be glad of any assistance Voltaire could give him in Prussia.

During his short stay at Rheinsberg, however—he was there for just a week—Voltaire learned no more than he knew on arrival. In the last letter received from Frederick in Brussels there was a hint of "gunpowder in June," and of the time being ripe for a complete change in the old political system. The first paragraph of the letter ran: "A most unforeseen event prevents me from opening my heart to you and chattering on as usual. The Emperor is dead."

✦ ✦ ✦

The Emperor of the Holy Roman Empire, Charles VI, had died as the result of eating mushrooms, it was said, on October twentieth, 1740. He left an empty treasury, a disorganized army, and the dubious expectation of his daughter, Maria Theresa, being able to enjoy her inheritance according to the provisions of the Pragmatic Sanction. Prussia had been induced to sign this document by a promise of support in claiming the succession to Jülich and Berg, but this promise had been broken. As soon as he heard of the Emperor's death Frederick sent for his foreign minister, Henry von Podewils, and General von Schwerin, who, like General von der Schulenberg, had voted against the death penalty for Von Katte at his trial in 1730. To these two men Frederick revealed an idea that had been incubating in his mind ever since he first thought seriously of kingship at Küstrin.

At Küstrin Frederick had told his friend Natzmer of Prussia's need for expansion. At Küstrin he had done research on the linen trade with Silesia, the prosperous Hapsburg province lying directly south of Frederick's habitat of the moment, its nose wedged in between a fold of Prussian territory. Silesia was rich in minerals, in agriculture and in population—all of them good things, all necessary to Prussia's future development. A claim to four Silesian duchies had been validated by Brandenburg in the sixteenth century and, in Frederick's opinion, this was the portion of Hapsburg domain to which he had the clearest title and of which he had the greatest need.

Podewils and Schwerin advised negotiation. In return for the province, Frederick should offer a guarantee for Austrian possessions in Germany and the Low Countries, the relinquishment of Jülich and Berg, and the support of Maria Theresa's husband, Francis of Tuscany, in the coming imperial election. Rival candidates would be Augustus of Saxony-Poland and Charles Albert of Bavaria, who had hardly waited for the breath to be out of the Emperor's body to claim all of Maria Theresa's inheritance for his wife, a daughter of an elder brother of Charles VI. Both of these contestants would be natural allies of Prussia.

But Frederick preferred to stand and act alone. If he was to bargain, he would bargain from a position of strength. His announced intention of occupying Silesia, a repetition of the sleight of hand performed in Herstal, caused hair to rise on the heads of his advisers. To dare Liége to come on was one thing; to dare Austria was another. For his timid henchmen, Frederick coolly analyzed the reaction of the Great Powers to his move. England was engaged in a trade war with Spain, a war that would be known to history as the War of Jenkins' Ear. She and her major colonial rival, France, would hold one another off. Holland would be indifferent. There remained only Russia, and in Russia the Czarina Anne was ill and likely to die.

As a matter of fact, Anne was already dead. The news of her passing was traveling to Berlin while Frederick was playing the flute for his guests at Rheinsberg, tantalizing Voltaire by his reticence, and telling Podewils to work hard on a manifesto, soon to be published to the world. Justification was a ministerial job; implementation was Frederick's portion; his orders to the army had already been given.

By November twenty-sixth the Rheinsberg house-party had dissolved, and Wilhelmina was back in Berlin, where the period of mourning for Frederick William being over, a series of brilliant fetes was given, a blind for what was going on in every Prussian barrack and in every quartermaster's office. The movement of troops could not be entirely concealed, but their final destination was kept secret until the Austrian Ambassador was handed Frederick's terms for the cession of Silesia. The terms were substantially those outlined by Podewils and Schwerin.

On December fourteenth Frederick appeared at a costume ball, wearing a domino, but not a mask. He drew a dancer aside whom he was going to send to England with his manifesto and gaily asked the man if his boots were greased. Two days later Frederick was in Silesia. As he crossed "his Rubicon"—Frederick could never miss the chance for a classical comparison—flags were flying, drums were beating. At the last moment the Prince of Anhalt-Dessau made a pitiful protest: was he, the creator of the Prussian army, to be left behind? It would be a pretty spectacle for the King of Prussia to go off to war with a tutor, Frederick said.

Though her husband had hurried home to Bayreuth to consult his ministers as to the stand the Franconian states would take in this crisis, Wilhelmina stayed on in Berlin, hoping to see Frederick again within the next few weeks. She had been as surprised as everyone else, though she had guessed that something big was in the making. On hearing of the Emperor's death, Wilhelmina asked Frederick's philosophic friend, Count Manteuffel, if he thought Frederick had imperial ambitions. She had never been able to forget the prediction of the Swedish palmist who had read her and her brother's childish hands, foretelling for one four royal suitors and for the other an imperial crown.

Just before Christmas Frederick wrote from Glogau, saying there had been no casualties and no resistance. The Silesians were glad to see him come and were only afraid he might leave. Soon he would enter Breslau, the capital of the province. If it were not for the mountains of Moravia, he and his perfect army might be standing now before the gates of Vienna!

Wilhelmina could not wait for Frederick's return, for her husband came to take her and Frederica home in January. She exulted in her brother's easy triumphs, and when she received a rueful letter from Voltaire, enclosing a poem which began, "Sister of Apollo, who has turned to Mars," she replied that Apollo and Mars were one. Frederick was the sort of wizard who could banish horror even from war.

A fortnight later Wilhelmina heard of a great battle fought in the snow near the town of Mollwitz on April twelfth, 1741, Frederick's first battle, his first of many victories.

I T had seemed at first as if the battle of Mollwitz was a defeat. The Prussian cavalry, a branch of the service which had been of only minor interest to Frederick William, collapsed; the infantry saved the day. Frederick was not there to see the long line of foot-soldiers move across the snowy field with the same, deadly, purposeful precision as though on parade at Tempelhof. On the advice of his generals, the King had gone to the rear to escape capture.

In the letter written to Wilhelmina a few days later, there was no mention of this humiliation, nor of the hours of agony Frederick spent until news of victory caught up with him. His account of the battle, however, was somber. There had been losses; among those whom Wilhelmina knew were General von der Schulenberg and one of the Schwedt cousins, who used to be invited to children's birthday parties at Charlottenburg. Wilhelmina's congratulations were in minor key, for she realized how frivolous her letter to Voltaire had been; victories could not be won without the shedding of blood.

A casualty that struck home to Bayreuth was the wounding of General von der Marwitz, the father of Wilhelmina's trio of graces, Dorothea, Albertine and Caroline. The General was so badly lamed by a ball in his thigh he was no longer fit for active service and was given the armchair command of all the troops in

Silesia. Dorothea was sent for to nurse him. She seemed glad to go, for both she and Albertine had enjoyed their trip to Berlin and had offended Wilhelmina somewhat by letting her see they thought Bayreuth dull after so much gaiety.

Two days before leaving, Dorothea came to Wilhelmina's room in great distress. The Margrave's fondness for her had apparently been noted in Prussia, for a scolding letter from the General told his daughter to put a stop to all this talk by leaving Wilhelmina's service and by marrying a man he would select for her. She could not survive a separation, Dorothea cried, nor could she bear the thought of marrying a stranger. Wilhelmina, sympathetic, deeply stirred, promised a permanent place in her household and all possible protection from the General's matrimonial schemes. Dorothea and the Margrave had shown such great restraint that the gossip of Berlin seemed groundless to Wilhelmina; it was just one of those indigenous plagues against which Frederick had warned his sister.

She was sister now to a very famous man. In May, less than a month after Mollwitz, France's most distinguished general, Marshal de Belle-Isle, called to pay his respects in Bayreuth. When King Louis XV heard of Frederick's venture he said, "the man must be crazy," but Belle-Isle had just been in Silesia to propose a treaty of alliance. While Cardinal Fleury was inclined to respect the Pragmatic Sanction, the Marshal represented a more vigorous, a more youthful, faction. And no one in France, neither young nor old, neither radical nor conservative, wanted to see Maria Theresa's husband emperor. If Francis were elected he might try to regain his duchy of Lorraine, which had been handed over to the father-in-law of Louis XV, Stanislaus Leszczinski.

There were many visitors to Frederick's headquarters at Breslau that spring. Britain sent as mediator a Lord Hyndford, whom Frederick promptly christened Lord Dog Foot. "I am dealing with a dozen dangerous Machiavellis here," Frederick wrote to Voltaire. As in one way or another the network of secret agreements underlying the offers made was revealed, Frederick's comment was even more cynical. "To play the part of honest man among rogues is risky," Henry von Podewils was told. "If there is anything to be gained by honesty, we will be honest, but if deceit is the order of the day, then the rascals will be fooled; we'll see to that."

Frederick had leapt into the jungle of European politics fully armed and undismayed. He had none of his father's timidity or indecision. He was unencumbered by the illusion that justice can prevail without enforcement. All Frederick's early training had conditioned him to walk warily and expect the worst.

In June, just as Maria Theresa was getting ready to go down the Danube to be crowned Queen of Hungary, Frederick signed an agreement with France, one of its provisions being mutual support of Charles Albert of Bavaria. When the Austrian ministers heard of the pact they all slumped down in their chairs about the council table, as though shot by a swiveled gun mounted in its center. A large indemnity, the Austrian Netherlands, the Hapsburg possessions in Italy, and finally all of Silesia itself was offered to Frederick if he would withdraw. He shrugged away the offers; he made solemn, poker-faced fun of the English negotiators.

French troops began to move into Austria in the late summer to cooperate with troops of the Bavarian claimant, the route of certain divisions passing through Bayreuth. It seemed as though Vienna would be taken, but at the last moment the allies veered away to capture Prague. Wilhelmina received a letter from the Dowager Empress, the mother of Maria Theresa, begging her to intercede with Frederick. She sent the letter on to him, asking what her reply should be. Word came back to say nothing definite. "For God's sake," Frederick urged, "don't let the Margrave do anything foolish."

Frederick's opinion of his brother-in-law's flair for politics was low. Somewhat earlier a plan had been submitted to him for Bayreuth to take under its protection the free city of Nürnberg, the Margrave having gone there and having been greeted by some of the leading citizens as their savior. This seemed to Frederick a foolhardy enterprise. The game was too complicated, he thought, to be judged from the sidelines. He, who was at the center, should direct its strategy.

But as the end which he and all others had foreseen drew near, Frederick asked himself whether he really wanted France to win, hands down. Would he be satisfied to see Austria vanish from the map and a French-subsidized Bavaria take its place? Saxony had also joined in the attack, hoping for its share of the spoils, and Frederick's grudge against Saxony endured.

On a night in October a very secret meeting was held at Klein Schnellendorf, a lonely Silesian castle halfway between Brieg and Neisse. Frederick met there the Austrian generalissimo and, once more, the English go-between, Lord Dog Foot, who had arranged the rendezvous. A temporary, unwritten armistice was agreed upon. Frederick was allowed to capture Neisse, with hardly a shot fired, and the Austrian army went off unscathed to menace Frederick's allies in Bohemia.

So successful were the Austrians that Prague was retaken on November twenty-sixth. Charles Albert, who had had himself crowned King, was forced to leave the country, his for only a matter of weeks. He retired to Munich, his enemies in hot pursuit; even there, in his homeland, it was impossible to hold them off. The only place of safety for the unfortunate man was Frankfurt. There Charles Albert could count on being elected Emperor with the help of France and Prussia.

As he passed through Bayreuth in January the Imperial Vagabond—the nickname was self-imposed—sent his compliments to Wilhelmina and her husband, but said he couldn't stop to see them. The Margrave mounted his horse and galloped after the shabby carriage in which Charles Albert was traveling. For a full half-hour the two men talked by the roadside. A gracious invitation to the ceremonies at Frankfurt was given.

With Frederick's admonition in mind, perhaps, it was decided to be as inconspicuous as possible and to stay for one day only. When the travelers arrived, after a wet winter journey over flooded roads, they were told the coronation had been put off for two weeks. Wilhelmina had merely brought a single costume for herself and for her ladies, Albertine von der Marwitz and Dorothea, who had hurried home to join the party; it consisted of a hooded cloak cut to conceal the lower part of the wearer's face. The two blond young men of the party charcoaled their eyebrows and put on black wigs. Thus disguised, the Bayreuthers witnessed the entry of the Emperor into the city, went to the theater and to masked balls, and were among the anonymous thousands who witnessed the coronation. Plenty of regalia was employed on this occasion, and plenty of holy oil was poured for anointment. Poor Charles Albert, however, was in no condition to enjoy the ceremony. He was suffering from a kidney stone and had to use his teeth to pull the ceremonial gloves over his gout-swollen fingers. On the day of his crowning, February twelfth, 1742, the Emperor's capital city of Munich was taken by the Austrians.

Seeing himself helpless to defend his own, Charles Albert and his backers cajoled the petty princes of the Empire. Day after day the resident representative of Bayreuth in Frankfurt was entertained by the Marshal de Belle-Isle, who headed the magnificent, free-spending, free-banqueting, French delegation. Madame de Belle-Isle and other distinguished folk came to call on Wilhelmina, who could no longer pretend she was just another sightseer. Her somewhat paranoid insistence on protocol came to the fore when a visit to the Empress was suggested. As Margravine of Bayreuth, Wilhelmina would only be entitled to sit on a footstool in the Empress's presence, and not in an armchair, as befitted the daughter and sister of a king. Wilhelmina only consented to the audience when assured that the imperial chair would be low and the footstool overstuffed.

The interview proved as baffling as most occasions where ceremony gets the upper hand. The Empress, very squat and very homely, was so shy that she trembled when she asked her visitor to sit down. There was a prolonged silence. When Wilhelmina ventured to murmur something in French the Empress said she did not understand and would prefer to speak German. This was probably untrue and only a convention forced on one who was the wife of a German Emperor. From that point on the two conversationalists lost all contact with one another, since each spoke a different dialect and neither spoke her idiom fluently.

A few days later Wilhelmina and her friends left Frankfurt. There had been so much to do there, and the ever sociable Margrave had enjoyed himself so thoroughly, that he had put his name to a treaty without carefully reading its contents. It was disconcerting to find that Bayreuth had promised to raise a regiment of eight hundred men for the Emperor and to support him, come what may. In return, the Margrave would receive the town of Rettwitz and the title of Marshal in the army of Franconia. These were dubious rewards, since Rettwitz was in Bohemia and would not be available until the kingdom had been reconquered; as for the army of Franconia, it only existed as yet on paper.

Frederick was worried when he heard of the treaty. Again he begged his relatives to ask his advice before taking any political step. They should look upon him, he suggested, as a wise old uncle, an East Indian merchant, who, having inside information, could tell them when to buy and when to sell their shares of stock.

Frederick was on his way to Moravia to make a diversion in favor of the Bavarians and French, for the pendulum had swung too far in the opposite direction. Austria was pushing ahead on every front, except the Silesian; soon reinforcements might come from Hungary, where Maria Theresa's personal appearance had had dramtic effect.

On May seventeenth, 1742, the enemy was met and defeated at Chotusitz. This time Frederick was present throughout the battle and in full command. He could be proud of the performance of his retrained cavalry. Peace was what he wanted now, a victor's peace. According to the document signed at Breslau in July, Frederick was granted the greater part of Silesia. He realized, of course, that this was only an interlude, for Maria Theresa was as determined and as courageous as he. As soon as she was able she would try to recover her purloined province.

In announcing to his allies, whose interests he had considered so little, his retirement from the war, it may have been a minor annoyance to Frederick to think that little Bayreuth, his sister's principality, had pledged more than it could deliver to the Emperor. Frederick, however, had already thought of benefiting the Emperor and himself by strengthening his ties with southern Germany. In this his sister and his brother-in-law could be of real assistance.

+ + +

Not long before the journey to Frankfurt there were visitors in Bayreuth. Three young, fatherless princes of Württemberg, who were being educated in Berlin, came for a fortnight in December. The eldest of the trio and heir to the dukedom, Charles Eugene, paid much attention to nine-year-old Frederica, who was five years his junior. Wilhelmina and the Margrave were amused by this childish flirtation and thought what a pretty pair their daughter and the Prince would make.

A few weeks later the boys' mother arrived. She was much less to Wilhelmina's taste than the young folk, a faded beauty, who liked to receive gentlemen in her bedchamber, where she had two bells of differing timbre beside her bed, one of which was rung for champagne to be brought and the other for tokay. Added to her flirtatiousness, the Duchess was an incessant, harsh-voiced talker. She suffered, Wilhelmina said, from "oral flux." At first amusing, she eventually wore you down by the persistent spray of her conversation.

The Duchess was on her way from Stuttgart, the capital of Württemberg, to see Frederick in Berlin. When she heard the King was still in Silesia, she wanted to stay in Bayreuth until his return. A good deal of polite pressure was needed to dislodge her so that her host and hostess could get off for Frankfurt. On their return, they received a formal offer of marriage from the guardians of the young Duke. The offer was endorsed by Frederick, who said he would supply the dowry and pay for the wedding. He would do as much for Wilhelmina's child as for one of his own. Though the family was Catholic, the match was a good one, Württemberg being the largest and richest of the Franconian states. The only drawback Frederick saw—and this he treated as a joke—was the Dowager Duchess. How such a freak and bore could produce such likable children, he could not understand!

Wilhelmina's response to the proposal was a tepid, a guarded, acceptance. It would be years, she pointed out, before a marriage could take place, and by that time the young Duke might not want to marry Frederica. "This has been known to happen," Wilhelmina reminded her brother, who had made such a determined if unsuccessful, resistance to being mated with a woman he did not fancy.

There the matter rested. For a full year there was no mention on either hand of Frederica's engagement.

After his return from Breslau Frederick devoted himself to business neglected during his campaign, his working day being as strenuous at home as in the field. He saw little of Elizabeth Christina, to whom he had given a pretty country house at Schönhausen. There she was to spend the greater part of a long life, ever loyal to "the dear master," ever hoping wistfully for a return to the happy days of Rheinsberg. The King and Queen met only in Berlin, where they sometimes dined together at Mon Bijou or appeared on such state occasions as the marriage of August William to the Queen's sister, Lousia of Brunswick-Bevern. At his brother's wedding Frederick appeared younger and gayer than the bridegroom, wearing a coat of silver tissue, his wife a gown of green Prussian velvet, product of Frederick's latest adventure in promoting industry.

A new opera, *Venus and Cupid*, was given by singers recruited in Italy. Though the new opera house on Unter den Linden was not yet ready because of wartime shortages, it was completed before the end of the year and was one of the finest in

Europe, with parking space in its courtyard for a thousand carriages and an underground water system for fire protection and for scenic effects on stage.

The plans for the opera house were sent to Wilhelmina, also those Knobblesdorf had drawn for a new wing at Charlottenburg to house the art collection of the Prince de Polignac, recently acquired in Paris. Wilhelmina was invited to view these wonders, but said she was not well enough to travel. In the early spring of 1743 she had had an abscess of the throat, but Frederick may have suspected her of being reluctant to talk with him further of the Württemberg marriage. He came quickly to the sour conclusion that somebody was trying to frustrate his plans when, in July, he heard of Duke Charles Eugene and his brothers being about to leave Berlin.

The rumor, for it was only a rumor, reached Frederick in Silesia. Unlike the Hapsburgs, who had never visited the province in the two hundred years they held it, Frederick was giving his new subjects much personal attention. Before long he might have to defend his acquisition, for the French had been defeated at Dettingen in June, and a new alliance had been formed between England and Austria, recognizing the ante-bellum frontiers of Hapsburg territories. At this moment it was unpleasant to hear of even a minor setback to the scheme for creating a south-German bloc friendly to Prussia and to the enfeebled Emperor.

Frederick wrote at once to Wilhelmina, asking if she had had anything to do with the Württemberg princes wanting to go home. Had anyone told her that he, Frederick, was no longer interested in a Bayreuth-Württemberg alliance? Had she passed this on to the boys' mother?

Certainly not, Wilhelmina replied. She would never take seriously the opinion of a third party in regard to Frederick's intentions. She would never dream of working against him in secret. But she repeated what she had said before: the marriage was only a dream of the future. It was too early as yet to set a definite pattern for the course of two young lives.

Frederick, as soon as he reached Berlin in August, saw to it that the Württembergers stayed where they were and the members of their household, who were responsible for the thought of their leaving, were pacified. He decided to visit Bayreuth as part of a tour reminiscent of the one made by Frederick William in 1730 to drum up imperial support. To please Wilhelmina, Frederick would take with him August William, for whom she felt a real affection, the star of his troupe of Italian singers, Porporino, and Voltaire, who had once more come to Berlin, unencumbered by Madame du Châtelet, and in hope of making further political capital out of his friendship with the King of Prussia.

SINCE their parting at Rheinsberg in the autumn of 1740 the temperature of friendship between King and poet had dropped by several degrees.

Voltaire was shocked by Frederick's invasion of Silesia. He hated war as the most highly organized form of human cruelty. Though elaborate congratulations had gone to the victor, Voltaire's flattery larded subtle criticisms; for example, "Your Majesty has done many things in a short time. . . . The only thing I dread is your coming to despise men too much. Millions of featherless, two-footed animals who people this earth, are at an immense distance from you both in mind and in estate. . . . There is yet another drawback: Your Majesty paints so well the noble deceits of politicians, the selfish attentions of courtiers that you will end by suspecting the affection of every man." All rhetoric aside, Voltaire was voicing his disappointment in Frederick as a disciple and was insisting on his own sincerity.

But sincerity in one who protested so much and so eloquently had become suspect. Frederick's image of the noble creator of noble works of art, naively expressed in his first letter to the master, had been severely damaged. Frederick had suspected Voltaire of trying to pump him at Rheinsberg, at a time when secrecy was all important. He was jolted by the presentation of an enormous bill for traveling expenses. To his trusty friend and secretary, Charles Étienne Jordan, Frederick complained that the entertainment of this one guest alone had cost him five hundred and thirty écus per day. "Never was royal jester so highly paid."

Frederick might fume, but he still considered Voltaire the greatest living writer of prose and verse, the greatest wit, one of the few to whom it was given "to make the mind laugh." In defense of his recent course of action, Frederick insisted on the duality of his nature. All that Rheinsberg represented was dear to him, but politics was the dreary, the necessary, business to which he had been born. Donkeys, Doric columns and kings had been created to bear the burdens of this world. When Voltaire sent a pacifist pamphlet, published recently at Amsterdam, Frederick endorsed its message; the scheme would be quite feasible, he wrote, if the consent of all of Europe and "a few other trifles" could be gained.

As for the Peace of Breslau, Frederick felt no need to apologize for any sort of peace to a philosopher, even though that philosopher happened to be a Frenchman. Unfortunately Voltaire's letter agreeing with these sentiments was opened by the police. It caused such an outcry in Paris that its authorship was disowned.

The French government, however, was itching to know what would be Frederick's next move. Voltaire might be a dubious character at home, but his connections abroad should not be wasted. The ministry suggested a second secret mission and agreed to the terms Voltaire proposed: a year's salary, plus eight thousand francs and the award of government contracts to a firm in which the poet was heavily invested. To make his acceptance of a standing invitation to visit Prussia plausible, Voltaire would pose as a refugee from persecution. A seat in the French Academy had become vacant on the death of Cardinal Fleury in his ninetieth year. Instead of Voltaire's being selected to fill the chair, it went to an obscure bishop, author of one dull book. As a final touch of verisimilitude, Voltaire's latest tragedy, *The Death of Ceasar*, was banned by the censor.

Hymning praise of his "adorable monarch" and comparing

[211]

Frederick to Tacitus and Xenophon, Voltaire journeyed to The Hague. There he took up residence in the Prussian Embassy, which was presided over by Otto von Podewils, a nephew of Frederick's foreign minister. Voltaire thought he had made an important discovery when he learned of Frederick's having negotiated a considerable loan from Dutch bankers; the news went back to Paris in cipher.

Voltaire's prominence in intellectual circles, however, was poor equipment for an undercover agent. His every move was discussed by friend and foe; before he had crossed the borders of France the secret of his mission was out. It was given further publicity by a Cologne newspaper. Frederick, who read newspapers and who was informed of what was being said in foreign capitals, was annoyed. He thought two could play at the game of hoodwink. He sent to his ambassador in Paris a letter from Voltaire in which the newly appointed tutor to the Dauphin, a churchman, was dubbed an ass. Frederick suggested this might be brought unobtrusively to the ass's attention. If the climate of France became too hot, Voltaire might be content to stay in Prussia.

To welcome his guest, Frederick arranged a select little dinner party for the evening of Voltaire's arrival. No hours spent at table could have been more gay and more harmonious. A few days later a set of questions on foreign policy was presented which Frederick dismissed with a wave of the hand. It would be as inappropriate, he declared, to talk politics with Voltaire as to offer a glass of physic to one's mistress. "I will talk only of poetry." After this rebuff, the invitation to go to Bayreuth with the King was offered as a consolation.

Wilhelmina had had sufficient warning to prepare a full program of entertainment for her guests. There was music, there were out-door dinner parties at the Hermitage, which was being enlarged and decorated by craftsmen newly arrived from Italy. A play was rehearsed, Racine's *Bajazet,* in which Wilhelmina appeared as Roxane and Voltaire as Acomat, the scheming vizier, dressed in a Chinese costume borrowed from the wardrobe of the palace theater. The Duchess of Württemberg, who, at Frederick's suggestion, had added herself to the party, sat up all of one night copying cantos of *La Pucelle*, which Voltaire had brought as a gift to his hostess.

The visit lasted for nine days, but during most of that time Frederick was absent. He went to Ansbach to meet with the Prince-Bishop of Würzburg, and to Kaiserhammer to inspect the forces of Emperor Charles VII. There was little for Voltaire to report to Paris, except that a strong Franconian league seemed unlikely; he himself had tried to inspire the Margrave to raise troops independently for France, but Wilhelmina's husband, though willing and pleasant spoken, lacked enterprise. For Wilhelmina, Voltaire felt a great admiration. She was gifted, she was witty, and her little daughter Frederica was "the most beautiful child in Europe." To a man whose life has been so insecure Bayreuth seemed an idyllic retreat, where one could enjoy all the pleasures of a great court, without the tiresome burden of etiquette.

Voltaire was so pleasantly occupied that for two weeks he forgot to write to Madame du Châtelet. As chief entertainer and most honored guest, he caught only an inkling of how dissatisfied Frederick and Wilhelmina were with one another.

✦ ✦ ✦

Before taking his leave Frederick composed some complimentary verses he left for Wilhelmina to discover on her writing table. His stay, he said, had been a hundred years too short for his pleasure and a hundred years too long for his business. To Minister von Podewils, Frederick confided, "I am afraid the Bayreuthers will not be with us." He had taken home with him an unpleasant impression of there being a pro-Austrian party at his sister's court.

Wilhelmina, on the other hand, was aggrieved by the small amount of time Frederick had spent with her. She felt the visit had been purely political. But what were Frederick's politics? He had told her nothing. She was still obsessed with the notion he wanted to be Emperor, and since Charles VII had been bed-ridden for the most part since his coronation, a new Emperor might soon be chosen. Wilhelmina wondered if her brother might not even change his religion to gain his end. She mentioned this to Count Cobenzl, an emissary from Vienna, who came frequently to Bayreuth, Wilhelmina's close connection with her brother being well known.

One member of Wilhelmina's circle who, if not actively pro-Austrian, was anti-Frederick, was Daniel de Superville, the physician who had come to Bayreuth at Frederick's instigation. Superville was not on hand for the autumn visit. He was busy at Erlangen with preparations for the opening of a university which would bear the Margrave's name, but which was the creation of his wife. A boy's academy, numbering only twenty-six students was the nucleus. At Erlangen, it was thought, there would be less interference from the conservative clergy than in the capital. Doctor de Superville, the university's appointed rector, had emphasized his liberal outlook by having an inaugural portrait painted of himself with his hand resting on volumes of Locke, Lucretius and Bayle.

On November third, 1743, Wilhelmina and her husband headed a procession of carriages moving down the principal avenue of Erlangen. Verses hailing the Margravine as the Minerva of Bayreuth were read, the most substantial feature of the exercises being a debate on two theses Wilhelmina had proposed, one dealing with the divisibility of matter, the other with the relation of matter to mind. When Frederick received an account of the ceremonies he poked a little tactless fun at the overambitious project of founding a university in Bayreuth. Wilhelmina, he said, should have pitted Medea—this was his pet name for the Duchess of Württemberg—against Superville and the entire faculty; he would back the Duchess to out-talk them all.

The Duchess, indeed! Wilhelmina's dislike of Medea was patent, but in the short time spent at the Hermitage Frederick had devoted much of his attention to making himself agreeable to the lady. It had been arranged for the young Duke and his mother to visit Bayreuth soon after Charles Eugene had reached his majority in January. Just before the birthday Frederick had a number of confidential talks with the boy and, for his benefit, wrote a graceful essay, "A Mirror for a Prince," in which there were a few discreet words on matrimony, but nothing so definite as to rouse antagonism. The result was that during the visit to Bayreuth Charles Eugene proposed of his own accord to Frederica, and the engagement for which Wilhelmina felt so little enthusiasm became official.

Other matchmaking plans to strengthen Prussia's position were under way. In Russia yet another Czarina reigned, Elizabeth, daughter of Peter the Great, who, with the help of a few personal friends and encouragement from the French ambassador, had pushed aside the infant successor of her cousin Anne. Being officially a virgin—though Elizabeth may have been married to one of her many lovers—the Czarina had appointed as heir to the throne her nephew Peter Ulrich, Duke of Holstein-Gastorp. The young man was in Petersburg and was being Russianized, but would be allowed a German wife. Frederick, who had been approached in regard to his two unmarried sisters, Ulrica and Amelia, could not stomach the idea of sending his own flesh and blood to a country where the mortality rate of royalty was so high. He was glad to suggest a substitute in the daughter of the Prince of Anhalt-Zerbst, a Prussian general, and the governor of Stettin. This fifteen-year-old girl, who, on being received into the Orthodox Church, would assume the name of Catherine, passed through Berlin with her parents en route to Russia. To make a deep impression upon her, Frederick exerted all the charm he had used to such effect on the Württembergers, mother and son. Ulrica, meanwhile, was safely and advantageously affianced to Adolph Frederick, Crown Prince of Sweden.

Wilhelmina received an announcement of Ulrica's betrothal which had been dictated to a secretary, Frederick apologizing for its not having been written by his own hand; the special cachet of their correspondence was its intimacy. The next letter in the series, however, was also dictated. Its tone, its content, were unlike anything that had ever passed between brother and sister.

✦ ✦ ✦

During Frederick's visit to Bayreuth, Caroline, the youngest of the Marwitz sisters, was at Carlsbad, where she had gone ostensibly to take a cure, but actually to meet and marry Count Schönburg, a very rich, a very handsome, young man, a palace chamberlain, whom all the unmarried ladies in Bayreuth had wanted for a husband. Since Caroline, unlike Dorothea and Albertine, was not officially a lady-in-waiting, Wilhelmina did not feel responsible for the elopement. She wrote to Frederick she might have sympathized entirely with the outraged feelings of General von der Marwitz, if the General had not wanted his two remaining daughters to come home at once to be properly married. A husband had been picked for Dorothea, Otto von Podewils, the Prussian ambassador with whom Voltaire had stayed at the Hague. Dorothea did not want to leave Bayreuth, and Wilhelmina asked Frederick not to interfere in case the General should appeal to him.

Whether it was negligence on Frederick's part, or whether, having heard the fairly common gossip that Dorothea was the Margrave's mistress, he thought it better for her to come home to Prussia, there was no answer, yes or no, to Wilhelmina's request. For two months Frederick continued to write of less significant and less urgent matters: of August William's wife being pregnant, of an amazing ballet dancer, La Barberina, who had just been engaged for the Berlin opera. Then, in April, word came from General von der Marwitz at Breslau, word which seemed to prove the existence of the Austrian party in Bayreuth which Frederick had suspected. Wilhelmina seemed to be its chief, for she was trying to marry her favorite lady-in-waiting to an officer in a regiment commanded by Francis of Tuscany, husband of Maria Theresa. Wilhelmina had written to the General, asking his consent to the match and offering to contribute to the dowry.

Frederick's secretary took his pen in hand to write at Frederick's dictation:

> Madame, my very dear sister: I am much surprised to learn from a letter from General von der Marwitz that you have been promoting a marriage between his eldest daughter and Count Burhauss. . . . I was all the more amazed because, of course you must remember the declared wish of our very dear father. When he gave you the Marwitz girls he stipulated they should not marry outside of this country, and in time they were to return here. . . . I hope, therefore, that your good sense and the feeling you have for me will prevent your going any further with this plan, which displeases me infinitely.

Frederick pointed out that if Dorothea persisted in marrying, she would suffer the same fate as Caroline and be cut off in her father's will, except for the very small amount required by Law. The letter continued on its stately way:

> I should be inconsolable if this unhappy affair should cause a rift between you and me, bound as we are by blood and affection—but I cannot recognize these foreign marriages. . . . In any case, I ask you to send the lady in question here. I will see to it she is well provided for.

A few days later Frederick wrote again, but only a shade less haughtily. He enclosed the letter from General von der Marwitz, who was in such poor health that the shock of Dorothea's marriage might put an end to him. Frederick hoped Wilhelmina would take pity on an elderly patriot, who was about to die as truly for his country as if he had fallen at Mollwitz.

But it was too late for an appeal to sentiment. Wilhelmina had already written to tell Frederick of Dorothea's marriage.

❧[*Chapter 24*]❧

THE marriage of Dorothea von der Marwitz to Count Burghauss, her old admirer, the man who had courted her when she was a girl of eighteen, took place on April eighth, 1744, with only a very few persons present. Neither of Dorothea's aunts, Flora and Madame von Sonsfeld, knew of what had happened. Madame von Sonsfeld, in fact, was ill in bed. It was she who had first suggested Dorothea's coming to Bayreuth, and it had been a satisfaction to her, no doubt, to watch the development of a close affection between her former pupil and her niece. When the journey to France was given up in 1739 because the Margrave's infatuation had become too obvious, Madame von Sonsfeld did her best to reconcile all three of the parties involved. Being old and infirm and spending most of her time in her room, the governess was probably unaware of gossip and of the change in Dorothea's attitude toward Wilhelmina.

Wilhelmina could no longer abide the insolence of the girl she had formed and for whom she still felt a bruised, unhappy love. If there was a disagreement between them now, Dorothea appealed at once to the Margrave. Her position was so well recognized that in the newspaper account of the inaugural ceremonies at Erlangen Dorothea was given special mention as a brilliant young woman who could have held her own in the debates.

Count Burghauss, on leave from the army, was also mentioned. In him Wilhelmina saw a solution to the problem of breaking off the liaison with the Margrave and at the same time keeping her promise to Dorothea, the promise of protection from the highhanded matchmaking of General von der Marwitz. Since Caroline's elopement stern letters, speaking of the duty children owed to their parents, were coming from Breslau.

In reviving an old romance Wilhelmina had to conquer a certain lack of enthusiasm on either hand. In writing to Frederick she took full responsibility for what she had done. She could not understand, she said, why Frederick should disinter a promise made to their father, and not to him. Dorothea did not want to marry a man she had never seen; she was twenty-seven now, and was certainly old enough to know her own mind. The General, indeed, had forced the issue by treating a mature woman as though she were a child. And, after all, was the matter so important? Wilhelmina begged Frederick not to "drive her to despair because of this bagatelle."

But bagatelle was too mild a term. "There is an old proverb," Frederick wrote, "that a person is judged by actions, not by words. If this is true, then you must know what I think of you. There is no need to go into particulars."

Frederick was on his way to the baths at Pyrmont as prelude to a strenuous summer. He had decided to ally himself again with France and re-enter the Franco-Austrian war. He might soon be fighting the army in which Count Burghauss held his commission.

From her mother Wilhelmina heard of the success of Frederick's course of treatments and sent congratulations. His health, Frederick replied coldly, was too small a matter for her interest. Wilhelmina tried to match Frederick's irony, but failed. She wrote abjectly in August, "You are still angry. . . . If I had known how you would feel, I would never have done it. But now it is done, and you have taken your revenge. . . . Don't leave me in my present state. Have pity on your poor sister, who only wants to make good her fault!"

When Frederick admitted grudgingly he could never forget their close relationship Wilhelmina took heart. She had by this time heard of the Prussian army's being in Bohemia. She let Frederick know she was praying for his success. It was Wilhelmina's misfortune, however, that a newspaper, published in Erlangen by a former professor at the Erlangen Academy, printed a mock-heroic account of the Prussian assault on Prague. Frederick, who had already cut off news from the paper for what he considered faulty reporting, was quick to take offense. "I don't know how I have earned this man's dislike," he wrote, "but I do know that in my country such an impertinence to one of my relatives would never to permitted."

It was useless for Wilhelmina to protest she had not seen the article, that she and her husband never read the newspapers. The journal would be suppressed, she promised, and the editor would be arrested, if he had not already removed himself to Nürnberg. "Let him go," was Frederick's disgusted rejoinder. "I only hope he has not misled your people!"

It would have been better if these devoted correspondents had ceased to write to one another altogether, but the habit of communication was too old, too strong, to be broken. There were periods of weeks and even months when no word passed between them.

Wilhelmina busied herself with the construction of an outdoor theater at the Hermitage and an opera house in the town, an exquisite example of rococo art, but her days were desolate. Albertine von der Marwitz had gone home to her father and was promptly married to Otto von Podewils. Dorothea remained in Bayreuth, but the old charm of her companionship was gone. Marriage had only confirmed Madame Burghauss's position as the Margrave's *belle amie*; Burghauss, absent at the war, was marked down as "the sort of man who is willing to wear second-hand clothing." Just before the end of the year General von der Marwitz died, leaving a will in which Albertine was named as heir to the bulk of her father's estate; only the small amount required by law was left to the other two sisters, and Frederick, who had been named executor, refused to pay these portions. Dorothea, embittered, let Wilhelmina see how greatly she had blundered.

In her loneliness, Wilhelmina took up again what had originally been a desultory pastime. It had occurred to her several years earlier to write the story of her life, but purely for her own amusement. She would give the manuscript to her daughter when Frederica was old enough to appreciate it, or she might "make a sacrifice to Vulcan," and feed it to the flames. There were models at hand of the genre Wilhelmina was attempting. Her great grandmother, the Electress Sophia, had written memoirs; Wilhelmina's library contained copies of all the best known reminiscences of the past century. Among them was one for which Wilhelmina felt a special affinity, the memoirs of Louise d'Orléans, Duchess of Montpensier, better known to posterity as La Grande Mademoiselle. Like Wilhelmina, this high-born lady, a cousin of Louis XIV of France, was courted ineffectually by various royal personages and in the end married beneath her.

Wilhelmina's tale of greatness unachieved was a tale of persecution and of her parents' bungling and cruelty. She lacked the high animal spirits of the French Princess, but had far greater creative gifts. Wilhelmina knew how to use contrast and suspense and how to develop character from a roughly static sketch to a rounded, moving personality. She had brought her story up to the year 1730, the crucial year of her imprisonment. In rewriting and extending it, Wilhelmina had in view an even more tragic denouement, her present estrangement from Frederick. Neither father nor mother had been spared in her earlier version; she tried now to show how Frederick's love for her had cooled, how with the years he had become hard hearted, calculating and tyrannical; a drastic metamorphosis, for in her opening pages she had written, "Never was there a greater tenderness than ours."

✦ ✦ ✦

While Wilhelmina was dealing thus sorrowfully with the past Frederick was battling with the present and, hedged by dangers, was trying to foresee the future. Before taking off on his dash to Prague, Frederick urged his principal ally, France, to wage a vigorous campaign in his rear. The support was feeble, chiefly because Louis XV had been pricked on by his mistress of the moment, Madame de Chateauroux, to lead his armies in person. He made the further mistake of falling ill. Prussian lines of communication were cut. Unlike the Silesians, the Slavic inhabitants of Bohemia were hostile. Peasants hid their corn, and they and their cattle vanished like mists into the forests. Frederick had to retreat through mountainous country into Silesia. The autumn rains were heavy, there was much sickness and desertion. Money was also running low. Frederick sent word to his confidential treasurer, Michael Fredersdorf, for all the gold and silver tableware and ornaments in the royal palaces to be removed secretly to the mint at dead of night. He also gave instructions for the government to be evacuated to Stettin in case of need.

The new year of 1745 opened with disaster. On January twentieth Charles VII died. The Imperial Vagabond, who had been an invalid during all of his three year tenure of office, was allowed by the kindness of Maria Theresa to close his eyes in his home city, Munich. Peace was made with Charles's youthful son, who was permitted to succeed his father as Elector of Bavaria in exchange for a promise to vote for Maria Theresa's husband as Emperor.

Frederick's ostensible reason for waging war was now gone, and he faced two new enemies, Saxony, which had gone over to the side of Austria, and a slowly mobilizing Russia, the Czarina's minister, Betuschev, being strongly anti-Prussian. Frederick's minister, Henry von Podewils, came close to nervous collapse when he heard of the Emperor's death. Though Frederick admitted that another spring might find him on his way to Avignon, where his distant Stuart cousins were living in exile, he exhorted Podewils not to be "a wet hen," and to remember how intrepid Maria Theresa had been when, four years earlier, it seemed as if Vienna might be taken. He was only able to keep his own courage up, he said, by giving "great cudgel blows to my soul."

No battle had been fought, however, and battle was the medicine which could kill or cure. On June third, 1745, Frederick lured an army of Austrians and Saxons across the Silesian border and thoroughly defeated it at Hohenfriedberg. To Wilhelmina, whom he had not heard from for three months, Frederick wrote a grimly exultant account of the numbers engaged, the huge amounts of matériel taken and the tally of prisoners. On the same day—this was something that had often happened in the past—she was writing to him to say, "You have wiped me from your mind."

Of his next victory, won at Soor in Bohemia, a desperate engagement, in which his horse was shot under him and his forces were outnumbered two to one, Frederick reported drily that, "We have beaten the Austrians, or rather the Imperialists, as it pleases you to call them." Very different were his words to Fredersdorf: "I hope the people at home will be satisfied with me, for I have done more than man can do." Wilhelmina, Frederick thought, could no longer appreciate his efforts. It so happened that she was about to offend him again.

The victory at Soor coincided roughly with the imperial election and coronation in late September. Frederick, as hereditary chamberlain of the Empire, should have been in Frankfurt to carry a ceremonial bowl of water in which the new Emperor, Francis of Tuscany, washed his hands. Maria Theresa, who had chosen not to be crowned as Empress, wishing to keep her hereditary titles to the fore, led the applause as her husband appeared in his regalia. On her way back to Vienna, she passed through a corner of Bayreuth. Wilhelmina went with her husband to pay her respects and was asked to preside at a dinner given the visitor. News of this event reached Berlin, where it was spoken of with flaming indignation by Sophia Dorothea. All her old animosity against Wilhelmina had revived. A letter came to Bayreuth that Wilhelmina said could only have been written to a bastard.

Frederick's comment was delayed for two months, a crowded two months, in which he had staved off an invasion of Prussia by Saxon and Russian troops, beating the enemy to an attack on Saxon soil. Detained in Bohemia, Frederick could not lead the army of reserves in person at Kesseldorf. The hero of the day was the Prince of Anhalt-Dessau, aged seventy-six. Old Snoutbeard, as he was sometimes called in derision because of his bristling mustache, was slow to move and Frederick had to use the spur of insult to get him started. Before the assault was made up an icy slope, for it was now early December, the Dessauer was heard to pray. He asked the Lord God to help him. "And if you won't do that, then at least don't help those rascals over there, the enemy."

Rising to his feet and waving his hat, the old man cried, "In the name of Jesus—march!" The men went singing up the slope, and a fortnight later peace was signed between Prussia, Austria and Saxony in Dresden.

"The interest you take in all that concerns the Queen of Hungary," Frederick wrote on December thirtieth, 1745, "gives me the opportunity of telling you we have just made a peace. I believe, my dear sister, this will be all the more pleasing to you because from now on your partiality need not be troubled by what remains of the old affection you once felt for me."

Wilhelmina was stung to a proud reply. She was glad of the peace, she declared, and thought it did Frederick greater credit than all his victories. "As for the Queen of Hungary, I have never had a partiality for her, or a particular interest in her fate. I respect her virtues, and think it right to value anyone who has them. My affection and concern for you is not lessened thereby, though you have made me see how little you believe in the truth of what I say."

✦ ✦ ✦

There were workers for accord within the family circle. Ulrica, now Crown Princess of Sweden, and August William were devoted to one another and, with a close brother-sister involvement of their own, considered the misunderstanding between Frederick and Wilhelmina "a mere lovers' quarrel." They also were familiar with their mother's temperament. Though absent from Berlin, Ulrica tried to tone down the denunciation of Wilhelmina's sins she was sure was echoing through Mon Bijou. Possibly August William let Frederick see one of the letters from Stockholm in which Ulrica said she was sure curiosity and the urgings of La Marwitz were responsible for Wilhelmina's visit to Maria Theresa.

A white flag of truce was hoisted. "I never suspected your heart of having anything to do with all the vexations you have caused me during the past three years," Frederick wrote. "I know you too well for that. I put the blame on the wretches who abuse your confidence and take a malicious delight in estranging you from those who love you tenderly. . . . Everybody knows the unworthy character of the creature whom I will not name for fear of soiling my pen. You alone have been blind. You are like the cuckold who is always the last to know what is going on under his own roof while the whole town is buzzing with the news. Forgive me, if I offend you."

For the first time the forbidden subject of marital infidelity had been mentioned. Wilhelmina ignored it in her reply, but, while accepting the offer of peace, she kept her defenses up. "You have been dearer to me than life, and it is because I loved you so much that I have suffered so fearfully from your coldness. . . . For some years now I have not found in you the brother I adored. . . . People used to say that Superville ran everything in Bayreuth; now they say it is Madame Burghauss, and if she were gone, it would be someone else."

Wilhelmina admitted to the accusations of weakness, arrogance, intrigue and frivolity, and she was afraid this unflattering talk had turned Frederick against her. There may once have been some truth in what was said, but not at present. "I am of an age"—Wilhelmina was thirty-seven—"when one no longer cares for boisterous pleasures. My health, which grows worse from day to day, forbids it. I like quiet talk with intelligent people, talk which has nothing to do with the powerful and exalted of this world."

Frederick was roused to a final blast. He rehearsed all his grievances, beginning with the marriage of "those disgraceful creatures," and ending with a new accusation, that the movement of enemy troops through Bayreuth had not been reported to him during the recent war. "All of Germany knew what you did, and if I had not loved you, I would have broken with you completely! . . . Don't deceive yourself and think I would allow people to speak ill of you to me. . . . No one begrudges you your pleasures. . . . On the contrary, I wish you all the good company you want . . . but to hell with the people who set us at one anothers' throats! . . . I would flay them without mercy, though I am not a cruel man. . . . And in spite of everything, I love you still!"

The burden of Frederick's next letter was: "Let us say no more." He filled what remained of his page with chitchat of the opera, of his singers and their outbreaks of temperament.

Wilhelmina's memoirs had progressed as far as the year 1742, the time when the first proposal for Frederica to marry Charles Eugene of Württemberg was made. She had no impulse to carry on beyond this point. The manuscript was laid aside, its conclusion an unfinished paragraph.

FREDERICK's hope, expressed to Fredersdorf, that the people at home would appreciate his superhuman labors was fulfilled. When the King returned from Dresden in December of 1745 he got a hero's welcome. The entire population of Berlin had turned out to cheer. There were tears in Frederick's eyes as he saluted to right and left. When he alighted from his carriage at the palace he turned to bow deeply, bareheaded, to the crowd, a slight and surprisingly youthful figure. Later Frederick would set a low value on demonstrations of mass emotion, but now, unsurfeited by praise, he found it sweet.

But homecoming had its sorrows. During Frederick's absence two of his most cherished friends of the Rheinsberg group had died, Césarion (Count Keyserlingk), and the charming and learned Charles Étienne Jordan. Now Jacques Duhan was dying. Frederick went to sit beside the bed of his old teacher, the noise of carousal in the streets penetrating the quiet of the sickroom. A few days later Duhan was gone.

At this time the thought of death was as insistent in Frederick's mind as it had been during his early prison days at Küstrin. Frederick was only thirty-four and would live for another forty-one years, but he could not foresee such length of days; the men of his family had a habit of dying in their early fifties. Frederick felt he had rounded the corner into old age. Time, therefore, was short, and there was much to do. The King had not been at home a week before he sent for his minister of justice, Samuel Cocceji, to begin a thorough renovation of the Prussian legal system. There still were monstrous punishments listed in the statute book; there were cases in the Berlin courts that had been dragging on for two hundred years. Frederick thought justice should be swift, fair, sensible and cheap.

Day by day the flood of administrative detail flowed in. Frederick could read twenty letters and, without referring to them a second time, dictate twenty replies. As his father had done before him, he jotted down comments on the margins of the reports which passed across his desk. All cases of capital punishment were reviewed by him and, except on very rare occasions, were dismissed by a pardon. Some could be dealt with summarily, for example, the case of a soldier, a cavalryman, who had been condemned to death for sodomy with his horse. "Transfer to the infantry," was the terse notation.

For Frederick's leisure there was his flute, which he practiced at odd moments four or five times a day, sometimes between bites of his breakfast. He was composing arias for the operas written by his concert master, Herr Graun, and a serenata for his mother's birthday. Frederick's accompanist was one Karl Philipp Emanuel Bach, whose father was the most famous organist in Germany, a composer also, though his work was considered so old fashioned that he was not to be compared to his contemporaries or to his gifted sons.

Frederick had often expressed a desire to meet Johann Sebastian Bach. One evening in May of 1747 the usual concert was about to begin when the King was handed a list of the travelers who had arrived in Berlin during the past twenty-four hours. "Old Bach is here," he announced with great satisfaction. The flutes and strings were laid aside. Word was sent for the visitor to come to the palace at once, without even stopping to change into his best clothes.

Frederick wanted to hear this great virtuoso play some new-fangled instruments he had recently bought from Gottfried Silbermann, instruments closely related to the cembalo, the strings, however, being struck instead of plucked. Frederick may or may not have known that Bach had had a hand in the production of these so-called pianofortes; he had tried one of the earliest models and had criticized the action as being too stiff for fingers used to caressing the keys of a well-tempered clavier.

The King and his musicians followed old Bach about as he tried first one piano and then another. A theme for improvisation was supplied by Frederick, and was later used in a composition, *The Musical Offering*, the composer sent from Leipzig. The day after Bach's arrival he played for his host on all the best organs in churches scattered throughout the city.

Somehow, in spite of all his other occupations—Frederick was still a voracious reader and rereader of the classics—he managed to continue his work on his *History of My Own Time*, which would not be published until after he was dead and which was dedicated to his brother and successor, August William. Frederick also began a *Memoir of the House of Brandenburg*, which he could expect to see in print in his own lifetime. Wilhelmina was asked to help in gathering material for this history of their family in Bayreuth. Other sites for research were Nürnberg, which had once belonged to the Hohenzollerns, and Berghohenzollern, the castle in Swabia, cradle of the race.

"It is too bad our ancestors wrote so little," Frederick complained to Wilhelmina. "They will only get a duodecimo from me instead of a folio."

Now that the nightmare of their misunderstanding was over Frederick enjoyed writing to his sister on any subject that strayed into his mind: fashions in coiffure, war and politics, silly novels, philosophy. His letters were frequent and had developed a more mellow tenderness than those of his youth. "How can I tell you what is in my heart," he wrote. "You say such lovely things to me!"

Wilhelmina was trying her hand, quite literally, at a new art. She was painting pastel portraits and, before she was through, would have a gallery of all the singers, all the musicians, in her employ. Frederick did not approve of this activity. He entertained many odd notions concerning health and was afraid long hours spent in bending over a table might be constipating. His own health was uncertain. Night sweats were so heavy that the sheets of his bed had to be hung out to dry in the morning. He was plagued by bleeding hemorrhoids and attacks of gout. Just after his thirty-fifth birthday Frederick suffered what was thought to be a stroke, though the effects were so transient that the diagnosis was questionable.

Wilhelmina could always match her brother in the number and variety of her ailments. She was very weak, she reported, and had no appetite. In June, 1747, she went to Carlsbad for a cure and promised to pay Frederick a visit as soon as she was well. He was anxious to have her see his new home, Sans Souci, the charming one-story mansion he had built on the Weinberg, just outside the gates of Potsdam. It stood on the summit of a slope which had been terraced for the growing of grapes. Greenhouses had been added to protect fig trees and other tender fruit bearers.

Frederick had never liked the austere and ugly Potsdam palace; it was haunted by almost as many unpleasant memories as Wusterhausen. Rheinsberg was too far from Berlin, Charlottenburg too near and too closely surrounded by houses of the nobility. The plans for Sans Souci were drawn by Frederick and, in spite of their architectural heresies, carried out by Knobblesdorf. Light and airy, decorated without and within by statues of the mythological beings Frederick was so fond of inserting in his verse, the new house was cheerful and, by royal standards, cozy.

The results of Wilhelmina's cure were mediocre. She protested that a visiting invalid, a walking skeleton, would only be a nuisance, but her protests were feeble. In August Wilhelmina arrived at Sans Souci. Seven years had gone by since she had seen the home of her youth, four since she had seen her brother. If there was a shadow left of the old disharmony, it vanished as Frederick and Wilhelmina rushed into one another's arms.

✦ ✦ ✦

"While I was with you," Wilhelmina wrote, "I was perfectly happy for almost the only time in my entire life." She had stored up sufficient vitality at Sans Souci to make a stop on her way home at the university town of Halle, where she had arranged to meet Lotte and her husband, the Duke and Duchess of Brunswick-Bevern. The distinguished visitors were serenaded by a chorus of university students and had a conference with the philosopher Christian Wolff.

The talk during this interview was well above the head of scatterbrained Lotte, whose vivaciousness was at the moment slightly subdued by her eleventh pregnancy. Wilhelmina introduced the subject of immortality. She had adopted Frederick's disbelief in an afterlife and had been sorry to gather from certain of Wolff's recent writings that he was no longer a staunch materialist. She was afraid the professor had been intimidated by the clergy; she was glad to report her fears were groundless to Frederick.

"What a little thing is man," was Frederick's rejoinder. "We are exposed to so many dangers that it is a wonder we survive. One moment of pleasure, one puff of gaiety, and the sponge is passed over all our troubles. Inconstancy, frivolity are the bases of our happiness. . . . We should congratulate ourselves on the misfortunes we escape and not let sad thoughts spoil the small joys that come our way."

The evanescence of human life was a theme to which Frederick returned again and again, always, with Wilhelmina's tendency to hypochondria in mind, pointing out the moral of contentment with one's lot. Wilhelmina responded as her brother hoped she would. She described the enjoyment she found now in simple things. She had witnessed and was profoundly impressed by a peasant passion play. She liked to see the girls and boys who worked on her estate dance to the rustic music of a harp. To Frederick, who collected jeweled snuff boxes, Wilhelmina sent one of home-dyed raffia, woven at the Hermitage.

At a single point the soothing exchange of comment and reflection was broken. Nothing had been said during Wilhelmina's

[231]

visit of the person who had been the cause of her quarrel with Frederick. Wilhelmina herself had made a point of telling her family how kind the Margrave had always been to her. The Countess Burghauss, however, was still in Bayreuth and still, with her husband, under Wilhelmina's roof.

After her return from Potsdam, plucking up her courage, Wilhelmina asked the couple to leave. There was an angry scene in which the Margrave bore no part, but he immediately handed over to his ex-mistress a house usually reserved for foreign ambassadors. This did not solve all of Dorothea's troubles. She had been ill, her husband had received no pay for two years, and they both were in desperate need of money.

Wilhelmina's conscience hurt her. She had made this marriage, but could not afford to endow it permanently. She turned to Frederick. Again she was in a labyrinth, she wrote, a labyrinth of her own making. She had begun with a misplaced friendship; she had ended with a misunderstanding with the one she loved best. Only Frederick could lead her out of the maze by releasing the money General von der Marwitz had willed his erring daughter. When this was done Dorothea would leave Bayreuth; Wilhelmina could promise that. "I beg this boon with clasped hands," she concluded.

"Princes are in this world to reward the thankless," Frederick replied. Burghauss had resources of his own and had probably lost them at the gambling table. The legacy, however, would be forthcoming as soon as the conditions for payment had been met. Wilhelmina was not to worry herself sick over this affair, for she had no reason now to feel remorse.

In one of her earlier letters Wilhelmina had expressed her contempt for the Christian concept of death by saying she was sure "the paradise of Biche and Folichon" would be hers. Folichon was her spaniel whom she had taken with her to Potsdam. Biche was Frederick's greyhound bitch, who had gone with him on his second Silesian campaign and was captured by the Austrians at Soör, along with two of Frederick's saddle horses and all of his personal belongings. Unlike the horses and the boxes of clothes and books, Biche was returned. She was let loose in Frederick's room, without his seeing her, and when she suddenly leapt up on the table by which he was sitting to lick his face, he burst into tears.

Not long after finis had been written to the Burghauss affair, Biche received the gift of a "sopha" and a feeding bowl from Folichon, with an accompanying letter, a declaration of love: "Yes, my lovely lady dog, I adore you . . . I languish at my mistress's feet . . . and will wag my tail a hundred times a day to your honor and glory." This was preceded by a short preamble, comparing dogs and human beings. Neither were automata, both were moved by similar emotions of love, jealousy, anger and greed. On the whole, dogs were more virtuous than men, since they were never inconstant and never ambitious.

Biche's reply took account of the veiled reference to what love of husband and brother had taught Wilhelmina. One must not distrust the emotions, it was pointed out, for without them men would stagnate and resemble more closely the vegetable than the animal world. Biche would always preserve the most essential organ, a loving heart. "Let us be wiser than human beings and not chase after the unattainable."

Thus master and mistress had their say.

✦ ✦ ✦

In the spring of 1748 Wilhelmina's daughter Frederica was approaching her sixteenth birthday. The most beautiful child in Europe had grown to be a beautiful girl, resembling her mother, but with a radiance of health and well being denied to Wilhelmina's youth. The wedding with the Prince of Württemberg, deferred for a year, was scheduled for the autumn. Wilhelmina was anxious to set a date that would be convenient for Frederick, for he had at first every intention of making the trip to Bayreuth, having ordered two elaborately embroidered coats and waistcoats for the occasion. Business of an international nature, however, kept him at home.

The long War of the Austrian Succession, begun by Prussia

and from which only Prussia had benefited, was over; a peace was in the making. According to an agreement between Russia, England and Holland, Russian troops were sent to the Rhine. Again, as in 1734, but with conscious intent of making herself useful to Frederick, Wilhelmina went to see the Cossacks. She was impressed by their exotic, oriental appearance; they resembled figures in the Chinese pavilion at Sans Souci, she reported to her brother. The horsemen were armed with bows, arrows and fourteen-foot lances. They also carried pistols, and when they shot from the saddle, their Tartar ponies at full gallop, they generally missed.

Frederick would be interested in these details, for he was sensitive to danger from the north, chiefly, perhaps, because he always thought of defense in terms of attack. Russia, with her vastness of territory and population, could not be invaded.

August William, who was recovering from a fever, was unable to represent Frederick at Frederica's wedding, and the two younger brothers, Henry and Ferdinand, were sent as substitutes. The Prussian princes made a dramatic entry into Bayreuth, riding with the bridegroom in a carriage drawn by six white horses. The wedding, on September twenty-sixth, 1748, was followed by a banquet, the traditional torch dance, performances at the opera, and a barbecue for the general public, at which an ox, two bucks and eight rams were roasted.

Wilhelmina was so exhausted she had to stay in bed the following day. Her parting with Frederica was grievous. The two had drawn very close to one another. After the eclipse of Dorothea and the death of Madame von Sonsfeld and her sister Flora in 1746 Frederica had been her mother's sole companion.

To Frederick, Wilhelmina confided her fears for her daughter's happiness. Charles Eugene was very much in love with his exquisite bride; he could be quite charming when he chose, but he was a spoiled child, fickle, violent, easily influenced by his entourage, who would want to keep their control over him at Frederica's expense. There was also the Dowager Duchess of Württemberg as mother-in-law, and the difference in religion.

The Bayreuth marriage had been performed by Parson Ellrodt, head of the Bayreuth Consistory, but when the young couple reached Stuttgart they would be remarried by a priest. Frederica's only guarantee for the future was her husband's passion, too hot, too purely physical to last. "When love goes," Wilhelmina prophesied—she had used "when" instead of "if"—"she will be wretched."

THE international tensions that had kept the King of Prussia from his niece's wedding in the fall of 1748 eased. Frederick could never feel secure, but for the time being allowed himself a little more liberty for writing and for musical composition. The history of Brandenburg was growing. It had reached the point where an editor and critic was needed, and the one and only candidate for that position was Voltaire.

During the past five years, however, the exchange of letters between disciple and master had been rare, Voltaire's silence being chiefly due to the influence of Madame du Châtelet. The Divine Émilie was justly offended by Frederick's failure to invite her to Prussia. Before each of the Berlin visits she had tried to keep her man at home by outbursts of temperament which included threats of suicide. If Voltaire went for a third time, he might never return!

In the interval the couple had made successful forays upon Paris. In 1746 Voltaire was elected to the French Academy, having already been appointed royal historiographer through the influence of Madame de Pompadour. The French King's latest and most powerful mistress might smile upon the poet, but the King himself was less benign. Feeling he had been cold-shouldered, Voltaire spent much time at Lunéville in Lorraine, where the father-in-law of Louis XV, Stanislaus Leszczinski, held court with all the trappings of royalty and little of its inconveniences.

But why Lunéville, Frederick inquired? Why not Berlin? Voltaire replied that Lunéville was near the healing waters of Plombières where he, who was now a semi-invalid, went frequently to patch up a broken-down machine containing "a soul devoted to Your Majesty." Voltaire, "a pretty corpse to drag to Berlin," had a disease which had deafened one of his ears, he said, and caused his teeth to drop out.

Come anyway, come with or without your teeth, Frederick rejoined. When Voltaire asked for some pills he had used to good effect when last in Prussia, Frederick sent a whole pound, enough, he said, to kill all the members of the five academies in France.

The correspondence had jerked back to life with vigor. Close-written pages, arabesqued with verse, went back and forth. A German, Frederick insisted, could not write good French poetry, or, for that matter, good French prose, without a tutor. "Listen, I am mad to see you! I want to study with you. This year"—it was now June, 1749—"I have the leisure, and God knows when I will have it again."

Though Voltaire would not come at once, he was definitely interested in a visit to Berlin, for Madame du Châtelet was pregnant. No one, least of all Frederick, suspected Voltaire of being the father of the unborn child, and a fatuous pretense was maintained that the Marquis du Châtelet had undertaken to add to his family after a lapse of more than sixteen years. Émilie's lover was the Marquis de Saint Lambert, a handsome young captain in the bodyguard of King Stanislaus. Émilie was forty-three years old, and she was miserably uncomfortable and apprehensive. Voltaire would not visit Frederick until after the baby was born and the mother was out of danger.

But, Frederick argued, Voltaire was not an obstetrician. "Madame du Châtelet can give birth without your help, and, if necessary, you can go back later."

"I am neither a begetter of children, a doctor, or a midwife,"

Voltaire replied, "but I am a friend, and even for Your Majesty I will not leave a woman who may die in September."

Frederick refused to give Voltaire's devotion the credit it deserved. He could no more believe in Voltaire's non-literary virtues than in his invalidism. Besides, Frederick had reason to be angry. Having heard that some of his own writings were being shown about in France and misrepresented, he, who had misused one of Voltaire's letters in 1743, blew off steam to Francesco Algarotti.

"Voltaire," Frederick grumbled, "has played me a mean trick. . . . It's a pity such a despicable soul is united with so much genius. He has all the pretty ways and the maliciousness of a monkey . . . but I only want to learn his French, so what do I care for his morals?"

Frederick was only a little less harsh when, in September, Voltaire's fears for Madame du Châtelet were realized. She died a few days after giving birth to a feeble baby girl, who survived for less than a month. Voltaire was bewildered by his grief and accused Saint Lambert of being a murderer. "I have lost a friend," he wrote to Frederick, "of twenty years standing, a great man, whose only fault was being a woman. . . . During her lifetime she was perhaps not fully appreciated. You would have judged her differently if you had had the privilege of knowing her. A female who could translate Newton and Vergil and who had all the good qualities of an honorable man should be mourned by you."

Frederick remarked to Algarotti that Voltaire's lamentations were so loud they would soon subside. He sent his condolences, however, and renewed his invitation.

It took eight months for Voltaire to discover how homeless he was in France, but in June of 1750 he set out for an indefinite stay in Prussia. Frederick had provided funds for the journey, a generous salary and the promise of one for Voltaire's niece, Madame Denis, if she would come to keep house for her uncle. Side benefits were a luxurious suite of rooms at Sans Souci, maintenance, the title of Royal Chamberlain, and a jeweled cross Voltaire could wear upon his coat, that of the Prussian Order of Merit. The services of Voltaire, who had been nominally a member of the household of Louis XV, were requested from the French government. In granting them, Louis said there would be one more madman at the Prussian court and one less at his own. The French foreign minister remarked to the Prussian ambassador at Paris, "I am afraid they [Frederick and Voltaire] won't get on—but this is strictly between you and me."

✦ ✦ ✦

The lure of yet another meeting with Voltaire was added to the constant urgings Wilhelmina received to come again to Sans Souci. She had been unable to do so in 1749 because she and her husband had had to go to Stuttgart, where their daughter badly needed their support. Though still her husband's darling and plaything, Frederica was surrounded by hostility. Attempts had been made to convert her to Catholicism. Charles Eugene was so rude to his wife's father and mother that it seemed as if he wanted to provoke an excuse for breaking off relations with them.

Nevertheless, a second and longer visit was made the following year. Wilhelmina wanted to be present for the birth of her grandchild, Augusta Louisa Charlotte, who was born on February nineteenth, 1750. Things went better this time. Charles Eugene had about-faced and was surprisingly amiable. He made much of his in-laws and gave a surrealist fete in their honor, at which his bewhiskered guardsmen were dressed as women and the masked ballet dancers made their entree riding on frogs, roosters and other animals. At the end of the procession came four live mules, laden with gifts for Frederica and her parents.

Wilhelmina made wicked fun, for Frederick's delectation, of the Dowager Duchess of Württemberg, who was so vain she hid her face under the sheet when extra candles were brought into the bedroom where she was entertaining a group of gentlemen. Wilhelmina herself, however, was conscious of changes in her own appearance. She had always wanted to look her best for

Frederick and confessed to him she sometimes spent an hour at her dressing table "trying to think of something to do to my poor face."

"You will see an old hag of a sister," she warned him before their reunion in August. "I am only fit to stand as an antique statue in a niche at Sans Souci. There I will represent an old sibyl, and everyone will look at me as a curiosity."

It was noted by those to whom the Margravine of Bayreuth was a curiosity that she used a great deal of rouge and white powder, but, unless one looked closely, one might take her for a woman in her late twenties. Frederick, also, in spite of his frequent illnesses, looked at least ten years younger than he actually was.

On arrival, Wilhelmina was given her choice of the operas she wanted to hear in Berlin, and one evening a great equestrian pageant, in which rode ancient Greeks, Romans, Carthaginians and Persians, was given in the palace square. The pleasantest hours for Wilhelmina, however, were those spent at Sans Souci, where Frederick's flute spoke sweetly and there were delicious little supper parties at which Wilhelmina was the only woman present. Elizabeth Christina had never been invited to the pleasure house on the Weinberg. She had faded out of her husband's life and even, it sometimes seemed, from his memory; unless Fredersdorf jogged his elbow, Frederick was apt to overlook the Queen in making up a family party at Charlottenburg.

Wilhelmina could hold her conversational own in the masculine group at Sans Souci, where there were a few new faces, among them that of Julien de la Mettrie, a physician, whose books, *A Natural History of the Soul* and *Man the Machine*, had led to his expulsion from France and Holland. La Mettrie was welcomed to Potsdam because his philosophy coincided with that of Frederick and his friends. All who met about the small round table in the dining room called themselves either atheists, free thinkers or deists. Irreverence of conventional piety was sure to rouse a laugh; clerical customs and terminology were turned upside down for humorous effect. "The Church" embraced everything which the Curia condemned. Sans Souci was a "monastery," where all were "brothers," where Wilhelmina was "Sister Guillemette," and Frederick was "Our Holy Abbot and Father in God."

When after three weeks Frederick left for a tour of Silesia, where, as impartial deist, he made a point of reconciling Protestant to Catholic, Wilhelmina went back to Berlin and was taken so ill she couldn't go home to Bayreuth with her husband. Her monastic brothers were attentive to her during a long convalescence. La Mettrie, a jolly madcap as well as a doctor, made her laugh by his antics; Voltaire came to her room to read aloud his latest play, *Rome Saved*.

A wistful standing invitation was proffered for Brother Voltaire to visit Bayreuth. He accepted joyfully for next spring, next year, for any time except the present. At least they could write to one another. In her first letter after their parting in December, Wilhelmina hoped their correspondence would not be as "meager as their respective persons."

Without Daniel de Superville, who had resigned as head of the Erlangen University and gone to Brunswick, without the Marwitz sisters, the Bayreuth circle had shrunk and desiccated. The gay news letters Sister Guillemette received from the Sans Souci Monastery were refreshing. Voltaire had been asked to provide a congenial companion for Wilhelmina. She had her eye on a woman who had spent much time at Cirey, Madame de Graffigny, author of a novel, *The Letters of a Peruvian Lady*, and a successful comedy which had just appeared in Paris. Voltaire may have thought a writer of fiction might tell tall tales of what life had been like with a pair of geniuses in a lonely country house in Lorraine, for he said Madame de Graffigny was now too elderly to be transplanted to Germany. In her place, he brought forward the name of a man he was anxious to remove from France, the Marquis d'Adhemar. D'Adhemar was courting Madame Denis, the niece Voltaire had selected as a prop for his old age and to whom he wrote letters, very different from those that went to Bayreuth, saying how homesick he was in Berlin. Wilhelmina was ready to accept any substitute from Voltaire's hand and only hoped the Marquis would arrive soon "to fill the gaps in our conversation, which is like Chinese music, made up of long pauses, ending in discordant tones."

A discordant tone was avoided by Voltaire when, late in January of 1751, he mentioned an affair he could not dismiss in silence since it was the talk of all Berlin. Voltaire, no doubt, wanted to present his version to Wilhelmina as antidote to what she may have heard from someone else.

✦ ✦ ✦

According to a clause in the Treaty of Dresden, certain Saxon government bonds were payable at par to Prussian subjects. Since 1745, these bonds had fallen in value, and there had been so much profiteering that their purchase by Prussians had been declared illegal. It continued, however, to flourish on the black market.

Voltaire, soon after his arrival in Berlin, engaged a Jewish moneylender, Abraham Hirschel, to buy bonds for him in Leipzig and Dresden. As security for the bills of exchange given him, Hirschel deposited some diamonds with Voltaire. The bonds were not forthcoming, payment was stopped on the bills, and when the agent was repossessed of his jewelry he declared certain gems had been replaced by false ones. Voltaire went to law.

"Brother Voltaire is doing penance here," the litigant announced cheerfully to Wilhelmina. "He is having the devil's own law suit with a Jew. One could make a comedy of this."

"Fie, fie, monsieur, for shame." Wilhelmina wagged a finger reproachfully in Voltaire's direction. Apollo engaged in a law suit—she had searched through all of mythology and could find no precedent! Yes, the story might be very funny on the stage, but she, for one, would not care to laugh at such a comedy. Great men should shine by their own light, and Wilhelmina only wanted to think of her friend Voltaire as surpassing all others in the Republic of Letters, even such famous poets as Racine and Corneille.

The phrase, the Republic of Letters, Wilhelmina had borrowed from a recent communication from Frederick, who was at Sans Souci while Voltaire was in Berlin. "From all I hear of the case," Frederick had written, "a rascal is trying to fool a cheat. It is a great pity intellect has so little influence on behavior and that a man so famous in the Republic of Letters should have such a despicable character."

Hitherto Frederick had never expressed his low opinion of Voltaire's character in writing to Wilhelmina, but now, knowing how fascinated she was by his troublesome guest, his tirade was repeated more than once. He didn't want to see Voltaire, or communicate with him, until after the suit had been settled; then he would give the offender a piece of his mind.

Wilhelmina made as light of the matter as possible. She had to admit to having heard in Berlin of Voltaire's sharpness in money matters, but she had never thought he would do anything dishonest. Since Voltaire was the chief instrument of Frederick's pleasure, his only, his irreplaceable distraction from work, she hoped this indiscretion would be soon forgiven.

Chief Justice Cocceji had been told to judge the suit of Voltaire versus Hirschel with absolute impartiality, even though one of the parties to it was a royal chamberlain. After a trial that lasted far longer, it seemed, than necessary, a verdict favorable to Voltaire was delivered.

Immediately letters of impish self-confidence and self-justification were received in Potsdam. To Frederick, Voltaire insisted he had done no wrong. Hirschel had solicited him to make some money. And, after all, no bonds had actually been bought. Voltaire spoke of himself as an unfortunate foreigner, an invalid, a recluse who had gone into exile for Frederick's sake. Without naming names, he hinted at a conspiracy of slander.

To Monsieur Darget, Frederick's secretary, who for the past two months had been bombarded with messages for the King,

Voltaire made a cocky prediction: he would be coming soon to Sans Souci; he hoped Fredersdorf would send a carriage for him. He would also like to change the location of his rooms in the palace and was counting on a good stove to keep him and his soup-pot warm.

But only a chill wind blew from Sans Souci. "I was glad to receive you as my guest," Frederick stated austerely, "because I admired your intellect, your talents and your knowledge. I took it for granted that a man of your age would be weary of literary feuds and would come here to find safe harbor."

After mentioning—for the first time, it was emphasized—Voltaire's interference in certain minor matters which did not concern him, after pointing out that the lawsuit had brought protests from the Saxon government, Frederick concluded with, "Until you came here I was able to keep peace in my household . . . I like gentle, unaggressive people, who don't act out in everyday life the passions one admires on the stage. . . . If you can make up your mind to live like a philosopher, then come to Sans Souci, but if you can't control yourself . . . it would be better for you to stay in Berlin."

It was obvious that Frederick could only be mollified by a more humble approach. Voltaire not only beat his breast, but laid it bare. "Your Majesty is absolutely right," he wrote. "At my age I have an incorrigible fault. I can never cure myself of the accursed impulse to forge ahead . . . I know there are a thousand times when one should hold one's tongue, and this was one. . . . Believe me, I am in despair and have never felt a more bitter sorrow. I have lightly tossed away the only reason for my being here. . . . I have offended the only man whom I had wanted to please."

Frederick, though still censorious, unbent a trifle. He said he was glad this miserable business was over. He hoped Voltaire would have no more quarrels with either the Old or the New Testament. By the end of March the poet was back at Sans Souci, seeming to Frederick "as gentle as a lamb and as amusing as Harlequin." Bits of humorous verse were tossed back and forth. Frederick had forgotten how marvelous mere table talk could be.

But the prospect for future serenity was dim. During Voltaire's absence, Frederick had seen much of Pierre Louis Moreau de Maupertuis, president of the Berlin Academy, a man whose integrity he prized, but who was a very dull companion. It was through Voltaire that Maupertuis had first come to Berlin, and the Laplander, as he was called in the Sans Souci Monastery because of his famous scientific expedition to the far north, had been a colleague of Madame du Châtelet. Lately, however, Maupertuis and Voltaire had got on one another's nerves. Each was jealous of the other's relations with Frederick.

Two unfortunate remarks had been reported, one to Frederick and the other to Voltaire, neither of which could be authenticated. Frederick had been told Voltaire called his editorial work "washing the King's dirty linen." La Mettrie had said to Voltaire that Frederick had spoken of "squeezing an orange and then throwing the skin away."

He was trying to keep a quiet mind, Voltaire wrote to Madame Denis, but it was hard to forget that orange skin. He was like the man who, having fallen out of the steeple of his village church, kept saying to himself on his way to earth, "So far, I'm quite all right."

Portions of Frederick's history of Brandenburg had been read aloud to the Berlin Academy and were serialized in its bulletin. The entire work was published in 1751. Frederick's narrative, slow paced in the opening chapters, picked up momentum with the period of the Thirty Years War. A century had gone by since the Peace of Westphalia, but the memory of the years of horror preceding the peace was still vivid. Frederick told a rousing tale of reconstruction under the Great Elector, his great-grandfather, who found Berlin a town of wooden shacks, pigs rooting in its streets, and left it a trim built city of stone. Of his grandfather, the first Frederick, the author had little good to say, except that a crown acquired for vain show had become an incentive to strength, to independence.

The last chapter of the history, dealing with the reign of Frederick William, must have been the most difficult to write. Frederick managed to give his father full credit for industry, for frugality, and for the wisdom to see that Prussia, small, weak and fragmented, needed a strong army to survive. Of the part he himself had been forced to play, he said nothing. "We pass over in silence the domestic troubles of this great monarch. One should have some indulgence for the faults of the children because of the virtues of their father."

Wilhelmina had written hundreds of pages on what Frederick

had so neatly glossed over. If she had needed to remind herself of a single detail of her sufferings, she had only to consult her memoirs, but they were now laid aside, untouched, unfinished. She actually liked to dream of herself back at Potsdam or Wusterhausen, Wilhelmina confided to her brother. They had had many troubles then and many worries, but at least they were together. It made her happy now to think of Frederick, but it also made her sad because she could do so little for him.

"I would like to be a general to shed my blood for you, or a minister to serve you well. I would like to be a tree, a statue, or a palace to add a little to your pleasure. I wish I had the gift of magic to give you world power, immortality, or perfect health . . . But after all this, I realize I am only an old, sick sister, who cannot even be your companion."

The social life of Bayreuth continued to resemble Chinese music, for the Marquis d'Adhemar, the enlivener Voltaire had undertaken to deliver promptly, seemed to be as coyly elusive as Voltaire himself. When Wilhelmina first came home from Potsdam in December, the weather was so cold she did not want to leave her room, but on Christmas Eve she was coaxed downstairs to see a performance in the palace theater. When the curtain went up only two figures were seen standing together on the stage, Frederica and Charles Eugene, who leapt over the footlights and ran forward with arms outstretched. The surprise visit lasted for a fortnight of bustle and play acting; when it was over drowsiness redescended.

Wilhelmina was pleased that her daughter and son-in-law shared a taste for theatricals, for any bond between them was worth strengthening. In March of 1751 their strongest tie dissolved: Wilhelmina's baby granddaughter died after only a year of life, and there seemed to be no likelihood of another child.

News from Stuttgart was often depressing; news from various correspondents in Berlin was laden with complaints, for Wilhelmina was felt to have so much influence with Frederick she was often used as intermediary. August William confided his love sorrows to her, his desire to divorce his unattractive wife and marry a beautiful young lady-in-waiting of Sophia Dorothea. This Frederick would not allow. Wilhelmina could not question the wisdom of Frederick's decision, but she assured him of August William's devotion. "He loves you. You can make what you will of him."

A similar, but less truthful, report was made after a visit from Henry, the next member of the family to feel the weight of Frederick's authority. Henry, now twenty-six years old, did not want to marry anyone at all, but was on his way to court a princess of Hesse-Cassel. "For several reasons," Frederick had declared, "he [Henry] should have a wife to bear his name—if you know what I mean." Wilhelmina knew what Frederick meant, though Henry's romantic attachments to various members of his own sex had not been mentioned specifically. She recognized in this younger brother a man of parts, of greater intelligence and force of character than August William, one who could be useful to Frederick if handled with tact.

The third brother, Ferdinand, was seldom heard from. He seemed so lacking in ambition he was quite content to play the colorless role of brother to Frederick the Great; the title had been invented by Voltaire, but was now in common use.

To Voltaire's admirer in Bayreuth, anxious to hear of peace and harmony at Potsdam, came a copy of *The Century of Louis XIV*, the history that had been so long in composition. Voltaire was also turning out articles for a philosophic dictionary to which others, including Frederick, might contribute. The most highly spiced numbers dealt with religion. "Brother Voltaire, as Your Royal Highness knows, only writes about God Almighty," Wilhelmina was informed. Later what was described as a "small book of devotions, written for our very Reverend Father in God, the Philosopher of Sans Souci," was sent, with a warning for Sister Guillemette to be careful in letting others view this work, since "the mysteries of the saints must not be exposed to profane eyes."

Even more welcome than elaborate foolery was a poem which arrived in October, 1752. Its subject was natural law as the source of human morality. Wilhelmina seized upon this as a matter for debate. She found the poem almost perfect, she said, though she felt it needed larger scope. The statement that God had implanted in man a conscience and a sense of justice seemed dubious to her. If justice were innate, then there would be no chicanery, and lawyers would starve to death. Virtues, Wilhelmina thought, were relative to the society in which they flourished. She would venture to say that self-love gave birth to the concept of justice as soon as human beings began to see there was no security in chaos. And from justice, conscience had been born.

Wilhelmina could hardly wait to know Voltaire's reaction to her views, but at this point the debate was broken short. No word came from Voltaire, who was again involved in a desperate contest that seemed to give all his psychological and moral theories the lie.

+ + +

For months, Voltaire had dreamed of getting his knife into the Laplander. The opportunity came at the 1752 spring session of the Academy. President de Maupertuis thought he had discovered a new law in mathematics, the principle of least action. His statement was courteously challenged by a foreign member of the assembly, a Swiss named König, now resident in Holland. König produced copies of two unpublished letters of Leibnitz as proof. Maupertuis was too pompous and too thin skinned to suffer contradiction; he instituted a superficial search for the original letters, which proved fruitless. König's copies were declared forgeries and, without so much as a vote being taken, König was expelled from the Academy.

There was a flurry of protest. And there was no doubt which side Voltaire would take in this controversy. He hated Maupertuis; he hated arbitrary action. An anonymous pamphlet, *Reply of an Academician of Berlin to an Academician of Paris*, was circulated. It had nothing to say of the scientific points involved in the Maupertuis-König dispute, but it flayed the President for high handedness. Within a very short time, the *Reply* was answered by a second publication, also anonymous, this time a *Letter of an Academician of Berlin to an Academician of Paris.* The *Letter* praised Maupertuis extravagantly and declared him to be an adopted son of Prussia and one of its glories.

Voltaire would have recognized the author, even if the royal eagle had not appeared on the title page of the second edition. He described his sensations to Madame Denis as he prepared for battle. "Coquettes, kings and poets are used to flattery, and this is the triple crown that Frederick wears . . . I haven't got a scepter, but I have a pen!" Voltaire was supping every evening with Frederick, just as usual, but he described their nightly sessions as "festivals of Damocles." The sword, he felt, was hanging over both their heads.

One evening in November Voltaire appeared with a manuscript, not too long to be read at a single sitting, *The Diatribe of Doctor Akakia, Physician to the Pope.* There really had been two sixteenth century doctors, father and son, whose family name was changed from Saint Malice to its Greek equivalent, Akakia. Voltaire's doctor, however, was purely imaginary. His diatribe was a presentation to the Inquisition of the writings of a silly young man, who pretended to be the president of a learned society, but was only fit to be the president of Bedlam. There followed a merciless ribbing of a book of essays by Maupertuis, in which he had let his imagination have its say on such questions as the feasibility of boring a hole through the earth, the establishment of a town in which only Latin should be spoken, and the examining of skulls of giants in the Antipodes to discover secrets of the human mind.

Frederick read and laughed, but said the thing was too cruel; it should not be published; some respect was due to the President of the Academy. To show he was in earnest, Frederick laid his copy of the manuscript on the fire.

A few days later *Dr. Akakia* was in print and was on sale in Potsdam. Frederick bristled. He bought up all copies available and had them burned. With great sternness Voltaire was told he would have to leave Prussia unless he stopped publishing libels. A written promise was required, in which, after pledging good behavior, Voltaire begged Frederick "to spare an old man, crushed with sickness and grief."

Frederick could not know how many copies of the satire had escaped the fire, but he wrote to Maupertuis, who was really ill with a chest complaint in Berlin, not to worry. There would be no further trouble.

A hope had been expressed, but not a fact. By the time Frederick came to his capital for Christmas, *Akakia* was there. The hobgoblin had also appeared in Paris on the selfsame day. For the Prussian editions, Voltaire had used the official stamp of approval obtained for another and quite innocuous essay.

"I am amazed by your effrontery," Frederick thundered. "After what you have done, which is as clear as day, you persist. . . . Don't think you can make people believe that black is white! If you go on, I will publish everything"—he meant Voltaire's pledge—"People will see that if your writings deserve monuments your deeds deserve a chain."

A stricken cry came back from Voltaire's well upholstered den in the Berlin palace: "Good God, sire, in my condition! I swear to you on my life, which I renounce without a pang, that all of this is due to a hideous calumny. I implore you to interrogate my staff"—Voltaire had both a secretary and valet—"What, you will judge me unheard! I demand liberty—and death!"

Frederick made no reply. On Christmas Eve there was another, an official, auto-da-fé of *Dr. Akakia*. The copies of the book were fed to the flames by the hangman; the spot chosen was a conspicuous point in the palace square, which was visible from Voltaire's window. Ashes of the bonfire were sent to President de Maupertuis.

Voltaire let Madame Denis know he would be with her soon. "The orange has been squeezed," he wrote, "one must think of saving the skin." But did he really want to go? And could Frederick really bear to lose him? Both parties to this strange relationship blew hot and cold.

On New Year's Day, 1753, an emotional, but dignified, letter of resignation was delivered to the King; with it was sent the chamberlain's key of office and the cross of the Order of Merit. Voltaire had written a verse on the paper in which the cross and key were wrapped:

> *These I received with tender joy.*
> *I give them back with sorrow.*
> *Thus a lover, still all a-fire with love,*
> *Gives back the picture of his mistress.*

An hour later Michael Fredersdorf, who had acted as messenger, brought back the insignia and a hint of reconciliation.

Voltaire stayed on, though he did not see his host again before the latter left for Sans Souci in February. In March Voltaire asked permission to visit Plombières. "You do not need the excuse of illness to quit my service," was the curt reply. "Go when you will, only before you go, return your contract of engagement, the key, the cross and the volume of verse I gave you."

The volume of verse was a collection of Frederick's poems, titled *Works of the Philosopher of Sans Souci,* of which only twelve copies had been printed and distributed. Most of the contents of the book was no better and no worse than the bulk of Frederick's poetry, except for a mock-heroic poem, *Palladion,* in which Frederick had succeeded in imitating Voltaire's *La Pucelle,* not merely in style, but in ribaldry. Louis XV had heard of *Palladion* and, through the French ambassador, had asked for a copy which Frederick modestly and prudently refused. He did not like to think of the uses to which Voltaire might put his naughty poem.

On March twentieth, Voltaire went to Sans Souci to say goodbye to Frederick. The farewell was touching, according to an account given by the departing guest in which he spoke again of Frederick as "his mistress." A few days later, however, Voltaire left Berlin with the cross, the key and the book of verse still in his possession.

✦ ✦ ✦

Wilhelmina had been kept abreast of each development in the Voltaire crisis. She knew there was no use saying black was white, but as long as there was any hope of compromise she tried to temper Frederick's wrath. What a loss Voltaire would be! One must make allowance for the artistic temperament, for age and feeble health. If Frederick turned the old man out, he would have nowhere to go, for France would not receive him. He would dwindle away like Tasso, or the blind English poet Milton.

But there was no sign of dwindling. Instead of going to Plombières, Voltaire went to Saxony. Wilhelmina heard from him at Leipzig, but only indirectly, through the Marquis d'Adhemar, who was at last a member of the Bayreuth household. Wilhelmina was allowed to see the letters and was much entertained by what they had to say of the quarrel with Maupertuis. Frederick was spoken of with respect, for it was plain the writer was angling for an invitation to Bayreuth.

Wilhelmina did not dare to be hospitable without consulting Frederick. He gave her in reply an extensive repetition of Voltaire's misdoings. Voltaire was "the greatest scoundrel in the universe," but it might be a good thing if he came to Bayreuth, for then Frederick, with Wilhelmina's permission, could send a messenger to collect the key, the cross and the book. It was the book that weighed most heavily on Frederick's mind.

Voltaire did not come to Bayreuth and did not stay long in Leipzig. He soon moved on to visit the Duchess of Saxe-Gotha, with whom he had been in correspondence. "Our rogue is in Gotha, making up to the Princess," Frederick commented. "If he stays long enough he will play her some sort of trick!" Voltaire's movements were being closely observed. Frederick learned that the poet expected to meet his niece, Madame Denis, in Frankfurt the first of June. Frankfurt was a free city, but the Prussian resident there, a man named Freytag, was ordered to go to Voltaire's hotel as soon as he arrived to collect the valuables.

The cross and key were handed over at once, but the book of poems was said to be in some luggage on its way from Leipzig.

Freytag, whom Voltaire later accused of having been a convict, made a brutally thorough search of everything in the room. Free city, or no, Voltaire was told he could not leave the grounds of the hotel until the luggage arrived; even when it had come and the poems had been confiscated, the pig-headed official continued to make difficulties. He said he would have to have the King's permission before the travelers—Madame Denis had by this time joined her uncle—could continue their journey. Since Frederick was in Silesia, permission was long acoming.

Late in June Wilhelmina received a fat bundle of mail from Frankfurt, stuffed with letters from Voltaire and Madame Denis which she was asked to send on to Frederick. Madame Denis was fairly restrained in what she had to say, but Voltaire let himself go in describing his captivity, his dying state, his niece's attack of convulsions, and the twelve soldiers Freytag had got the Frankfurt government to station at their door.

"But I can't help pitying him," Wilhelmina confessed to Frederick. "A man reduced to despair will do anything. You may think, dear brother, I go too far in his defense, merely because of his wit."

"You would never believe, dear sister," Frederick replied, "how these sort of people play to the gallery. All their convulsions, their illnesses, their despairs, are faked."

Frederick, however, had given word to let the prisoners go.

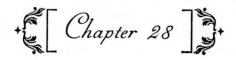

Chapter 28

Not long after the bonfire in the palace square at Berlin there was a conflagration in Bayreuth. At eight o'clock on the evening of January twenty-sixth, 1753, fire broke out in three places at once in the palace. It seemed to have been a case of arson, and Wilhelmina, who was able to save her jewels, her boxes of letters, and Folichon, took this sadly as another proof of her unpopularity. The military and members of the court had tried to fight the blaze, but the townspeople gave little help.

Wilhelmina wrote to Frederick, lying on a sofa in the house of her theatrical director, Monsieur de Montperni, surrounded by piles of salvage. All of the Margrave's belongings had been destroyed; Wilhelmina begged Frederick to send a flute and some music to his brother-in-law, though the poor man was so busy he had little time to amuse himself. As a result of the fire the lamentable state of finances in Bayreuth had to be mentioned once more. They would have been out of debt in a few years, Wilhelmina confided ruefully, but now it was absolutely hopeless.

Frederick sent not only flutes and music but a gift of a hundred thousand thalers, which, he pointed out, had been taken not from state funds, but from private income, an unspoken criticism of the way affairs had been handled in Bayreuth. August William, Henry and Ferdinand would also help, and Eeka and her husband should be appealed to since their son would inherit Bayreuth if the Margrave died without a male heir.

It would take time to rebuild. Though the octagonal tower and chapel of the old residence still stood, a new site was chosen where buildings, already in existence, could be altered or thrown together to make a larger unit. After a week under Monsieur de Montperni's roof Wilhelmina moved to one of the houses that would be incorporated into the new palace. Her health was even worse than usual that winter. She suffered from violent, prostrating headaches. Wilhelmina's host, Montperni, had been very ill recently and was brought back to health by the ministrations of a peasant woman, who used no medicines, but had a mysterious healing power.

Wilhelmina, who was willing to try anything to ease her pain, began a series of treatments which at first seemed to have great effect. At the time of day she had been told the healer would be concentrating on her case, the patient felt a curious tingling sensation in her head, as though ants were crawling around inside it. She became warm, relaxed and drowsy. After a sleep which lasted for an hour or more there was marked improvement.

But Frederick was alarmed. "For God's sake," he wrote, "don't put yourself into the hands of a quack. One never knows what they will do next. I will be very uneasy until I hear from you again."

Frederick's protests were all the more vigorous because he sometimes had to repress a penchant for the occult and the unreasonable in himself. Wilhelmina hastened to say she didn't really believe in the powers of her "witch." The relief from the headaches was brief, the healer giving as excuse the Margravine's lack of faith. Frederick's personal physician, Dr. Cothenius, made a trip to Bayreuth and put the patient on a cure of vegetables and mineral water.

All she wanted from Cothenius, Wilhelmina declared, was to make her well enough to get to Sans Souci again. She was able to visit Frederick in the autumn, and the following spring he came to the Hermitage for several days. These were quiet, family visits, though during Frederick's stay in Bayreuth a performance was given of the latest opera for which Wilhelminia had supplied the libretto and several arias. After Frederick was gone, Wilhelmina walked through the rooms where he had been and wept because they seemed so empty. She had looked so frail Frederick was quick to endorse a scheme for which Wilhelmina gave her husband credit. They would spend the coming winter in southern France and in the spring would make the tour of Italy they had planned and given up in 1739.

Again the argument of economy was used; again it seemed as if a marital quarrel might keep the travelers at home. In August Frederica suddenly appeared in Bayreuth, without her husband, whom she accused of humiliating her by installing a mistress in the palace at Stuttgart. Charles Eugene arrived two days later. After much persuasion, peace of a sort was made. The first stop of the tour, however, had to be in the Württemberg capital to make sure Charles Eugene had kept his promise of sending his "fraulein" away.

This was hardly a happy send-off. There was better luck a few days later when a stop was made at Colmar in Alsace. There Wilhelmina met Voltaire, and two accounts of their meeting, differing in detail, went off in opposite directions. To his friends in France whom he wanted to impress, Voltaire wrote of being surprised by an invitation from the Margravine to meet her and her husband at an inn outside the town. They talked for eight hours without stopping. "She overwhelmed me with kindness; she made me a beautiful present; she insisted on seeing my niece. In one word, she had but a single thought, to make up for all the evil done me in her brother's name. One has to admit that women are worth a great deal more than men."

To Frederick, Wilhelmina wrote it was she who was surprised. She heard a noise in the corridor and, looking out, found it was Voltaire being helped up the stairs by two servants. He seemed so feeble he could hardly walk. When he spoke with sorrow of

Frederick, Wilhelmina did not have the heart to scold him. She found Madame Denis, who came to call with her uncle the following day, overly fat and overly self-important.

The truth lay somewhere between the two versions. Though Wilhelmina, at Frederick's request, had refrained from writing to Voltaire, she had heard from him once directly in the past year, and often indirectly through the Marquis d'Adhemar. She may even have chosen to stop at Colmar because she thought she might be surprised. It was a mistake, however, to play on Frederick's sympathies by mentioning her guest's difficulty in climbing stairs. "Voltaire is an old comedian," Frederick growled.

The friends met once more at Lyon. Though Voltaire was not supposed to be officially in France, he thought of settling somewhere at a discreet distance from Paris and Versailles. Wilhelmina met her old acquaintance, the Marshal de Belle-Isle, also the Duke de Richelieu and Cardinal Tencin, both of whom were friends of Madame de Pompadour. When Voltaire called on the Cardinal he was received with such menacing frigidity that he left at once for Switzerland. After he was gone Wilhelmina enjoyed the society of a group of Jesuit missionaries, who had been in China and who had written a thirty volume history of that mysterious and artistically fashionable country. To Sans Souci went a set of the Fathers' books. They were received with thanks and a warning: individual Jesuits might be charming, but their order was an abomination. "I speak not as a heretic, but as a philosopher," Frederick wrote.

Avignon had been chosen as the spot where Wilhelmina would spend the winter while her husband returned to attend to business in Bayreuth. From December until March an intense cold endured all over Europe. The Rhone was frozen over; Wilhelmina had to sleep in her fur-lined pelisse and shuddered to see some kilted Scotch Highlanders going about bare kneed and breaking the ice in the river to bathe. These were followers of Charles Edward Stuart, Wilhelmina's very distant cousin, who nine years earlier had made his adventurous and disastrous attempt to unseat the House of Hanover. Wilhelmina would have liked to meet her bonny relative, but he had been expelled from France by the Treaty of Aix-la-Chapelle and not even his intimate friend and "prime minister," Lord Dunbar, knew where he was.

In spite of the cold, in spite of frequent physical collapse, Wilhelmina saw all the sights of Avignon and the surrounding region—the Fountain of Vaucluse, the Pont du Gard, the antiquities of Nîmes, Orange and Vienne. By the first of April the Margrave had returned. The travelers descended to the coast, took boat at Antibes for Genoa, and from there went to Pisa, Florence and Rome. They traveled incognito, as the Count and Countess de la Marche; the only princely houses they visited were those of such great art collectors as Cardinal Albani. Wilhelmina kept a diary throughout her trip, which, like most travel diaries, was a mere itinerary and catalogue of her enthusiams. For a semi-invalid to have seen and admired so many pictures, so many statues, so many historic monuments, was a stupendous achievement. Wilhelminia was determined to miss nothing, though, as she told Frederick, she was sometimes so feeble she had "to creep on all fours in and out of the ruins."

It went without saying that the effect of ruins on one who had herself built a ruined Roman theater at the Hermitage was overpowering. Here were authentic relics of the Ancient World, relics also of the story-book land to which Frederick and Wilhelmina had been introduced in childhood. Travelers' tales of the discovery of Herculaneum had reached Bayreuth in 1748. Wilhelmina pushed bravely southward, guided by a famous scholar and scientist, Charles de la Condamine, to explore the excavations. While in Naples, she painted a watercolor of Vesuvius in eruption. On her way north, Bologna, Venice and Verona were visited, her cicerone in Venice being Francesco Algarotti.

"I am like a blind woman," Wilhelmina wrote to Frederick, "who has just been taught to see and has gained thereby a new organ of appreciation. What I have witnessed in Italy surpasses all I had been told. I am often bewitched and wonder if I have been dreaming."

Frederick's reaction to his sister's superlatives was somewhat astringent, for, as he himself admitted, he was envious. Wilhelmina was reminded that contemporary Italy was "an old courtesan who thinks herself as beautiful as in her prime. Everything there—art, music, and learning—has declined. Italy is politically impotent, and the Pope is a mere pensioner of the great powers." Not until later did Wilhelmina tell Frederick of her papal audience. She had found Pope Benedict XIV, who had been legate in France and who had met and admired Voltaire, so congenial that she was afraid Frederick might believe a rumor which had reached Berlin of her and her husband's having gone over to the Roman Church.

"Ah, if you had only been with me," Wilhelmina sighed. She was back again in Bayreuth in August of 1755, heavily laden with mementos of her tour, many of which were intended for Frederick. En route Wilhelmina had sent to Potsdam an antique statue and a wall painting Frederick declared a fake, since it seemed to be painted in oil, a medium unknown to the ancients. Undiscouraged by his skepticism, Wilhelmina set to work on a plaster model for him of the Palatine and Capitoline hills of Rome. She wove a wreath for her hero of laurel, picked at the tomb of Vergil at Posillipo.

This Frederick refused to accept with the seriousness intended. He was embarrassed by the gift, he said, until he remembered how French cooks are apt to garnish their tasty dishes of boiled ham with sprigs of laurel. "I am no hero to myself," he added, with a rare humility. "I am only a poor fellow, a mixture of good and evil, and often dissatisfied with what I am able to accomplish."

✦ ✦ ✦

In September Frederick returned from his annual tour of Silesia to find a letter from Wilhelmina which spoke of war. She had heard war talk in Italy and France. European gazettes were carrying news of the dispatch to America of a British army under General Edward Braddock to attack Crown Point, Fort Niagara, and Fort Duquesne, at the junction of the Monongahela and Allegheny rivers. Wilhelmina was told not to worry. It was a long way from the Ohio to the Spree. War was like a great lady who travels slowly and in style. She was on the ocean now; she had not yet come to land.

During the next few months, however, Frederick's optimism faded. He had drawn up in 1752 another political survey of Europe, which took for granted the undying enmity of France and Austria. Early in 1756 a diplomatic revolution took place. Reasons for a landslide shift in alliances were, as always, complicated, but certain personal factors were involved, chief among them being the reputation Frederick had gained for daring and acquisitive success. A new minister had been appointed in Austria, Baron von Kaunitz, who, while ambassador to France, had cultivated the acquaintance of the Pompadour; in Russia the ministry had been anti-Prussian since the days of the Second Silesian War; but the carelessly disrespectful remarks Frederick had made about the King of France's mistress and the sex life and drinking habits of the Czarina Elizabeth had played their part in the formation of an accord between Russia, Austria and France.

Frederick, well aware of the danger of this combination, had found an unusual ally in England. George II detested his nephew, but he, as well as his ministers, saw the likelihood of Hanover's being lost if Lady War landed at a European port. A defensive pact was signed at Westminster on January sixteenth, 1756. Two months later Frederick's twelve-year-old alliance with France ran out. He tried to renew the agreement, but without success.

Information obtained by spies in Vienna and Dresden convinced Frederick an attack on him was planned for 1757. He was never one to allow the enemy to strike the first blow and, never having known defeat, was almost childishly confident of success. Minister von Podewils advised caution and was snubbed. August William, Henry and Ferdinand demurred and were told to stay at home if they had no stomach for a fight.

[261]

During the Silesian campaigns Frederick had told Wilhelmina nothing; now she was to know everything. In June Frederick asked what her neighbors in Franconia were up to; he was sure she had ways of finding out. "Let me know their doings and, above all, the movement of troops. . . . We have one foot in the stirrup here, and the other will follow soon."

Austria was also mobilizing. Before taking the field, Frederick asked Maria Theresa what was the object of her preparations and whether she intended to attack him this year or the next. No satisfactory answer could be obtained. The Russo-Austrian alliance was denied, though the denial was purely technical. Only signatures were lacking to the agreement, and Frederick knew one of its terms to be the return to Austria of Silesia. On August twenty-eighth, 1756, a Prussian army was on the march in the direction of Bayreuth.

"I am about to pay our fat neighbor a visit," Frederick announced to Wilhelmina.

Chapter 29

THE fat neighbor to whom Frederick had referred at the beginning of what was to be a bloody and grueling seven years war was Augustus III of Saxony-Poland. Though his name did not appear in the Grand Alliance, there was no doubt where the sympathies of Augustus lay; his wife was an Austrian archduchess, his daughter was married to the Dauphin of France. It was Saxony's ill luck to be the gateway to Bohemia, and it was there Frederick intended to strike. Augustus protested the Prussian invasion, but made no resistance. The small Saxon army retreated to the Bohemian border and capitulated after Frederick had defeated the Austrians at Lobositz on October Fourth, 1756.

Augustus fled to Warsaw, and Frederick settled down to spend the winter in Dresden, the wonder city he had visited as a boy. His rivals in the town, he told Wilhelmina, were a wicked fairy, a dwarf and a wizard. The wicked fairy was the Queen-Electress Maria Josepha, who had grown no prettier since first encountered some twenty-eight years earlier; the dwarf was her son, the Electoral Prince, a spindling offshoot of the tree which had borne Augustus the Strong; the wizard was the French ambassador, Count Charles de Broglie. Those who wished to keep a foot in either camp visited Frederick in the morning and the captive establishment in the afternoon. Frederick made use of documents taken from the Dresden archives in drawing up a manifesto proving Vienna's intention of attacking him.

Wilhelmina had been ill with "a headache all over her body." The news of Lobositz brought her back from death to life, she said. That she should rejoice to hear of a battle proved her a better Frederickian than Christian. The little she had been able to tell her brother of her neighbors was depressing. Three weeks before the first shot was fired at Lobositz, Frederick was declared a peacebreaker by the Imperial Diet. Though Bayreuth, and possibly Ansbach, would remain neutral, the rest of Franconia would send troops against him.

Let them come, was Frederick's jaunty reply. He was enjoying the Dresden picture galleries and, though the opera was poor, had heard some fine oratorios sung in Catholic churches; church music was for Frederick a new musical enthusiasm. He was saving all his strength for the spring, for then the "crazy" French, the "wild" Russians and the "great stupid" Hungarians would hunt him as if he were a stag. But Wilhelmina was not to worry. The mere thought of taking his enemies by the ears and knocking their heads together gave Frederick the health of an athlete. He had never been so well. "You'll see, dear sister! I will be able to embrace you yet and thank you for the stout spirit you have lent me."

There was tonic here for Wilhelmina, but there was also bravado. In January Frederick made a quick trip to Berlin and while there drew up secret instructions in case of his death or capture. If he was killed, the war effort must go on as if nothing had happened; if he was taken prisoner, no attention should be paid to anything he wrote from prison. A king was king only as long as he was free. Frederick had given similar instructions before his first Silesian campaign, but then his heart was really light.

Spring came. There was a costly victory outside of Prague in May and a defeat at Kolin in June. Frederick was cruelly surprised by his first military disaster, a disaster for which he felt he had no one but himself to blame. He did not try to deceive

Wilhelmina as to the seriousness of his situation. It was not for the moment desperate, for Russia, always slow to mobilize, had not yet come into the picture. Before she did, Frederick would try to make peace with France. Wilhelmina could help. She could approach the Marshal de Belle-Isle, whom she had encountered recently in France, through the French delegate to the Imperial Diet. "If peace comes from your hand," Frederick wrote, "it will be doubly dear, and you yourself will have had the honor of saving Germany."

Wilhelmina sent off a courier at once to Frankfurt, but she had a suggestion of her own to make. After the return from Italy an Academy of Arts and Sciences was founded in Bayreuth. At its head was a Frenchman whom Wilhelmina had met on her travels, Louis Alexandre Mirabeau de Riquetti. Mirabeau was a cousin of the Abbé de Bernis, French foreign secretary and close associate of the Pompadour. Wilhelmina proposed that through these two a bribe should be offered to the favorite.

His sister, Frederick exclaimed, was his second self, but much more clever! Mirabeau was soon on his way to France and had been authorized to dangle a half-million francs before the Pompadour's nose. The negotiations, however, were to be very secret, so that nothing should be heard of them in England.

For weeks Wilhelmina was tantalized by reports of Mirabeau's minor successes and major frustrations in Paris. Meanwhile war news thundered in her ears. She, who had been so bored she could hardly keep her eyes open at military reviews, followed the movement of armies on her map. Wilhelmina had by heart the details of each engagement. The French were attacking Friesland; the Russians were besieging Memel; the Swedish Ricksdag had declared war, in spite of an attempt by sister Ulrica to set up a royal dictatorship.

Frederick, who wrote he was like a traveler surrounded by brigands, all of them intent on plunder, had to withdraw from Bohemia. The retreat was to be made in two sections, he leading the main body, a smaller army under August William moving in his rear to protect the town of Zittau, which was the base of Prussian supplies and ammunition. The maneuver was hopelessly bungled. Zittau was taken and burned by the Austrians. When Frederick arrived at the appointed rendezvous August William was already there, with only a fraction of his hungry and exhausted army. White with rage, Frederick refused to speak to his brother. He sent word that August William deserved a court martial and would never again be given the command of so much as a platoon. Wilhelmina heard of this sorry business from both parties and spoke a soft word for the one who had gone back to Prussia in disgrace.

But never, never in all the years, had Wilhelmina felt so close, so utterly at one with Frederick. She had made a new connection with France. Soon after the defeat at Kolin the brother and sister learned of the death of their mother, whose health had been failing for the past year. Letters of condolence came from Voltaire; he wrote from Les Délices, an estate he had bought near Geneva. Voltaire advised an appeal to the Duke of Richelieu, wrote to the Duke himself, and also to Cardinal Tencin, who had treated him with such discourtesy at Lyon.

Wilhelmina was touched and grateful. She became the medium through which letters were exchanged with Frederick. To her old friend, Wilhelmina poured out the anxieties, the despair, she tried to conceal from her brother. What subjects for tragedies were piling up today! "The state I am in is worse than death. I see the greatest man of the century, my brother, the one I love, at the end of his resources . . . I have never prided myself on being much of a philosopher, for I have found nothing in philosophy to soothe the sorrows of my soul—nothing except the advice to escape sorrow by ceasing to live." Wilhelmina had just received some verses from Frederick, an epistle in which he spoke of suicide. He had often told her he would not survive defeat, and she was sure she could not survive his death.

Voltaire, who did not hesitate to speak ill of Frederick to others and who blamed Frederick for the renewal of war, was moved to tears by Wilhelmina's letters. He wanted Frederick to communicate directly with Richelieu, and a disguised Prussian officer was sent into the French camp, but to no effect.

The time had come for daring. In September Wilhelmina was told she might hear nothing for the next six weeks, and then she would hear only in cipher. Less than half the time went by, and there was news, good news. At Rossbach near Magdeburg, in a battle lasting only an hour and a half, Frederick was victor. He could not allow himself to rest, however, for winter was coming on and Breslau had been taken by the Austrians.

Hurrying back to Silesia, Frederick made a speech to his officers at Leuthen on the evening of December fourth, 1757, a speech which for generations would quicken the pulses of German patriots. Frederick spoke of past heroisms, of the danger of Silesia's being lost, of the strength of the enemy which enormously outnumbered the Prussian forces. The action he contemplated seemed doomed to failure, but it must succeed. If there was anyone here who wished to hand in his resignation now it would be accepted without comment or future reprisal.

No one stirred; there was complete silence in the room. Frederick laughed and said he knew his brave companions would not fail him. But now the challenge had been accepted: it must be followed through. Any regiment faltering on the morrow would lose its standards and be retired to garrison duty.

At Leuthen, as at Kesseldorf, the troops went into action singing, their song a doxology dating from the Wars of Religion. Victory was again prodigious. These two engagements, Rossbach and Leuthen, only a month apart, made Frederick the hero, not merely of his invalid sister, but of all Europe. A traveler from Prussia was mobbed on landing in England by admirers, each of them brandishing a picture of Frederick, all clamoring to know which was the best likeness; victory ribbons were worn in Dresden, and even in Vienna. An extraordinary tribute was paid in France. The Marshal de Belle-Isle told Madame de Pompadour that, after Rossbach, one might expect the conqueror to arrive in Paris any day. "Then at last I'll see a king," the Pompadour said.

Frederick himself was carried away. "This will bring peace," he exulted to Wilhelmina. "This spring I will clasp you in my arms."

✦ ✦ ✦

But as he prepared to spend his second winter away from home, in retaken Breslau, Frederick knew he had spoken too soon. The Russians had yet to be beaten; they had overrun East Prussia. The Swedes were in Pomerania.

Frederick sent for one of his Sans Souci friends, the Marquis d'Argens, to keep him company. Later he acquired a new companion for his scanty leisure, a young Swiss scholar, Henry de Catt, whom he had met on a short trip into Holland in 1755. On the boat from Wesel to Utrecht, Frederick had passed himself off as a musician, the conductor of the King of Poland's orchestra. De Catt had wondered how a concert master could speak with such authority of public affairs. He was not completely surprised by an invitation to Potsdam two months later; illness forced him to decline. In 1758 De Catt heard from Frederick again and jumped at the chance of becoming better acquainted with the victor of Rossbach and Leuthen.

After arriving at Breslau toward the end of March, De Catt was given a salary and the function of reader, but in the late afternoon hours spent with the King, Frederick did most of the reading, or rather the reciting, for he knew by heart whole sections of tragedies of Racine, which he declaimed so loudly and so fervently that the valet in the next room sometimes came in, thinking he had been called. The valet told De Catt he wondered at times if His Majesty was quite right in the head.

De Catt had no such qualms. His chief trouble was in keeping up with the rapid dartings of Frederick's mind. Now Frederick was sketching the strategy of a battle, or the ground plan of Sans Souci, now he was trying to shake De Catt's faith in the immortality of the soul. The King delivered historical and literary judgments; he gave medical advice and wrote verses addressed to a young lady of Breslau whom he had never seen, but whom De

Catt fancied. In the record kept by the Swiss each afternoon's session was fresh adventure.

Frederick, who declared himself an old fogey now, a reader of old books, liked to speak of the past. He spoke often of his quarrel with Voltaire, but De Catt noted how eagerly a letter, coming from Switzerland via Bayreuth, was torn open. The searing experiences of youth were often mentioned, the climax of the account being the day when the grenadiers held Frederick's head against the window bars at Küstrin. His father, wonderfully intelligent in practical affairs and wonderfully endowed to deal with them, was a just man—but how terrible!

Having spoken of his father, Frederick told De Catt of a dream he had the following night. "My father entered my room with six soldiers. He ordered them to tie me up and to take me to Magdeburg. 'But why?' I asked of my sister of Bayreuth. 'It's because,' she said, 'you do not love your father.'"

This was a recurrent dream. Each time that Frederick experienced it he woke dripping with sweat. His rational credo did not allow interpretation of his nightmares, but De Catt could see he was fascinated by the subject. If his father played the part of Nemesis in the world of sleep, Wilhelmina was ever the wise counselor. To her, Frederick said, he owed all of his success in life, for she had inspired him to work and to educate himself by reading. Her influence on him as a child had caused him to creep out of his bed at night and read by candlelight.

One night in May Frederick dreamed he saw his dead mother coming out of her tomb, led by Wilhelmina and August William. He ran to her and would have kissed her hand, but his father held him back. Frederick awoke, as usual, in great physical distress. Shortly after came news of the death of August William, who had hidden himself away from the world and his humiliation at his country estate, Oranienburg. The Prince complained of headache one day and was dead the next. An autopsy revealed a blood clot in the brain.

Frederick wrote of his dismay to Wilhelmina, for he had been fond of his brother and had even begun to think the disaster at Zittau was not altogether August William's fault. One death suggested another, a more hideous, loss. Frederick had not heard from Wilhelmina for several weeks. This might have been due to the recent occupation of Bayreuth by Austrian troops, but Frederick could not be sure.

"Oh you, the dearest of my family," he wrote, "you, the most deeply rooted in my heart of anyone in this world . . . take care of yourself. . . . Don't fear for us. You'll see, we'll come through all our trials!" Frederick had a feeling Wilhelmina might not be well enough to write herself. If this was so, he begged her to get one of her household to send him word, a single sentence would do. Anything was better than uncertainty.

But Wilhelmina had already written herself, and with greatest difficulty. After years of ill health and hypochondria, of baffling, constantly shifting symptoms, the disease which had killed both of her parents, firmly fixed in her inheritance by inbreeding, had declared itself. She had, without mentioning her state to Frederick, been bedridden for months. Wilhelmina's face, her legs, and her hands were swollen; she could hardly hold a pen.

"Good God, what a handwriting!" Frederick exclaimed with horror. "You must have been a hundred times worse than they had told me."

In the interval news of the invalid had come from Henry— Henry, who had distinguished himself throughout the war and had been put in command of an army to drive the enemy out of Franconia. Henry had dined with the Margrave in Bayreuth and had seen Wilhelmina. He had told Frederick she was dying.

But Frederick would not let her die. "Think of this," he wrote with passionate intensity, "and make yourself believe it; there is no happiness for me in life without you. My life depends on yours . . . I am not paying you pretty compliments; this comes from the bottom of my heart. . . . Only by caring for yourself can you prove your love for me." Frederick was forcing his will upon Wilhelmina with the same determination as he forced his soldiers to win for him, or die.

Of the next letter only the signature was in the familiar hand. Wilhelmina had hardly had the strength to dictate her message, "not to a King, but to the one I love . . . I have been in hell," she had whispered, "but more in spirit than in flesh. To keep me from knowing of our loss"—she was referring to August William's death—"the Margrave kept back what you have written, and I believed the very worst. Now that I have your dear letters they have softened the grief I feel for my brother." She gave details of her illness, for it was no use trying to conceal them any longer. She could not believe in a miracle of recovery for herself, but she could believe in a miraculous victory for Frederick.

The unwelcome guests, the Austrians, had vanished from Bayreuth, after cutting down orchards of ripening fruit and trampling the grain. The French were no longer a serious menace, but the Russians had penetrated deeply into Prussia. They had reached Küstrin. Frederick, going to meet them, saw the town of his imprisonment and apprenticeship a ruin. After a long day of ferocious fighting at nearby Zorndorf, the enemy left the field, but losses had been so heavy neither side could claim a victory.

Frederick spent a few days at Tamsel, the beautiful estate where he had once played at being in love with Eleanora von Wreech. She was a widow now, with grown children; she had fled before the Russians. Her house stood empty. When Frederick arrived the body of a dead peasant woman was lying in the garden. Frederick wrote sadly to the mistress of Tamsel, saying he would do something for her and for her people when he could and when the Russians had been driven from the province. To Wilhelmina he wrote with groundless optimism that the war might end this year.

A glimmer of improvement was his reward. An abscess had broken in Wilhelmina's side. Frederick, remembering how his father had come back to life after a similar episode, wrote: "I have been in despair over your illness, but something tells me you will get well. I beg you on bended knee—do everything you can to conquer this sickness, eat, take your medicine, obey your doctor blindly." Again he was pressing her hard to do his will. To keep her spirits up he enclosed "some foolishness" he had written, the verses dashed off at Breslau for De Catt's sweetheart.

De Catt saw Frederick at work on yet another poem, the first sketch of which was read aloud and which was polished and repolished with unusual care. Sent off on October twelfth, 1758, this last *Epistle to My Sister of Bayreuth* was never read by the one to whom it was addressed. Wilhelmina had died on the fourteenth, holding one of Frederick's letters in her crippled hand. On the day of her death, Frederick was defeated at Hochkirch in Saxony. He was in great danger; a bullet flattened the snuff box in his breast pocket, but the hope he had expressed in his poem of going down into the Underworld hand in hand with his sister was unrealized.

There was some preparation for the terrible news, a letter from the Marquis d'Adhemar, but when the word came at two o'clock on the morning of the seventeenth Henry de Catt was sent for. He went to Frederick's room and stayed there for three hours, saying what he could, listening to Frederick's wild and, at times, incoherent grief. For four days the shutters of the room were kept closed, and no one saw the King except his reader. Frederick's officers were worried, so was De Catt, who had been shown a small ivory box hung on a chain about Frederick's neck. It contained opium pills, a last resort in case of capture. Frederick had spoken of it as his final consolation.

On October twentieth Henry arrived with his army. Seeing his brother may have been a comfort, but it was also a call to action. To make good what had been lost in the recent defeat, Frederick had to leave his darkened room. Life swept him on.

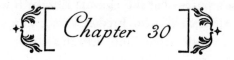

AN EPILOGUE

THE defeat at Hochkirch was not the last that Frederick
had to suffer. Each year after Wilhelmina's death the
chances for Prussian victory became more desperate. Survival was the final aim. By the winter of 1761 Frederick faced the
prospect of asking for peace on enemy terms. But from which
enemy? On every front Prussia was outnumbered. The quality of
Prussian armies had declined; they were now made up of clumsy
recruits or foreigners of dubious loyalty. With a new ministry in
England, Lord Bute having taken the place of the war lord William Pitt, there was danger of English subsidies being withdrawn.

To Henry, who had become one of his most valued and reliable generals, Frederick wrote, "The more I reflect on events, the
more I conclude how right the Romans were to consecrate a
golden statue to Fortune." But though Frederick's outlook
might be fatalistic, though he had never completely renounced
what his father had once termed "the damnable and godless
doctrine of predestination," nothing had been left to chance.
Frederick had negotiated with the Tartars of the Crimea to attack Russia, and with the Turks to attack the Austrians in Hungary. If this spring an offensive was not begun in either sector,
Prussia would have to yield.

But before the end of the year came a whisper—one could

hardly call it a report—that the Czarina Elizabeth was ill. Of the three women adversaries, who, Frederick said, were maenads, trying to tear him limb from limb, Elizabeth was the one most feared and most reviled. Frederick's word for her was "that infamous bitch of the North." He made a wager with his stable-mate, Henry de Catt, on Elizabeth's recovery, he taking the positive, De Catt the negative, side. The loser would have to produce a gift.

One day in February of 1762 De Catt was received with a low bow and the words, "You have won." Elizabeth had died of a stroke on January fifth. Frederick handed the Swiss an epitaph he had just written:

> Oh passer-by, here Messalina lies,
> The concubine of Russian and Cossack.
> Having worn them out, she leaves this earthly sphere
> To hunt for lovers in the realms of death.

De Catt may have expected a more substantial present than a verse, but he, who had seen Frederick pass through so many trials, could rejoice in his triumph.

Triumph it would be, for the successor to Elizabeth was said to adore the Prussian King. Peter, late of Holstein-Gastorp, now of all the Russias, spoke of Frederick as his master; his bodyguard was drilled and uniformed *à la Prusse*; Frederick's miniature, set in a ring, sparkled on the young Czar's finger.

Before the month was out a Russian envoy arrived to offer not only peace but an alliance. The help Frederick needed so badly had only just begun to materialize when word came of yet another dethronement in Russia and yet another assassination. Peter's partiality for Frederick had helped to weigh the scales against him, and Peter's wife, Catherine, who may or may not have connived at his murder, had stepped into his shoes.

Frederick had last seen the new Russian potentate when, a provincial miss from Stettin, she came to Berlin on her way to Saint Petersburg. The effort he had made to charm her then was not entirely wasted now, for though Russian troops were withdrawn and the lyric note vanished from diplomatic correspondence, peace was maintained. The following spring there was peace all over Europe, a peace which assured the possession of Silesia to Frederick for the third time. Fortune, which had done so much for him in the past, had favored him again.

On March thirtieth, 1763, the streets of Berlin were crowded. A welcome comparable to that at the close of the Second Silesian War was planned, but Frederick could not face it. He slipped into the city in a closed carriage and reached the palace by an obscure route. Though he was only fifty-one, Frederick was an old man, his bright brown hair gone gray, his body wasted. Only the big blue eyes were unchanged; they stood out more prominently than ever from the bony structure of his face.

The royal family had gathered to greet the King. There were few left of Frederick's generation, and the younger folk had changed so greatly they had to be introduced to him. Elizabeth Christina took an uncertain step in her husband's direction. Frederick spoke the only words that came to his mind after seven years. "Madame has grown stouter," he said.

The feeling of coming home to a strange place, where all he saw were strangers, where only the walls and buildings were familiar, was strong in Frederick. A great task lay ahead of him, a task comparable to that of the Great Elector, the ancestor whom Frederick admired so much. This war had not lasted for thirty years, a generation, but it had left burnt towns and broken walls, unsown fields and empty farmhouses.

Frederick took up his burden. That during the next few years he was able to rebuild his country and in his spare time write an ambitious historical work, many political treatises, and many thousands of facile and undistinguished hexameters was proof of his vitality. Frederick's *History of the Seven Years War* was a continuation of his *History of My Own Time*. Like Caesar in his *Commentaries*, Frederick spoke to posterity in the third person. Politics was his theme; he did not often allow himself to stray far from it, but when his account reached the disastrous year of 1758, he turned aside to speak of Wilhelmina and what her loss had meant to him.

"She was a Princess of rare worth," Frederick wrote. "She had a cultivated mind. . . an intellect equal to any, and a special talent for all the arts. To mention only her gifts, however, is to give too little praise. Nobility of soul, sweetness of character were added to her superior mind. . . . She often suffered from the ingratitude of those she had loaded with favors. . . . The most affectionate, the most faithful friendship, united the King and this noble sister. Their ties had been formed in early childhood, the same upbringing, the same feelings having drawn them close together." Frederick concluded his paragraph by saying the ancient Romans would have seen more than a chronological link between the defeat at Hochkirch and the death of Wilhelmina, but such superstition was inadmissible today.

This stately and restrained tribute was not the first that Frederick had attempted. In the early weeks of his sorrow he went over and over his last poem to Wilhelmina and found it inadequate. He could not even bear to read a eulogy sent him by the Marquis d'Adhemar. Frederick wrote to Voltaire, Voltaire who was the only one who could do justice to Wilhelmina. "Never forget her," he urged. "Gather all your strength to raise a monument to her. You only have to do her justice. Without going beyond the truth you will find many and beautiful things to say."

For once Frederick was dissatisfied with Voltaire's response to a poetic challenge. In his *Ode to Her Royal Highness, the Margravine of Bayreuth,* Wilhelmina was represented as the heroic sister of a hero. "I wanted something stronger," Frederick complained, "something more public. Let all Europe weep with me a virtue too little known." He would prefer there to be no mention of himself. Wilhelmina should stand on her own pedestal.

Voltaire tried again. His second effort was received in March of 1759, and Frederick declared it to be the first real comfort he had had in the past six months.

[276]

Wilhelmina's death had gone far toward reconciling the two beings she considered so superior to all others, though they continued to rail at one another, and during the darkest period of the war their correspondence all but ceased. Only time could modify their resentments and give them a less distorted view of one another. Established safely in Switzerland, Voltaire was bolder in asserting his beliefs. His denunciation of the legal murder of Jean Calas in 1762 and the protection he gave to other Protestant victims of religious bigotry roused Frederick's enthusiasm. He interpreted rightly Voltaire's slogan of *écrasez l'infâme* as a call to crush intolerance, not to destroy a particular church or sect.

From a poem of Voltaire, written long before their first meeting, Frederick took the inspiration for a concrete memorial to Wilhelmina. Voltaire had described the Temple of Friendship as hidden away in a secluded spot, far from the noisy traffic of the world. The lines had never been forgotten; in his last poem to his sister Frederick had said how strange it was such a temple existed only in the mind of a poet. In 1768, in a quiet corner of the Sans Souci grounds, work was begun on a small circular temple, its Corinthian columns decorated by plaques representing all the most famous friends of antiquity. At the rear of the shrine, against a screen of marble, a statue of Wilhelmina was placed, an idealized portrait. She was shown seated in a chair, under one arm a lap dog, which might have been Folichon, or one of Folichon's predecessors or successors. In her lap was a book, open, as though it had just fallen from her hand.

Frederick sent for a Bayreuth architect, Charles von Gontard, to carry out his design, and for Bayreuth sculptors to carve the statue, though Wilhelmina's principality was no longer an artistic center. A year after his wife's death the Margrave remarried, the bride chosen being Wilhelmina's niece, the twenty-two year old daughter of Lotte of Brunswick-Bevern. A son and heir, object of the marriage, did not materialize; the Margrave lived only four years longer. With his passing, all the activities which he and Wilhelmina had fostered slowed to a standstill. When Bayreuth was united with Ansbach in 1769 it became a mere province of its larger neighbor.

A few artists remained, however, and found a patroness in Frederica, Duchess of Württemberg. Wilhelmina's daughter had only kept up the pretense of reconciliation with her husband while her mother lived. She left Stuttgart and, until her father died, lived at Neustadt on the Aisch, but this was still too near to her hated husband. Having inherited Fantasie, a hunting lodge, one of the minor margravial residences Wilhelmina had beautified, Frederica came back to spend the rest of her life in Bayreuth.

In 1773 the Duchess was in Switzerland. She paid a two day visit to Voltaire at Ferney. He was struck by her resemblance to her mother, and when he spoke of Wilhelmina, Frederica burst into tears. The years with her mother had been the happiest of her life, she exclaimed. Voltaire also wept.

And Frederick, when he heard of the visit, said he would have mingled his tears with theirs, if he had been there. To the old man at Ferney, Frederick sent a drawing of his temple and compared it to the one Cicero intended to build for his beloved daughter Tullia. To no other human being had he raised a monument. "I go there often," Frederick concluded simply, "to think of my great loss and the happiness I once enjoyed."

✦ APPENDIX ✦

❖[*Significant Dates*]❖

Birth of Wilhelmina   *July 3, 1709*

Birth of Frederick   *January 24, 1712*

Death of Frederick I of Prussia   *February 25, 1713*

Accession of Frederick William I   *February 25, 1713*

Death of Queen Anne of England   *August 10, 1714*

Accession of George I   *August 10, 1714*

Pomeranian Campaign of Frederick William I

April–December, 1715

Promulgation of Pragmatic Sanction   *1724*

Death of George I   *June 21, 1727*

Accession of George II   *June 21, 1727*

Frederick's visit to Dresden   *February, 1728*

Frederick's arrest at Wesel   *August 12, 1730*

Execution of Von Katte   *November 11, 1730*

Wilhelmina's marriage   *November 20, 1731*

Birth of Wilhelmina's daughter, Elizabeth Frederica Sophia

August 30, 1732

Frederick's marriage to Elizabeth Christina of Brunswick-Bevern

June 6, 1733

War of the Polish Succession   *1733–1735*

Rhine Campaign and illness of Frederick William I   *Autumn, 1734*

Death of George Frederick Charles (Wilhelmina's father-in-law)

May 7, 1735

Death of Frederick William I   *May 31, 1740*

Accession of Frederick II   *May 31, 1740*

Death of Emperor Charles VI   *October 20, 1740*

Frederick invades Silesia   *December 16, 1740*

Election of Charles Albert of Bavaria as Emperor Charles VII

January 24, 1742

Peace of Breslau (Prussia and Austria)   *July 28, 1742*

Marriage of Dorothea von der Marwitz to Count Burghauss

April 8, 1744

Frederick re-enters War of Austrian Succession   *August 8, 1744*

SIGNIFICANT DATES

Peace of Dresden (Prussia, Austria, Saxony) *December 25, 1745*

Marriage of Wilhelmina's daughter, Frederica, to Charles Eugene of Württemberg *September 26, 1748*

Voltaire's stay in Prussia *1750–1753*

Wilhelmina's travels in France and Italy
October, 1754—August, 1755

Beginning of Seven Years War; Frederick invades Saxony
August 28, 1756

Death of Wilhelmina *October 14, 1758*

Defeat of Hochkirch *October 14, 1758*

Building of Temple of Friendship *1768*

✛✛✛

CHILDREN OF FREDERICK WILLIAM I & SOPHIA DOROTHEA

(Married November 28, 1706)

SOPHIA FREDERICA WILHELMINA, *July 3, 1709—October 14, 1758*

Frederick Louis, *November 22, 1707—May 5, 1708*

Frederick William, *August 16, 1710—July 31, 1711*

FREDERICK II, *January 21, 1712—August 17, 1786*

Charlotte Albertine, *May 5, 1713—June, 1714*

Frederica Louise (Eeka), *September 28, 1714—February 4, 1784*

Philippine Charlotte (Lotte), *March 13, 1716—February 16, 1801*

Louis Charles William, *March 3, 1717—August 31, 1719*

Sophia Dorothea Maria, *January 25, 1719—November 13, 1765*

Louise Ulrica, *July 24, 1720—July 2, 1782*

August William, *August 9, 1722—June 12, 1758*

Anne Amelia, *November 9, 1723—March 30, 1787*

Frederick Henry Louis, *January 18, 1726—August 3, 1802*

August Ferdinand, *May 23, 1730—May 2, 1813*

⁜[*Notes and Comments*]⁜

ABBREVIATIONS USED

Forschungen zur Brandenburgischen und Preussischen Geschichte.
FBPG

Förster, Friedrich. *Urkundenbuch zu der Lebensgeschichte Friedrich Wilhelm's I.* 2 vols. Potsdam, 1834, 1835.   *Urkundenbuch*

Friedrich der Grosse und Wilhelmine von Bayreuth. Berlin, 1924.
Vol. I: *Jugendbriefe*   *Jugendbriefe*
Vol. II: *Briefe der Königzeit*   *Königzeit*

Hohenzollern Jahrbuch, 1898–1918.   *HJB*

Mémoires de Frédérique Sophie Wilhelmine, Margravine de Bareith. Leipzig, 1889.   *Mémoires*

Oeuvres de Frédéric le Grand, ed. J. D. E. Preuss. Berlin, 1846–1857.
Oeuvres

Pöllnitz, Baron von. *Mémoires pour servir à l'histoire des Quatre Derniers Souverains de la Maison de Brandenbourg Royale de Prusse.* Berlin, 1791.   *Memoires pour servir*

Publicationen aus den Königlichen Preussischen Staatsarchiven   *PKPS*

Voltaire, Francois Marie Arouet de. *Correspondance*, ed. Theodore Besterman. 94 vols. Geneva, 1953–1963.   *Voltaire*

CHAPTER I

CHIEF SOURCES: *Mémoires*, pp. 1–32; Letters of Sophia Dorothea and Wilhelmina to Frederick William in *HJB,* 1913, pp. 212 ff.

Pesne's remark to Frederick, quoted in the opening paragraph, appears in *Jugendbriefe*, p. 313.

The childhood picture of Frederick and Wilhelmina now hangs in the Charlottenburg Museum in West Berlin. It is often said to have been painted in 1715, but an article by Paul Seidel in *HJB*, 1911, dates it a year earlier. The fact that Frederick is represented still in petticoats is an argument in favor of the earlier date. Pesne, who painted all of the royal family many times over, did a portrait of one of Frederick's elder brothers in which the same Negro page appears as in the joint picture. This page is mentioned in contemporary descriptions of the Prussian court and probably came to Hanover as part of Sophia Dorothea's elegant trousseau. Her father George I took a number of Negro servants with him to London in 1714.

CHAPTER II

CHIEF SOURCES: *Mémoires*, pp. 32–38; Letters, *HJB*, 1913, pp. 220–28; George Schnath, *Briefwechsel der Kurfürstin Sophia von Hanover mit dem Preussischen Königshaus*, Berlin, 1927.

Literature concerning the Prisoner of Ahlden is copious, contemporary items being *Le Roman Octavia*, by Anton Ulrich von Wolfenbuttel (1707) and Baron Pöllnitz's *Histoire secrète de la duchesse d'Hanover, épouse de George I* (1732). Eloquent love letters of the unhappy lady to Count Königsmarck, often quoted, and appearing in the *Revue des Deux Mondes*, in 1914, are now thought to be forgeries.

The account Wilhelmina gives in her memoirs of the visit of Peter the Great to Berlin is flamboyant, but not more so than that of Baron von Pöllnitz in his *Mémoires pour servir*, pp. 64 ff. Peter's destructiveness as a guest is noted in the *Diary of John Evelyn*, Vol. I, p. 362. Evelyn's house at Deptford was rented by the Czar for three months in 1698. Peter had never seen a wheelbarrow and was so fascinated he had himself pushed about in one to the utter ruin of the box hedges of garden beds. Evelyn's servant wrote nervously, "There is a large company here —and nasty!" After Peter was gone the house and premises were inspected by the King's surveyor, Sir Christopher Wren, and the King's head gardener; £150 was allowed by the crown for damages.

CHAPTER III

CHIEF SOURCES: Otto Krauske, "Vom Hofe Friedrich Wilhelm's I," *HJB*, 1903, pp. 175–210; Adolf Stockfuss, *500 Jahre Berliner Geschichte*, Berlin, 1900, pp. 316 ff.; Frederick's letters to has father, *Oeuvres*, Vol. XXVII, Pt. III; Wilhelmina's letters, *HJB*, 1913, p. 217.

The visitor to Berlin in 1717 cited in the first paragraph was Johann Michael von Loen, a lawyer (Gustav B. Volz, *Friedrich der Grosse in Spiegel seiner Zeit*, Berlin, 1901, Vol. I, pp. 22 ff.). Von Loen tells an anecdote, that was apparently going the rounds, of little Fritz's remarking as he passed a barred window of the treasury where gold pieces were stored, "How happy these poor prisoners would be if they could get out!" The grownups walking with Frederick laughed, but the King, who was also of the party, was not amused.

The stories of Frederick's being taught Latin and of his getting out of bed to read at night are taken from Heinrich de Catt, *Unterhaltungen mit Friedrich dem Grossen* in *PKPS*, Vol. XXII, p. 71.

CHAPTER IV

CHIEF SOURCES: *Mémoires*, pp. 38–76. Letters, *HJB*, 1913, p. 229.

The letters of Frederick William to the Prince of Anhalt-Dessau (*Die Briefe König Friedrich Wilhem's I an den Fürsten Leopold zu Anhalt-Dessau*, Berlin, 1905), though dealing mainly with military affairs, depict the rugged personalities of these two devoted friends. Sophia Dorothea, the lifelong enemy of the Prince and of Grumbkow, must have supplied her daughter with some of the less credible anecdotes concerning them that appear in the early pages of the *Mémoires*. One of her ladies-in-waiting, who was first imprisoned and then exiled on their account, Madame von Blaspil, was recalled by Frederick after he became king and was appointed governess to his younger sisters.

CHAPTER V

CHIEF SOURCES: *Mémoires*, pp. 67–82; Letters, *HJB*, 1913, p. 225; Reinhold Koser, *Friedrich der Gross als Kronprinz*, Berlin & Stuttgart, 1912, pp. 5–8; Förster, *Urkundenbuch*, Vol. II, pp. 5–13.

The dog who figures in Wilhelmina's story of the ink went to Bayreuth with her when she married and lived to a ripe old age. Frederick, Wilhelmina and also Sophia Dorothea were pet lovers. Dogs appear in many of the pictures painted of them. Frederick's most famous dog was Biche, who was captured by the Austrians at the battle of Soor and who corresponded with Wilhelmina's dog, Folichon, as described in Chapter 25 of this book. A small pack of greyhounds companioned Frederick's old age. They were tenderly nursed through illnesses and are buried in the gardens of Sans Souci.

Though Sophia Dorothea mentions her mother frequently in her letters to her husband, nothing is said of the life and death of the Prisoner of Ahlden in Wilhelmina's memoirs. One wonders if this was one subject that was taboo between mother and daughter.

CHAPTER VI

CHIEF SOURCES: *Mémoires*, pp. 78–85; Förster, *Urkundenbuch*, Vol. II, pp. 5–197; August Hermann Francke, *Neue Beitrage zur Geschichte August Hermann Francke's*, Halle, 1875; Johann Anastasius Freylinghausen, *Sieben Tage am Hofe Friedrich Wilhelm's I*, Berlin, 1900.

Jochen Klepper's *In Tormentis Pinxit* considers Frederick William as an artist and reproduces examples of his painting, which are strong, crude and interesting from a psychological point of view.

Frederick's letter to Jacques Égide Duhan appears on p. 269 of *Oeuvres*, Vol. XVI. Frederick's library was hidden in the house of Counselor von Peyne and was gloatingly catalogued by its youthful owner.

CHAPTER VII

CHIEF SOURCES: Paul Haake, "Der Besuch des Preussischen Soldatenkönigs in Dresden," 1728 in *FBPG*, Vol. XLVII; *Mémoires*, pp. 86–88, 104; Otto R. Gervais, *Die Frauen um Friedrich den Grossen*, Vienna, 1933, pp. 135–63; *Jugendbriefe*, p. 64.

The account of the visit to Dresden given in *FBPG*, Vol. XLVII, is based on an unpublished journal which was in the Berlin Archives in 1935.

Frederick's illness after the visit is attributed to syphilis by certain writers, but there is no reliable evidence on which to base such a diagnosis. Whether La Orczelska was actually Frederick's mistress is also uncertain. Wilhelmina's statement to that effect in the *Mémoires* may have been due to his boasting and to her jealousy. Sophia Dorothea also disapproved of the young lady and of her masquerading as a man (Letters, *HJB*, 1913, p. 234).

Aurora Königsmarck, sister of the lover of the Prisoner of Ahlden, came to Saxony to look for her brother after his mysterious disappearance at Hanover on July first, 1698. Her search came to nothing, but she thus met Augustus the Strong, the patron of Königsmarck, and became the mother of Maurice de Saxe, Marshal of France and, among other achievements, ancestor of the novelist, Georges Sand.

CHAPTER VIII

CHIEF SOURCES: *Mémoires*, pp. 104–20; Frederick's letter to his father and its reply, *Oeuvres*, Vol. XXVII, Pt. III, pp. 9–10; Otto Gervais, *Die Frauen um Friedrich den Grossen*, Vienna, 1933, pp. 135–63.

Frederick Louis, Prince of Wales, who died in 1751 and who was the father of George III, returned with interest the dislike of his parents. He caricatured them in his *Histoire du Prince Titi* (1735); he gave life-long encouragement to the opposition in Parliament. The Prince may have been maligned in the memoirs of Lord Hervey and the letters of Horace Walpole, but he does not seem to have been an attractive character, and it is doubtful if Wilhelmina would have been happy as his wife.

CHAPTER IX

CHIEF SOURCES: *Mémoires*, pp. 121–57; Sir Richard Lodge, *Great Britain and Prussia in the Eighteenth Century*, Oxford, 1923; *Der Kronprinzen Prozess*, Berlin, 1936, p. 185.

Frederick, in his *Mémoires pour servir à l'histoire de la Maison de Brandenbourg* (*Oeuvres*, Vol. I), declares Seckendorf to have been the greatest enemy of the Prussian state during the reign of Frederick William. The feelings of Seckendorf, who was still alive when the book was published—he lived to be a hundred and died in 1763—were hurt. Seckendorf visited Bayreuth in 1751, and Wilhelmina thought him much more "pretty" after having lost all his teeth. During the Seven Years War Seckendorf, aged ninety-five, was taken prisoner by a Prussian patrol and was interned at his estate, Meuselwitz, for several months.

CHAPTER X

CHIEF SOURCES: *Mémoires*, pp. 163–80; Wilhelm Oncken, "Sir Charles Hotham und Friederich Wilhelm I im Jahre 1730," *FBPG*, Vols. VII, VIII; William Proctor, A *Short Journal of His Polish Majesty's*

Camp at Radewitz, London, 1737; *Der Kronprinzen Prozess*, Berlin, 1936, pp. 39 ff; L. G. Friedrick Raumer, *Beitrage zur neueren Geschichte*, Vol. III, pp. 506–16; unpublished letters of Sir Charles Hotham, Guy Dickens, Dr. Villa, Ambassador Reichenbach, General von Grumbkow and others in London Bureau of Records.

At this time the Brunswick representative in Berlin was writing particularly full news letters home, since Brunswick was interested in a marriage alliance with Prussia. The letters, which begin in 1728 and run to 1731, have been edited by Richard Wolff for the *Schriften des Vereins fur die Geschichte Berlin's*. They are extremely discreet, but unfriendly in tone to Frederick William. The King's treatment of his son is only hinted at, but there is frequent mention of cruel punishments in the army and in the royal household.

CHAPTER XI

CHIEF SOURCES: *Der Kronprinzen Prozess*, Berlin, 1936, pp. 1–100.
Frederick told his reader, Henry de Catt, in 1758 that he destroyed some of the records of his trial after his accession. Many, however, remained in the archives. Those collected in the *Kronprinzen Prozess* give an accurate account of the attempt to escape and its aftermath. Some are actual transcripts of what was said at the hearings of the many people involved.

CHAPTER XII

CHIEF SOURCES: *Mémoires*, pp. 182–208; Pöllnitz, *Mémoires pour servir*, pp. 230–42; unpublished letters in the London Bureau of Records.
Baron von Pöllnitz, a gossipy journalist who was rewarded for his writings by many royal persons, says that Grumbkow saw through the ruse of the substituted letters and told Frederick William that women were more tricky than the serpent in the Garden of Eden.

Frederick told De Catt of Madame von Kamecke's courageous affront to Frederick William, but said she stood between him and the younger children whom the King was going to beat and who had hidden themselves under the table. Frederick, who was not an eye witness, may have confused what happened at the palace on August twenty-ninth, 1730, with what happened to him when his father found him studying Latin as a child.

CHAPTER XIII

CHIEF SOURCES: *Mémoires*, pp. 209–34; Letters, *Oeuvres*, Vol. XXVII, pp. 1–3; *Jugendbriefe*, pp. 66–68, 454–58; *Der Kronprinzen Prozess*, Berlin, 1936, pp. 136–42.

NOTES AND COMMENTS

Since practically all of the letters of Frederick and Wilhelmina given in *Oeuvres*, Vol. XXVII, appear in the much larger German collection, *Jugendbriefe* and *Briefe der Konigzeit*, only the latter are noted from here on, though for purposes of translation the French originals have been used whenever possible.

Theodor Fontanne in his *Wanderungen durch die Mark Brandenburg* chattily and charmingly describes many places mentioned in this story, notably Wusterhausen. He gives an account of Katte's execution and burial (pp. 227–45). Fontanne was present at an opening of Katte's tomb one hundred and fifty years after the young man's death. He saw the skull of the severed head, the ribbon with which Katte's hair had been tied, the blue silk shroud in which the body had been wrapped.

CHAPTER XIV

CHIEF SOURCES: *Mémoires*, pp. 238–95; *Jugendbriefe*, pp. 70–79; unpublished letters in the London Bureau of Public Records.

Something comparable to a court martial was held before Wilhelmina was told she must marry the Prince of Bayreuth. Frederick William consulted eight ministers and asked them if a man was justified in forcing his daughter to wed against her will. Only one of the parsons, the chaplain of the garrison church at Potsdam, said yes. (Richard Fester, *Die Bayreuther Schwester Friedrich's des Grossen*, Berlin, 1902, p. 51.)

The report of the Brunswick repesentative mentioned in the notes to Chapter 10 gives a few colorful details of Wilhelmina's wedding which Wilhelmina overlooked in writing her memoirs.

CHAPTER XV

CHIEF SOURCES: *Der Kronprinzen Prozess*, Berlin, 1936, pp. 144–84; Förster, *Urkundenbuch*, Vol. III, pp. 1–75; Frederick's letters to Frederick William, *Oeuvres*, Vol. XXVII, Pt. III, pp. 23–51.

Frederick William's opinion of predestination was solidly based on a childhood fear of hell fire. He also thought it disruptive to military morale, for what if a soldier should say to himself, "I am destined to desert?" Frederick's first religious instructor, Parson Andrëa, was dismissed because of his Calvinist leanings.

In his first letter to Voltaire (*Voltaire*, Vol. V, p. 212) Frederick mentions a woman he loved who had fostered his feeling for poetry. This might have been La Orczelska, but it was more likely to have been Frau von Wreech.

CHAPTER XVI

CHIEF SOURCES: *Mémories*, pp. 297–328; *Jugendbriefe*, pp. 79–86; Frederick's correspondence with Grumbkow in *PKPS*, Vol. LXXII, pp.

1–44; Frederick's letters to his father, *Oeuvres*, Vol. XXVII, Pt. III, pp. 53–58.

CHAPTER XVII

CHIEF SOURCES: *Mémoires*, pp. 333–423; *Jugendbriefe*, pp. 92–146, 278; Grumbkow's letters, *PKPS*, Vol. LXXII, pp. 45–103; *Urkundenbuch*, Vol. III, pp. 85–126.

Doris Ritter was married to the Commissioner of Berlin Cabs and was paid a pension for life by Frederick. Voltaire in his *Vie Privée* (p. 39) reports having seen Doris in 1750 and thinking her too gaunt and unattractive to have suffered for a king.

CHAPTER XVIII

CHIEF SOURCES: *Mémoires*, pp. 424–91; *Jugendbriefe*, pp. 149–284; Christoph Louis Seckendorf, *Journal secret*, Tübingen, 1811, pp. 9–20.

The Seckendorf who kept the *Journal secret* was not the Austrian ambassador, but his nephew, Christoph Louis, who was left behind in Berlin to act as informant after the ambassador's recall. The journal was first published in 1811 in the same volume as the German edition of Wilhelmina's memoirs.

A journal Frederick kept during the Rhine compaign of 1734 is published in *FBPG*, Vol. IV. Since it was meant for Frederick William's eye it has none of the usual graces of Frederick's literary style.

CHAPTER XIX

CHIEF SOURCES: *Mémoires*, pp. 491–503; *Jugendbriefe*, pp. 284–345; Friedrich Wilhelm von Hahnke, *Elizabeth Christine,* Berlin, 1848, pp. 32–37; Hans Droysen, "Rheinsberg," *HJB*, 1916; *Voltaire*, Vol. V, p. 212; Christoph Louis Seckendorf, *Journal secret*, Tübingen, 1811, pp. 147–49; Otto Gervais, *Die Frauen um Friedrich den Grossen*, Vienna, 1933, pp. 243–73.

Wilhelmina's mad sister-in-law Charlotte was the grandmother of the Duke of Saxe-Weimar who was Goethe's patron.

The letters of Baron von Bielfeld give an idyllic picture of life at Rheinsberg. Bielfeld first met Frederick when Frederick, unknown to his father, was inducted into a Masonic Lodge in Brunswick in 1738. He was later appointed tutor to Frederick's youngest brother Ferdinand and became the chancellor of all Prussian universities. Bielfeld admired Elizabeth Christina and even thought that she was beautiful.

Werner Langer's *Friedrich der Grosse und die geistige Welt Frankreich's* describes Frederick's intellectual development during this period. Frederick's correspondence with Manteuffel and Suhm appears in

Oeuvres, Vol. XXV. It was to Manteuffel that Frederick confided his feeling—or lack of feeling—for Elizabeth Christina.

CHAPTER XX

CHIEF SOURCES: *Mémoires*, pp. 546–59; *Jugendbriefe*, pp. 415–49; Hans Koser, "Aus den letzten Tagen König Friedrich-Wilhelm's I," *HJB*, 1904; Baron von Bielfeld, *Letters*, pp. 118–41; Frederick's letters to his wife, *Oeuvres*, Vol. XXV, pp. 7–14; Pöllnitz, *Mémoires pour servir*, pp. 330–78.

Frederick's political essay, *Considerations sur l'état présent du corps politique de l'Europe* and his *Antimachiavel* are in *Oeuvres*, Vol. III.

As finale to his unsuccessful diplomatic career, Frederick William, in April of 1739, turned to France and obtained a treaty guaranteeing him part, but not all, of Berg.

CHAPTER XXI

CHIEF SOURCES: *Mémoires*, pp. 559–66; *Königzeit*, pp. 21–38; *Voltaire*, Vol. X; Frederick, *Politische Correspondenz*, Vol. I, pp. 90–147.

Wilhelmina in her memoirs says that Frederick did not write to her for six weeks after his accession, an example of how unreliable her memory could be when her emotions were involved, for there are several letters of this period given in *Königzeit*.

CHAPTER XXII

CHIEF SOURCES: *Mémoires*, pp. 566–84; *Königzeit*, pp. 38–57; *Politische Correspondenz*, Vol. VI, pp. 244 ff.

Adrien Fauchier-Magnan's *The Small German Courts in the Eighteenth Century* gives the background of the Württemberg marriage. Charles Eugene is chiefly known to history as the founder of a military school where the poet Schiller was an unhappy and rebellious pupil.

CHAPTER XXIII

CHIEF SOURCES: *Voltaire*, Vols. XII, XIII; *Königzeit*, pp. 61–75; Richard Fester, *Die Bayreuther Schwester Friedrich's des Grossen*, Berlin, 1902, pp. 111–122.

Letters from Voltaire to Wilhelmina were found in the mid-nineteenth century in a miscellaneous manuscript belonging to the Von Miedel family in Bayreuth. They had been acquired through the purchase of the library of Wilhelmina's daughter Frederica, after Frederica's death in 1780. The letters appear in the Besterman collection of Voltaire's correspondence and also in a book by Georg Horn, *Voltaire und die Markgräfin von Bayreuth* (1865). An English translation was brought out in 1888.

Catherine the Great describes her meeting with Frederick in her memoirs. Her parents had gone to dine at the palace without her, but Frederick sent for her and would not sit down to table until she had arrived (Otto Gervais, *Die Frauen um Friedrich dem Grossen*, Berlin, 1933, pp. 388 ff.)

Frederick and Wilhelmina's youngest sister Amelia had a love affair, real or imaginary, with one of Frederick's officers, Freiherr von Trenck. Frederick put an end to the affair by having Trenck arrested after the battle of Soor. Amelia never married and was appointed Abbess of Quedlinburg in 1756. She was odd, musically gifted, and considered by some to be a witch.

CHAPTER XXIV

CHIEF SOURCES: *Königzeit*, pp. 77–100; Leopold von Ranke, *Abhandlungen und Versuche*, Leipzig, 1872, Vol. XXIV, pp. 57 ff.; J. G. Droysen, *Geschichte der Preussischen Politik*, Leipzig, 1873, Pt. IV, pp. 33–96; Hans Droysen, "Die handschriftliche Uberlieferungen der Mémoires von der Markgräfin von Bayreuth," *FBPG*, Vol. XXXII, pp. 191–205; Gustav Berthold Volz, "Wilhelmine von Bayreuth und ihre Denkwurdigkeiten," *FBPG*, 1924, Vol. XXXVI, pp. 164 ff.

Johann Gustav Droysen, Wilhelmina's most hostile nineteenth century critic, maintains that she continued to work on her memoirs after her reconciliation with Frederick, writing with one hand slander, with the other letters of tender sentiment. Gustav Volz disproves this theory, his best arguments being internal evidence offered by the texts of the various manuscripts. Droysen considered Wilhelmina a borderline psychotic. He suggests the interesting, but unproved, hypothesis that she was unwilling to part with Dorothea von der Marwitz because she was no longer able to have sexual relations with her husband and took satisfaction in Dorothea's acting as her substitute in this respect.

Frederick's letters to his factotum, Fredersdorf, are fascinating because they reveal a new personality. Written in German only a little less grotesque than that of Frederick William, the letters show Frederick to be a gossipy fellow, who likes his little joke and can quote peasant wisdom. After Frederick's death and perhaps while he was still alive, the King became a figure in folklore. Heinz Diewerge's *Der Alte Fritz im Folksmund* is a collection of unwritten and apochryphal anecdotes in which "Old Fritz" always has the last, smart word. Frederick loved Fredersdorf and trusted him with all his personal expenditures and the management of his theater and opera. He gave his friend, during the latter's long and ultimately fatal illness, frequent medical advice and scolded him affectionately for failure to do what he was told.

NOTES AND COMMENTS

CHAPTER XXV

CHIEF SOURCES: *Königzeit*, pp. 101–53; Frederick's marginal comments, *Die Randbemerkungen Friedrich's des Grossen*, Potsdam, 1948; Ernest Eugene Helm, *Music at the Court of Frederick the Great,* Norman, Okla., 1960; Gustav B. Volz, *Das Sans Souci Friedrich's des Grossen*, Berlin, 1936.

Frederick's music, like his writing of verse, was a pastime, but one that he took very seriously. His standard of performance was so high that he could easily have made a living as a professional flutist. His and Wilhelmina's compositions are charmingly reminiscent of Vivaldi, an influence that came to Frederick through his flute teacher, J. J. Quantz.

CHAPTER XXVI

CHIEF SOURCES: *Voltaire*, Vols. XVII–XX; *Königzeit*, pp. 154–95; Georg Horn, *The Margravine of Bayreuth and Voltaire*, London, 1888; Frederick's letter to Algarotti, *Oeuvres*, Vol. XVIII, p. 74.

The reason for Frederick's diatribe against Voltaire to Algarotti is obscure, though it is obvious from the content that it had something to do with Voltaire's use of Frederick's writings in France.

Wilhelmina's visit to Sans Souci in 1750 is mentioned in the diary of Count Lehndorf (*Dreissig Jahre am Hofe Friedrich's des Grossen*). Lehndorf, who was court chamberlain to Elizabeth Christina, looked upon Wilhelmina as a foreigner, for she had not been in Berlin for seven years. Her close resemblance to Frederick is noted, and she is spoken of with a jealous hostility as one of the King's inner circle of wits and intellectuals. Voltaire, of course, belonged to the same coterie and shared the same unpopularity.

CHAPTER XXVII

CHIEF SOURCES: *Königzeit*, pp. 206–41; *Voltaire*, Vols. XX–XXII.

Frederick's *Mémoires pour servir à l'histoire de la Maison de Brandenbourg* is in *Oeuvres*, Vol. I, his *Palladion* in *Oeuvres*, Vol. XI. *Palladion* tells the story, in mock-heroic terms, of Frederick's secretary, Claude Étienne Darget, being carried off by the Austrians during the Second Silesian War; a case of mistaken identity; he was thought to have been the Marquis de Valori, the French ambassador. There are some scurrilous remarks on the mores of monks. Various theological personages appear, among them Calvin, Luther and Saint Hedwig, the Hohenzollern saint in whose honor the first Catholic church was built in Berlin by Frederick.

Frederick's three brothers were devoted to one another and united to form the nucleus of a feeble, a very feeble, opposition to Frederick's regime. Except in wartime there was little for the brothers to do. They dabbled in the arts—August William painted and Henry played the violin; they gave elaborate parties for one another and their coterie. Henry's marriage was even less successful than that of August William, for he would have nothing to do with his charming wife, Wilhelmina of Hesse-Cassel, and turned Rheinsberg, which Frederick had given him, into a bachelor hall. Count Lehndorf's diary, mentioned above, is full of coy references to his passionate friendship for Henry.

CHAPTER XXVIII

CHIEF SOURCES: *Königzeit*, pp. 241–326; Wilhelmina's journal of her Italian tour and letters to Frederick in Mary Burrell, *Thoughts for Enthusiasts at Bayreuth*, Chiswick, 1888; *Voltaire*, Vol. XXV; Frederick, *Histoire de Mon Temps* in *Oeuvres*, Vol. II.

Charles Marie de la Condamine, Wilhelmina's guide in southern Italy, had been sent in 1735 to measure a degree of the meridian in South America at the same time Maupertuis was making a similar observation in Lapland. He also descended and explored the Amazon.

CHAPTER XXIX

CHIEF SOURCES: *Königzeit*, pp. 325–448; *Voltaire*, Vol. XXXII; Georg Horn, *The Margravine of Bayreuth and Voltaire*, pp. 99–183; Heinrich de Catt, *Unterhaltungen mit Friedrich dem Grossen* in *PKPS*, Vol. XXII, pp. 4–197; Frederick's speech to his officers at Leuthen in *Oeuvres*, Vol. XXVII, Pt. III, pp. 283 ff.

Wilhelmina was not particularly pleased by the new palace of Bayreuth and called it a stable. It was her home for only three years. During that time she was so preoccupied with the war and with her failing health that she neglected to install her library. The books which had been saved from the fire were found after her death, piled up on the floor of a vacant room, covered with dust and fallen plaster; they had been left to the University of Erlangen.

Wilhelmina made two wills, one in 1748 and one shortly before she died. She left Dorothea Burghauss a pair of silver candlesticks and a gold etui. There was no mention in either document of the disposal of her memoirs. Wilhelmina asked to have Frederick's letters buried with her, but this wish was disregarded.

CHAPTER XXX

CHIEF SOURCES: Heinrich de Catt, *Unterhaltungen* in *PKPS*, Vol. XXII, pp. 450 ff.; Ernst Ahasuerus Heinrich Lehndorf, *Dreissig Jahre am Hofe Friedrich's des Grossen*, Gotha, 1907, pp. 457 ff.; Frederick, *Histoire de la Guerre de sept ans* in *Oeuvres*, Vol. IV, pp. 252–53;

Voltaire, Vol. LXXXVI; Frederick's verses to Wilhelmina in *Oeuvres*, Vol. XII.

Voltaire not only spoke ill of Frederick, but was suspected of being the author of various scandalous attacks published in Frederick's lifetime and of which he took no notice. After Voltaire's death his *Mémoires pour servir à la vie de Monsieur de Voltaire écrits par lui même* were published. In later editions this work was titled *La vie privée du Roi de Prusse*. It accuses Frederick, *inter alia*, of being sexually impotent and a pederast. Frederick must have read the *Mémoires*, but nevertheless wrote a sincere eulogy of the great man lost to literature.

Frederica of Württemberg took an interest in the new German literature, particularly in Wieland and Goethe. She lived to see Bayreuth governed by her cousin, the Margrave of Ansbach, Eeka's son, and was buried beside her parents in the palace chapel in 1780.

✦[*Bibliography*]✦

Acta Borussica, Denkmaler der Preussischen Staats Verwaltung in 18 Jahrhundert. Vols. I, III. Berlin, 1901.

Acton, Lord. "Confessions of Frederick the Great" in *Essays on Church and State*, ed. Douglas Woodruff, London, 1952.

Anonymous. *Briefe eines Preussischen Feldpredigers verschiedene Characterzüge Friedrich's des Einzigen betreffend.* Potsdam, 1791.

Anonymous. *Chronischische Aufzeichnungen einers Berliners von 1704–1758, Verein für die Geschichte Berlins—Schriften.* Vol. XXXVI. Berlin, 1898.

Arnheim, Dr. Fritz. "Aus Briefen der Kronprinzessen Ulrike von Schweden an die Königin Mutter, Sophie Dorothee, 1745–1748" in *Forschungen zur Brandenburgischen und Preussische Geschichte.* Vol. II. Leipzig, 1889.

Bac, Ferdinand, *La ville de Porcelaine.* Paris, 1934.

Baldensperger, Fernand. "Frederic II appreciateur de Racine," in *Études d'Histoire.* Paris, 1907.

Bielfeld, Baron. *Letters of Baron Bielfeld.* 4 vols. London, 1768.

Boileau, Nicolas. *L'art Poetique.* Paris, 1856.

Boyer, Jean Baptiste de. *Mémoires du Marquis d'Argens.* Paris, 1941.

Borkowski, Heinrich. "Erzieher und Erziehung, König Friedrich Wilhelm's I" in *Hohenzollern Jahrbuch*, 1904.

Bracker, Elizabeth. "Markgräfin Wilhelmine von Bayreuth und die geistige Welt Frankreichs" in *Erlanger Abhandlungen sur mittleren und neureren Geschichte*, 1940.

Broglie, Charles Jacques Victor Albert, Duc de. *Frederic II et Louis XV, 1742–1744.* Paris, 1885.

Buchner, Gerhard, and Dittrich, Georg. *Rheinsberg und Sanssouci.* Leipzig, 1927.

Burrell, Mary. *Thoughts for Enthusiasts at Bayreuth.* Chiswick, 1888.

Catt, Heinrich de. *Unterhaltungen mit Friedrich dem Grossen, Memoiren und Tagebücher* in *Publicationen aus den Preussischen Staatsarchiven.* Vol. XXII. Leipzig, 1884.

Colombier, Pierre du. "Antoine Pesne, premier peintre des Rois de Prusse" in *Le Correspondant* (March 25, 1959).

"Correspondance de Sophie-Dorothée Princesse electorale de Hanovre avec le Comte de Königsmarck" in *Revue des deux Mondes* (April, 1914).

Cuthell, Edith E. *Wilhelmina, Margravine of Bayreuth.* 2 vols. New York, 1902.

———. *A Vagabond Courtier, from the Letters and Memoirs of Baron Charles Louis von Pöllnitz.* London, 1913.

Diewerge, Heinz. *Der Alte Fritz im Folksmund.* Munich, 1937.

Droysen, Hans. "Aus den Briefen der Königin Sophie Dorothée" in *Hohenzollern Jahrbuch.* 1913.

———. "Friedrich Wilhelm's I und der Philosoph Christian Wolff" in *Forschungen zur Brandenburgischen und Preussischen Geschichte.* Vol. XXIII. Leipzig, 1910.

BIBLIOGRAPHY

———. "Friederike, Markgräfin von Ansbach, eine Schwester Friedrich des Grossen" in *Hohenzollern Jahrbuch*, 1911.

———. "Rheinsberg, 1736–1740" in *Hohenzollern Jahrbuch*, 1916.

———. "Vom Hofe König Friedrich's I aus den Jahren 1709–1711" in *Hohenzollern Jahrbuch*, 1915.

———. "Die handschriftliche Uberlieferungen der Mémoires von der Markgräfin von Bayreuth" in *Forschungen zur Brandenburgischen und Preussischen Geschichte*. Vol. XXXII.

Droysen, Johann Gustav. *Geschichte der Preussischen Politik*. Part IV. Leipzig, 1873.

Ergang, Robert. *The Potsdam Führer*. New York, 1941.

Erman, Jean Pierre. *Mémoires pour servir à l'histoire de Sophie Charlotte, Reine de Prusse*. Berlin, 1801.

Fassmann, David. *Leben und Thaten des Allerdurchlauchstigsten Königs von Preussen, Friedrick Wilhelmi*. Berlin, 1735.

Fauchier-Magnan, Adrien. *The Small German Courts in the Eighteenth Century*. London, 1958.

Fester, Richard. *Die Bayreuther Schwester Friedrich's des Grossen*. Berlin, 1902.

———. "Markgräfin Wilhelmine und die Kunst am Bayreuthen Hofe" in *Hohenzollern Jahrbuch*, 1902.

Fontanne, Theodor. *Wanderungen durch die Mark Brandenburg*. Zurich, 1960.

Förster, Dr. Friedrich. *Friedrich Wilhelm I, König von Preussen*. 3 vols. Potsdam, 1834, 1835.

———. *Urkundenbuch zu der Lebensgeschichte Friedrich Wilhelm's I*. 2 vols. Potsdam, 1834, 1835.

Franckc, August Hermann. *Neue Beitrage zur Geschichte August Hermann Francke's*, ed. D. G. Kramer. Halle, 1875.

Freimark, Hans. *Die Anormalen Männer und Frauengestalten in den Memoiren der Markgräfin von Bayreuth*. Berlin, 1909.

Frederick II. *Briefwechsel Friedrich's des Grossen mit Grumbkow und Maupertuis* in *Publicationen aus den Königlichen Preussichen Staatsarchiven*. Vol. LXXII. Leipzig, 1898.

———. *Die Briefe Friedrich's des Grossen an seinen vormaligen Kammerdiener, Fredersdorf*. Berlin, 1926.

———. *Die Randbermerkungen Friedrich's des Grossen*, ed. Georg Borchardt. Potsdam, 1948.

———. *Friedrich der Grosse und Wilhelmine von Bayreuth*. Vol. I, *Jugendbriefe*; Vol. II, *Briefe der Königzeit*. Berlin, 1924.

———. *Friedrich's des Grossen Briefe und Gedichte an Luise Eleonore von Wreech, 1731–1761*. Marburg, 1952.

———. *Oeuvres de Frédéric le Grand*. Berlin, 1846–1857.

———. *Politische Correspondenz*. Berlin, 1879–1936.

——— and Von Katte. *Der Kronprinzen Prozess*. Berlin, 1936.

Frederick William I. *Die Briefe König Friedrich Wilhelm's I an den Fürsten Leopold zu Anhalt-Dessau*. Berlin, 1905.

———. "Briefe an Hermann Reinhold Pauli" in *Abhandlungen der historische-philologischen Klasse der Königlichen Gesellschaft der Wissenschaften zu Göttingen*. Vol. XXXIX. Göttingen, 1893.

BIBLIOGRAPHY

Freylinghausen, Johann Anastasius. *Sieben Tage am Hofe Freidrich Wilhelm's I*. Berlin, 1900.

Gaxotte, Pierre. *Frédéric II*. Paris, 1936.

Gervais, Otto R. *Die Frauen um Friedrich den Grossen*. Berlin, 1933.

Gleichen-Russwurm, Alexander von. *Die Markgräfin von Baireuth*. Stuttgart, 1925.

Gooch, George Peabody. *Frederick the Great, the Ruler, the Writer, the Man*. New York, 1947.

————. *Courts and Cabinets*. London, 1944.

Haake, Paul. "Der Besuch der Preussischen Soldaten Königs in Dresden, 1728" in *Forschungen zur Brandenburgischen und Preussischen Geschichte*. Vol. XLVII, 1935.

Hahnke, Friedrich Wilhelm von. *Elizabeth Christine, Königin von Preussen*. Berlin, 1848.

Hartmann, Karl. *Geschichte der Stadt Bayreuth in der Markgrafenzeit*. Bayreuth, 1949.

Hegemann, Werner. *Das Jugendbuch vom Grossen König*. Hellerau, 1930.

Helm, Ernest Eugene. *Music at the Court of Frederick the Great*. Norman: University of Oklahoma, 1960.

Hildebrand, Dr. Arnold. "Frauenbildnisse des Preussischen Hofmalers Antoine Pesne" in *Velhagen und Klasung Monatshefte*. July, 1936.

Horn, Georg. *The Margravine of Bayreuth and Voltaire*. London, 1888.

Hübsch, Georg. *Der fürstliche Lustsitz Eremitage bei Baireuth*. Bayreuth, 1924.

Kaltenborn, Rudolph W. von. *Briefe eines alten Preussischen Officier's verschiedenen Characterzüge Friedrich's des Einzigen betreffend*. Hohenzollern, 1790.

Klepper, Jochen. *In Tormentis Pinxit*. Stuttgart, 1959.

Koser, Reinhold. *Geschichte Friederich's des Grossen*. 4 vols. Berlin and Stuttgart, 1912.

————. *Friedrich der Grosse als Kronprinz*. Stuttgart, 1886.

————. *Aus der Korrespondenz der französischen Gesandschaft zu Berlin, 1746–1756* in *Forschungen sur Brandenburgischen und Preussischen Geschichte*. Vol. VII, 1894.

————. "Aus den letzten Tagen König Friedrich-Wilhelm's I" in *Hohenzollern Jahrbuch*, 1904.

Krauske, Otto. "Vom Hofe Friedrich Wilhelm's I" in *Hohenzollern Jahrbuch*, 1903.

Langer, Werner. "Friedrich der Grosse und die geistige Welt Frankreich's" in *Hamburger Studien zu Volkstum und Kultur der Romanen*. Hamburg, 1932.

Lavisse, Ernest. *La Jeunesse du Grand Frédéric*. Paris, 1891.

————. *Le Grand Frédéric avant l'avennement*. Paris, 1893.

Lehndorf, Ernst Ahasuerus Heinrich von. *Dreissig Jahre am Hofe Friedrich's des Grossen*. Gotha, 1907.

Lodge, Sir Richard. *Great Britain and Prussia in the Eighteenth Century*. Oxford, 1923.

London Bureau of Records. Unpublished letters of Sir Charles Hotham, Villa, Grumbkow, Reichenbach and others.

Markgräfin Wilhelmine von Bayreuth und ihre Welt, Ausstellung im Neuen Schloss Bayreuth, Sommer, 1959. Munich, 1959.

Marriott, J. A. R., and Robertson, C. Grant. *The Evolution of Prussia.* Oxford, 1917.

Mauvillon, E. de. *Life of Frederick William King of Prussia.* London, 1750.

Montpensier, Mademoiselle de. *Memoirs.* 3 vols. London, 1848.

Müller, Ernst. "Briefe der Kronprinzen Friedrich an Hans Christoph von Haacke, 1732–1738" in *Forschungen zur Brandenburgischen und Preussischen Geschichte.* Vol. XL. Leipzig, 1927.

Nicolai, Friedrich. *Anekdoten von König Friedrich II von Preussen.* Halle, 1788.

Oncken, Wilhelm. "Sir Charles Hotham und Friedrich Wilhelm I im Jahre 1730" in *Forschungen zur Brandenburgischen und Preussischen Geschichte.* Vol. VII. Leipzig, 1894.

Oppeln-Bronikowski, Friedrich von. "Eros als Schicksal bei Friedrich dem Grossen und bei Stendhal" in *Psychoanalytische Bewegung* (July, 1930).

Pöllnitz, Baron von. *Histoire secrète de la Duchesse d'Hanover, épouse de George I.* London, 1732.

———. *Lettres et Mémoires.* Amsterdam, 1737.

———. *Mémoires pour servir à l'histoire des quatre Derniers Souverains de la Maison de Brandenbourg Royale de Prusse.* Berlin, 1791.

———. *La Saxe Galante.* Frankfurt, 1734.

Proctor, William. *A Short Journal of His Polish Majesty's Camp at Radewitz in the Year, 1730.* London, 1737.

Ranke, Leopold von. *Abhandlungen und Versuche, Erste Sammlung.* Leipzig, 1872.

———. *Memoirs of the House of Brandenburg and History of Prussia.* London, 1849.

Raumer, Friedrich von. *Beitrage zur neueren Geschichte aus dem britischen und französichen Reichsarchiv.* Vol. III. Leipzig, 1839.

Reck-Malleczewen, Fritz. *Sophie Dorothée.* Berlin, 1936.

Recueil des instructions données aux ambassadeurs et ministres de France depuis les traités de Westphalia jusqu'à la Révolution française. Vol. XVI. Paris, 1884–1962.

Sainte-Beuve, C. A. de. "La Margrave de Baireuth" in *Causeries de Lundi.* Vol. XII. Paris, 1857.

Scarron, Paul. *Le Roman Comique.* 2 vols. Paris, 1857.

Schiedermair, Ludwig. *Bayreuther Festspiele im Zeitalter des Absolutismus.* Leipzig, 1908.

Schnaith, Georg. *Briefwechsel der Kurfürstin Sophie von Hanover mit dem Preussischen Königshaus,* 1927.

Seckendorf, Baron Christoph Louis de. *Journal Secret.* Tübingen, 1811.

Seidel, Paul. "Die Kingerbildnisse Friedrich's des Grossen und seiner Brüder" in *Hohenzollern Jahrbuch,* 1911.

Seydewitz, Thea von. *Ernst Christoph, Graf Manteuffel.* Dresden, 1926.

BIBLIOGRAPHY

Spranger, Eduard. "Der Philosoph von Sanssouci" in *Abhandlungen der Preussischen Akademie der Wissenschaften*. Berlin, 1942.

Stockfuss, Adolf. *500 Jahre Berliner Geschichte*. Berlin, 1900.

Thiebault, Dieudonné. *Mes Souvenirs de vingt ans de séjour à Berlin*. Paris, 1804.

Toland, J. *An Account of the Courts of Prussia and Hanover*. London, 1706.

Valori, Henri Zozime de, *Mémoires des Négociations du Marquis de Valori*. Paris, 1820.

Voltaire, François Marie Arouet de. *Correspondance*, ed. Theodore Besterman. Geneva, 1953–1963. 94 vols.

———. *Mémoires pour servir à la vie de Monsieur de Voltaire, écrits par lui même*. Paris, 1784.

Volz, Gustav Berthold. *Friedrich der Gross im Spiegel seiner Zeit*. 2 vols. Berlin, 1901.

———. *Das Sans Souci Friedrich's des Grossen*. Berlin, 1926.

———. "Die Krisis in der Jugend Friedrich's des Grossen" in *Historische Zeitschrift*, 1917.

———. "Die Markgräfin Wilhemine von Bayreuth und ihre Denkwurdigkeiten" in *Forschungen zur Brandenburgischen und Preussischen Geschichte*. Vol. XXXVI. Leipzig, 1924.

Voss, Sophie Marie Gräfin von. *Neun und sechsig Jahre am Preussischen Hofe*. Leipzig, 1876.

Weber, Karl von. *Aus vier Jahrhunderten*. 2 vols. Leipzig, 1861.

Weigel, T. O. *Die Herzogin von Ahlden*. Leipzig, 1852.

Wilhelmina. *Mémoires de Frédérique Sophie Wilhelmine, Margrave de Bareith, soeur de Frédérique le Grand*. Leipzig, 1889.

Wolff, Richard. "Vom Berliner Hofe zur Zeit Friedrich Wilhelm's I" in *Schriften des Vereins fur die Geschichte Berlin*. Berlin, 1914.

Zimmermann, J. G., Ritter von. *Über Friedrich den Grossen und meine Unterredungen mit ihm*. Leipzig, 1788.

⊹[*Index*]⊹

Adhémar, Marquis d', 241, 247, 253, 258, 272, 276
Adolf Frederick, Crown Prince of Sweden, 215
Ahlden, Prisoner of, *see* Sophia Dorothea of Brunswick-Celle
Albani, Cardinal, 259
Albert the Bear, 26
Albert, Prince of Culmbach, 144
Alexis, Czarevitch of Russia, 27
Algarotti, Francesco, 191, 195, 238, 259, 300
Amelia, Princess, daughter of George II of England, 6, 39, 83
Andrëa, Parson, 21, 296
Anhalt-Dessau, Prince Leopold of, 26, 27, 29, 46, 47, 58, 111, 161, 188, 191, 198, 224, 292
Anhalt-Zerbst, Prince of, 215
Anna, Duchess of Courland, 27
Anne, Czarina of Russia, 112, 136, 170, 180, 198
Anne, Princess, daughter of George II, 154, 155
Anne, Queen of England, 6
Anne Amelia, sister of Frederick and Wilhelmina, 39, 124, 194, 215, 299
Ansbach, Frederick Charles Alexander, Margrave of, 302
Ansbach, Margrave of, "Eeka's" husband, 72, 86, 141, 192
Apollo, 171, 199, 242
Argens, Marquis de, 268
August William, brother of Frederick and Wilhelmina, 49, 69, 167, 172, 191, 194, 207, 209, 224, 225, 229, 234, 247, 248, 256, 261, 265, 266, 269, 270, 271, 301
Augusta Louisa Charlotte, Wilhelmina's grandchild, 239, 247
Augustus II, Elector of Saxony, King of Poland, "the Strong," 52, 54–61, 66, 75, 78, 83, 85, 112, 124, 153, 155, 174, 263, 294

Augustus III, Elector of Saxony, King of Poland, son of Augustus the Strong, 56, 153, 180, 197, 263
Augustus Ferdinand, brother of Frederick and Wilhelmina, 83, 167, 194, 234, 248, 256, 162, 297

Bach, Johann Sebastian, 228, 229
Bach, Karl Philipp Emanuel, 228
Barberina, La, 216
Bayle, 214
Belle-Isle, Madame de, 204
Belle-Isle, Marshal de, 201, 204, 258, 265, 267
Benedict XIV, Pope, 260
Bernis, Abbé de, 265
Betuschev, 222
Biche, 232, 233, 293
Bielfeld, Baron von, 297
Bielinska, Countess, 56
Blaspil, Madame de, 293
Boileau, 119
Borcke, Field Marshal von, 76, 117
Braddock, General William, 260
Brandenburg-Schwedt, Dowager Margravine of, 27
Brandenburg-Schwedt, Margrave of, 27, 28, 29, 77, 78, 116, 162, 166
Broglie, Count Charles de, 263
Brunswick-Bevern, Dowager Duchess of, 147, 152, 156
Brunswick-Bevern, Duchess of, Frederick's mother-in-law, 120, 146
Brunswick-Bevern, Duke of, Frederick's father-in-law, 120, 146, 160
Brunswick-Bevern, Princess Louisa of, 207
Buddenbrock, Colonel von, 94, 98
Bufardin, 61
Burghauss, Count, 184, 217, 218, 232
Burghauss, Countess, *see* Dorothea von der Marwitz
Burgundy, Duke of, 23
Bute, Lord, 293

INDEX

Caesar, 275
Calas, Jean, 277
Calvin, 300
Carlyle, Thomas, viii
Caroline, Queen of England, 65, 67, 68, 76, 81, 84, 177
Catherine I, Czarina of Russia, wife of Peter the Great, 15–17
Catherine II, Czarina of Russia, "the Great," 215, 274, 299
Catt, Henry de, 268, 269, 272, 274, 292, 295
"Césarion," see Count Keyserlingk
Charlemagne, 192
Charles VI, Emperor, 40, 46, 52, 112, 150, 196, 197
Charles VII, Emperor, 197, 203, 204, 213, 214, 222
Charles XII, King of Sweden, 9, 64, 159
Charles Albert of Bavaria, see Charles VII
Charles Eugene, Duke of Württemberg, 206, 208, 215, 233–235, 239, 247, 257, 298
Charles, Prince, Duke of Brunswick-Bevern, "Lotte's" husband, 123, 156
Charlotte of Bayreuth, Duchess of Saxe-Weimar, 144, 157, 169, 297
Charlotte, Queen of Prussia, 10, 12, 33, 60
Chateauroux, Madame de, 222
Châtelet, Marquis de, 177, 237
Châtelet, Marquise de, 177, 178, 193, 196, 209, 213, 236–238, 245
Chesterfield, Lord, 121
Chétardie, Marquis de, 167
Chotusitz, Battle of, 205
Christine Eberhardine, wife of Augustus the Strong, 54, 55
Cicero, 173, 193, 278
Cirey, 177, 178
Cobenzl, Count, 214
Cocceji, Samuel, 228, 243
Condamine, Charles Marie de la, 259, 301
Conti, Prince of, 54
Corneille, 243
Courland, Duke of, 180

Croze, Mathurin Vizyierre de la, 13, 18, 173, 174, 195

Darget, Claude Étienne, 243, 300
Degenfeld-Schönburg, Count, 153
Denis, Madame, 238, 241, 245, 250, 251, 253, 254, 258
Derschau, Colonel von, 97
Descartes, 174, 175
Dickens, Guy, 83, 86, 87, 88, 91, 116, 121
Diewerge, Henry, 299
Droysen, Johann Gustav, 299
Duhan, Jacques Égide, 18, 22, 23, 50, 51, 111, 152, 174, 175, 191, 227, 293
Dunbar, Lord, 259

"Eeka," see Frederica Louise, Margravine of Ansbach
Eisenach, Princess of, 134
Elizabeth Christina of Brunswick-Bevern, Queen of Prussia, Frederick's wife, 134, 145, 146, 148, 153, 154, 162, 170, 172, 173, 185, 186, 188, 189, 194, 195, 207, 240, 275, 297, 298
Elizabeth, Czarina of Russia, 215, 261, 274
Elizabeth Frederica Sophia, Duchess of Württemberg, Wilhelmina's daughter, 150, 160, 169, 194, 199, 206, 207, 213, 215, 221, 226, 233–235, 239, 247, 257, 278, 298, 302
Ellrodt, Parson, 235
Émilie, the Divine, see Marquise du Châtelet
Erlangen, 183, 184, 220, 241, 301
Eugene, Prince of Savoy, 26, 46, 47, 161, 162, 163, 167, 226
Evelyn, John, 292
Eversmann, 46, 116, 118

Fauchier-Magnan, Adrien, 298
Feldmann, Bombardier, 47
Fénelon, Abbé, 23, 144
Fester, Richard, vii
Fink, Countess, 102
Finkenstein, Count Fink von, 18, 24, 64, 65, 69, 76, 77

Flemming, Count and Countess, 55, 60

Fleury, Cardinal, 181, 196, 201, 211

Folichon, 232, 277

Fontanne, Theodor, 296

Förster, Friedrich, 291

Francis I, King of France, 83

Francis of Lorraine and Tuscany, Emperor, husband of Maria Theresa, 182, 197, 201, 216, 223

Francke, August Gotthold, 48–51, 57

Frederica, *see* Elizabeth Frederica Sophia

Frederica Louise, Margravine of Ansbach, sister of Frederick and Wilhelmina, 10, 30, 31, 72, 86, 92, 123, 141, 150, 151, 192

Frederica Sophia Wilhelmina, *see* Wilhelmina

Frederick, Prince, Margrave of Bayreuth, Wilhelmina's husband, 78, 108, 109, 116, 117, 120–124, 142, 144, 155, 160, 163, 164, 169, 179, 183–185, 195, 199, 201, 202, 203, 213, 218, 232, 241, 255, 259, 270, 271, 277, 296

Frederick I, King of Prussia, 4, 9, 11, 17, 78, 140

Frederick II, Crown Prince, King of Prussia, "the Great," portrait painted (1736), 3; born (Jan. 24, 1712), 7; his marriage with his English cousin planned, 6; his portrait painted with Wilhelmina, 7; thought timid by his parents, 8; hand read by Swedish palmist, 10; educated by tutors, 18, 19; writes childish letters to his father, 19; criticizes his father's habits, 21; beaten for declining mensa, 22; his early love of reading, 23, 24; his regime at Potsdam, 36, 37; refuses gift at Magdeburg, 37; plays the flute, 21, 38, 194, 198, 228, 240, 300; has private language with Wilhelmina, 39; feels his father's growing hostility, 41; catechized by pietists, 49, 50; promises Duhan a pension, 50; collects a library, 51; visits Dresden (1728), 53–58; is ill after visit to Dresden, 58, 293; writes secretly to Queen Caroline, 66; attempts a reconciliation with his father, 66, 67; plays duets with Doris Ritter, 69, 70; makes a friend of Von Keith, 70; persecuted by father, 72–74; publicly beaten, 75; his friendship with Von Katte, 75; persuaded by Wilhelmina not to escape to England, 79; writes letter to Sir Charles Hotham, 83; visits the camp at Radewitz, 84–87; begs Hotham not to leave Prussia, 88; quarrels with Wilhelmina, 89; attempts to escape during tour of Southern Germany (1730), 91–98; writes to Wilhelmina from prison, 109, 110, 119; examined at Küstrin, 112; witnesses execution of Von Katte, 114, 115; visited in prison by Pastor Müller, 129, 130; works in Office of Administration, 130; writes first political essay, 132; corresponds with Grumbkow concerning marriage, 133, 136, 145–148; is reconciled with father, 134, 135; flirts with Eleanora von Wreech, 137, 138; reunited with Wilhelmina at her wedding ball, 139; has low opinion of his brother-in-law, 140; asks Wilhelmina for a talisman, 148; engaged to Elizabeth Christina of Brunswick-Bevern, 146, 148; accepts money from Austria, 152; married (June 12, 1733), 156; asks father's permission to fight in War of Polish Succession, 159; his secret meeting with Wilhelmina, 163; observes Rhine campaign, 163; reaction to his father's illness, 165; visits Wilhelmina openly, 165; plans for kingship foiled by his father's recovery, 166–168; sent on mission to East Prussia, 170, 171; given Rheinsberg by his father, 171; his life at Rheinsberg, 171–173; his opinion of his wife, 172; corresponds with Wilhelmina on philosophy, 174, 175; correspondence with Voltaire begun, 176; subsidized by Czarina Anne, 180; writes political pamphlet and begins *Antimachiavel*, 180, 181; predicts he and Wilhelmina will die together, 182; visits East Prussia with

Frederick II (*continued*)

his father, 185; advises Wilhelmina not to come to Berlin during her father's illness, 187; is treated affectionately by dying father, 187, 188.

As King, recognizes Elizabeth Christina as Queen, 189; early reforms of his reign, 190, 191; visits Wilhelmina (1740), 191; enforces claim to Herstel, 192; meets Voltaire, 192; visited by Wilhelmina and Voltaire at Rheinsberg, 194–196; invades Silesia, 198; thinks victory of Mollwitz a defeat, 200; allies himself with France and Bavaria, 202; concludes secret armistice with Austria, 203; wins battle of Chotusitz, 205; makes peace with Austria at Breslau (July, 1742), 205; promotes engagement of Wilhelmina's daughter to the Duke of Württemberg, 206, 207; appears with wife at wedding of August William, 207; visits Wilhelmina with Voltaire (1743), 209–213; his attitude toward Voltaire, 210, 211; suspects Wilhelmina of being pro-Austrian, 213; arranges marriages of Ulrica and Catherine the Great of Russia, 215; accuses Wilhelmina of disloyalty, 219; fights and wins Second Silesian War, 222–224; reconciled to Wilhelmina, 225, 226; welcomed by populace after Peace of Dresden, 227; visited by J. S. Bach, 228; writes a history of Brandenburg, 229, 246; his ill health, 230; visited by Wilhelmina at Sans Souci (1747), 230; helps Dorothea Burghauss financially at Wilhelmina's request, 232; writes letter of Biche to Folichon, 233; urges Voltaire to settle in Prussia, 236–239; visited by Wilhelmina (1750), 239–241; his reaction to Voltaire's law suit, 243; defends Maupertuis in his quarrel with Voltaire, 250, 251; burns copies of *Dr. Akakia*, 250; parts with Voltaire, 252; orders Voltaire's arrest at Frankfurt, 253; sends money for rebuilding Bayreuth palace, 255; scolds Wilhelmina for consulting a faith healer, 256; envies Wilhelmina her trip to Italy, 260; reassures Wilhelmina as to threat of war, 261; invades Saxony and Bohemia (1756), 262; defeats Austrians at Lobositz, 263; spends winter in Dresden, 263, 264; gives instructions in case of death or capture, 264; defeated at Kolin, 264; asks Wilhelmina's help in secret negotiations with France, 265; dismisses August William from the army, 266; wins battles of Rossbach and Leuthen, 267; has Henry de Catt as companion during war, 268–272; recounts dreams, 269; hears of death of August William, 269; fears for Wilhelmina, 270, 271; hears of Wilhelmina's death, 272; defeated at Hochkirch, 272; saved from defeat by death of Czarina Elizabeth, 274; returns to Berlin (1763), 275; includes tribute to Wilhelmina in his history of Seven Years War, 276; asks Voltaire to write an ode to Wilhelmina's memory, 276; builds Temple of Friendship as a memorial to Wilhelmina, 277, 278.

Frederick Augustus, *see* Augustus the Strong

Frederick Barbarossa, 26

Frederick Louis of Hanover, Duke of Gloucester, Prince of Wales, 5, 6, 28, 63, 68, 79, 81, 89, 133, 154, 157, 294

Frederick William I, King of Prussia, father of Frederick and Wilhelmina, 4, 5, 8, 9, 11–13, 14, 15, 17, 18–23, 26, 27, 30, 31, 32, 33, 34, 37, 38, 39–42, 44, 45–49, 51, 52, 57, 65–68, 70, 72, 73, 78, 80, 81, 84, 86, 88, 92, 94, 95–98, 104, 107, 110, 111, 112–114, 116, 118, 121, 123, 125, 129, 130, 134, 135, 141, 146, 149, 150, 154, 157, 161–168, 170, 171, 181, 182, 185–188, 191, 200, 246, 269, 292, 298

Frederick William of Brandenburg,

"the Great Elector," 9, 246, 275
Fredersdorf, Michael, 195, 222, 223, 227, 240, 244, 252, 299
Freylinghausen, Johann Anastasius, 48–51
Freytag, 253, 254

George Augustus of Hanover, King George II of England, 5, 6, 12, 45, 65, 74, 81, 92, 112, 187, 261
George Frederick Charles, Margrave of Bayreuth, Wilhelmina's father-in-law, 140, 141, 143, 144, 150, 151, 152, 153, 157, 160, 162, 166, 168, 169
George Louis of Hanover, King George I of England, 6, 12, 34, 35, 36, 39, 40, 44, 291
Gloucester, Duke of, *see* Frederick Louis of Hanover
Gooch, George Peabody, vii
Gontard, Charles von, 277
Gotha, Princess of, 134
Graffigny, Madame de, 241
Graun, Herr, 228
Grumbkow, Field Marshal General von, 26, 27, 29, 39, 46, 52, 76, 77, 81, 82, 83, 84, 88, 98, 102, 106, 116, 117–119, 125, 131–138, 145–148, 152–155, 157, 172, 176, 185, 191, 292, 295
Grummersbach, 90, 94
Guelph, 6, 39, 154
Gundling, Jacob, 20, 21, 46

Hans Wurst, 154
Hapsburg, 26, 40, 46, 197
Hedwig, Saint, 300
Henry IV, King of France, 176
Henry VIII, King of England, 83
Henry Louis, brother of Frederick and Wilhelmina, 167, 194, 234, 248, 256, 261, 270, 272, 273, 301
Hermitage, The, 170, 175, 180, 220, 231, 259
Herrenhausen, 40, 41, 42
Herstel, 192, 198
Hervey, Lord, 294
Hesse-Beck, Count Charles of, 84
Hille, Herr, 131, 132, 133, 135, 147

Hirschel, Abraham, 242, 243
Hochkirch, Battle of, 272, 273, 276
Hohenfriedberg, Battle of, 222
Hohenzollern, 3, 6, 7, 23, 26, 39, 55, 72, 78, 140, 229
Holstein-Gastorp, Peter Ulrich of, *see* Peter III, Czar of Russia
Holy Roman Empire, 40
Horn, George, 299
Hotham, Sir Charles, 81, 82, 83, 86, 87, 88, 101, 116
Hoym, Count, 86
Hubert, Saint, 66
Hyndford, Lord, 201, **203**

Ingersleben, Lieutenant von, 69, **113**
Iris, 119

James I, King of England, 6
Joan of Arc, 177
Jordan, Charles Étienne, 173, 189, 195, 227
Jülich and Berg, 40, 47, 71, 181, 197

Kadettenkorps, The, 9, 13, 16, 19, 36
Kalkstein, Colonel Christopher William von, 18, 21, 50, 69
Kamecke, Madame von, 98, 106, 112, 295
Katte, Captain von, 91, 93
Katte, Hans Hermann von, 75, 76, 85, 87, 90, 91, 92, 93, 96, 98, 99, 102, 103, 104, 106, 110, 113–115, 116, 129, 130, 133, 135, 191, 197, 296
Kaunitz, Baron von, 261
Keith, brother of Peter Christopher, 93–96
Keith, James, 170
Keith, Peter Christopher von, 70, 75, 90, 93, 96, 97, 113, 191
Kesseldorf, Battle of, 224, 267
Keyserlingk, Count Dietrich von, 69, 178, 180, 195, 227
Kilmansegge, Sophia Charlotte von, Lady Darlington, 12, 32, 33, 34
Klein Schnellendorf, 203
Kleist, General von, 163
Klepper, Jochen, 293
Knesebeck, Fräulein von, **12**

Knobblesdorf, 180, 190, 195, 208, 230
Knyphausen, Herr von, 80
Kolin, Battle of, 264, 266
König, 249
Königsmarck, Aurora, 56, 296
Königsmarck, Count, 11, 292
Koser, Reinhold, vii
Küstrin, 98, 108, 109, 114, 116, 122, 129–140, 145, 197, 269, 271

Lancret, 180
Lange, Werner, 297
Laplander, the, see Maupertuis
La Rochefoucauld, 168
Lehndorf, Count, 297, 300
Leibnitz, 13
Lepell, General, 130
Leszczinski, Stanislaus, King of Poland, 153, 159, 167, 171, 180, 201, 236
Letti, Mademoiselle, 5, 13, 28, 29, 30, 31, 32, 34
Leute, Herr Hofrat, 111
Leuthen, Battle of, 267, 268
Liége, Prince Bishop, 192
Lobositz, Battle of, 263
Locke, John, 177, 224
Loen, Johann Michael von, 292
"Lotte," see Phillipine Charlotte
Louis XIV, King of France, 4, 57, 221
Louis XV, King of France, 153, 201, 222, 236, 252, 261
Louis Charles William, brother of Frederick and Wilhelmina, 30, 31
Louise d'Orléans, Duchess of Montpensier, 221
Louise Ulrica, Crown Princess of Sweden, sister of Frederick and Wilhelmina, 194, 215, 224, 225, 265
Lucretius, 214
Luther, Martin, 21, 300

Machiavelli, 181, 185, 196
Manteuffel, Count, 174, 199, 297, 298
Marcus Aurelius, 173
Maria Anna, sister of Maria Theresa, 133
Maria Josepha, Crown Princess, Electress of Saxony, Queen of Poland, 56, 59, 263
Maria Theresa, Archduchess of Austria,

Queen of Hungary and Bohemia, Empress, 46, 71, 87, 133, 182, 197, 202, 205, 216, 222, 223, 224, 225, 262
Marwitz, Albertine von der, 170, 183, 184, 195, 200, 204, 216, 220
Marwitz, Caroline von der, 170, 183, 200, 216, 219
Marwitz, Dorothea von der, Countess Burghauss, 141, 161, 166, 170, 180, 183, 184, 195, 200, 201, 204, 216–221, 225, 232, 299, 301
Marwitz, General von der, 141, 200, 216, 217, 219, 220, 232
Maupertuis, Pierre Louis Moreau de, 195, 245, 249–251, 301
Maurice of Saxony, 56
Mecklenburg, Duchess of, 136
Mermann, Frau, 29, 108, 110
Mettrie, Julien de la, 240, 241, 245
Milton, 253
Mirabeau de Riquetti, Louis Alexandre, 265
Molière, 55, 144
Mollwitz, Battle of, 199, 200, 217
Mon Bijou, 14, 20, 27, 56, 61, 99, 101, 103, 122, 194, 207, 225
Montperni, Monsieur de, 255, 265
Morien, Baroness, 172
Müller, Pastor, 129, 130

Napoleon, vii
Natzmer, Count von, 132
Natzmer, Marshal, 102
Neuberg, Count Palatine of, 40, 47
Newton, 177, 238

Orczelska, Maria Ann, Countess, 56, 58–61, 84, 137, 294, 296
Osnaburg, Bishop of, 44

Pepin, 192
Pesne, Antoine, 3, 6, 9, 171, 194, 291
Peter I, Czar of Russia, "the Great," 14–17, 27, 36, 74, 106, 180, 215, 292
Peter III, Czar of Russia, 215, 274
Philip II, King of Spain, 106
Phillipine Charlotte, Duchess of Brunswick-Bevern, sister of Frederick and

INDEX

Wilhelmina, 10, 30, 120, 123, 153, 154, 156, 157, 162, 172, 231, 277

Pitt, William, 273

Podewils, Count Henry von, 191, 197, 198, 202, 213, 222, 261

Podewils, Count Otto von, 212, 216, 220

Polignac, Prince de, 208

Pöllnitz, Baron, 292

Pöllnitz, Fraulein von, 33

Pompadour, Madame de, 236, 255, 261, 265, 267

Porporino, 209

Potsdam Guard, 4, 17, 46, 182

Pragmatic Sanction, 46, 153, 197, 201

Quantz, J. J., 61, 152, 300

Racine, 168, 212, 268

Radewitz, 83–85

Ramen, Frau, 103, 106, 108

Ranke, Leopold von, viii

Ravenstein, 74

Reichenbach, Herr von, 81, 84, 88

Rettwitz, 205

Rhinebeck, Parson, 102, 116

Rheinsberg, 171–173, 175, 178, 180, 182, 186, 188, 194–198, 207, 210, 211, 230

Richelieu, Duc de, 258, 266, 267

Ritter, Cantor, 69, 70, 111

Ritter, Doris, 69, 70, 92, 111, 113, 152, 297

Rochow, Colonel von, 69, 84, 85, 93, 94, 95, 98

Rohwedel, Lieutenant von, 132

Roloff, Parson, 187

Rossbach, Battle of, 267, 268

Roucoulle, Madame de, 5, 32, 72, 185

Rudowski, Count, 56, 61

Saint Lambert, Marquis de, 237, 238

Sand, Georges, 294

Sans Souci, 230, 231, 234, 238, 240, 241, 252, 268, 277

Saxe-Gotha, Duchess of, 253

Saxe-Weimar, Duke of, 169, 297

Scarron, 39

Schiller, 298

Schönburg, Count von, 216

Schönhausen, 207

Schöning, General von, 137

Schulenberg, Ehrengarde Melusina von der, Duchess of Kendal, 12, 34

Schulenberg, General von der, 113, 136, 137, 163, 197, 200

Schwerin, General von, 197, 198

Seckendorf, Count Charles Louis von, 297

Seckendorf, Count Frederick Henry von, 45–47, 52, 57, 58, 71, 84, 92, 94, 96, 134, 145, 152–155, 182, 294

Seide, Paul, 291

Senning, Major, 50

Silbermann, Gottfried, 228

Silesia, 197, 198, 201, 205, 206, 210, 222, 241, 254, 267, 275

Sonsfeld, Flora von, 141, 151, 161, 166, 218, 234

Sonsfeld, Madame von, "Sonsine," 33, 35, 42, 50, 64, 79, 82, 90, 101, 108, 109, 117, 118, 141, 161, 183, 218, 234

Soor, Battle of, 223, 232

Sophia Dorothea of Brunswick-Celle, 11, 12, 43, 44, 56, 292

Sophia Dorothea, Margravine of Brandenburg-Schwedt, sister of Frederick and Wilhelmina, 30, 108, 109, 116, 162, 167

Sophia Dorothea, Queen of Prussia, mother of Frederick and Wilhelmina, 4, 5, 7, 8, 10–14, 16, 20, 26–29, 31, 33–35, 39, 41, 42, 43, 44, 48, 53, 60, 61, 62, 63–69, 72, 73, 76–78, 81–83, 88, 98, 99, 100, 101–107, 108, 109, 112, 116, 118, 120, 121, 123, 141, 153, 154, 167, 187, 194, 223, 266, 269, 291, 293, 294

Sophia, Dowager Electress of Hanover, 6, 12, 43, 44, 56

Spaen, Lieutenant von, 113

Spandau Prison, 32, 98, 108, 111, 152

Stuart, Charles Edward, "Bonnie Prince Charlie," 258

Suhm, Count von, 66, 67, 75, 174–176, 180, 297

Sulzbach, Count von, 47

Superville, Daniel de, 182, 214, 225, 241

Tabagie, the, 20, 21, 46, 111, 154, 182
Tacitus, 212
Tamsel, 137, 138, 151, 271
Tasso, 253
Telemachus, 23, 24, 53
Tencin, Cardinal, 258, 266
Tettau, Mademoiselle von, 172
Thulmeyer, Herr von, 118
Townsend, Lord, 40, 82
Trenck, Freiherr von, 299

Ulrica, *see* Louise Ulrica

Valori, Marquis de, 300
Vergil, 238, 260
Villa, Dr., 78, 79, 80
Vivaldi, 300
Voight, Baron, 141, 142
Voltaire, Marie François Arouet de, 176–178, 185, 186, 191, 192–194, 196, 199, 201, 209, 210–213, 236–239, 241, 242–245, 248, 249–253, 257, 258, 266, 276, 277, 296, 297, 299, 300, 302
Volz, Gustav, 299

Waldow, Colonel von, 94, 98
Wales, Prince of, *see* Frederick Louis of Hanover
Walpole, Horace, 294
Wartensleben, General Field Marshal von, 114
Watteau, 38, 180
Weissenfels, Duke of, 63–65, 71, 77, 78, 85, 105, 116
Wilhelmina, Crown Princess of Prussia, Margravine of Bayreuth, birth (July 3, 1709), 3; precocity, 3, 19; her parents' favorite, 5; early education, 5; "engaged" to her cousin, Frederick of Hanover, 5; her portrait painted with Frederick by Pesne, 7; defends Frederick, 7, 8; hand read by a Swedish palmist, 10; tutored by Vizyierre de la Croze, 13, 14; meets Peter the Great, 14–17; writes letters to her father, 18, 20; her marriage with the Margrave of Schwedt suggested, 28; beaten by Letti, 29; ill with dysentery and scarlet fever, 30; 31; asks for a grown-up dress, 31; her new governess, Madame von Sonsfeld, 33; inspected by visitors from Hanover, 33, 34; meets her grandfather, 34, 35; has a private language with Frederick, 39; hides an inkwell in her pocket, 42, 43; her dislike of pietists, 51; obtains an invitation for Frederick to visit Dresden (1728), 53; thinks she is promised to Augustus the Strong, 60; disapproves of La Orczelska, 61; resists engagement to Duke of Weissenfels, 63–69; is willing to marry Prince of Wales, 68, 69; is jealous of Frederick's friends, 70, 90; persecuted by her father, 72, 73; ill with small-pox, 73; her marriage to the Prince of Bayreuth proposed, 78; persuades Frederick not to escape to England, 79; forgiven by her father, 84; quarrels with Frederick, 89; talks with Von Katte and Grumbkow of Frederick, 99–101; learns of Frederick's and Katte's arrest, 101, 102; destroys and forges letters to Frederick, 103, 104; is beaten by her father, 105–107; her imprisonment, 108–110; hears of Katte's death, 110; consents to marry Prince of Bayreuth, 117, 118; meets her future husband, 120; her betrothal and marriage, 121–125; reunion with Frederick, 125; finds her marriage settlement inadequate, 140, 141; her wedding journey, 141–143; her first impressions of Bayreuth, 143–145; her pregnancy, 141, 149; visited by her father, 150; birth of her daughter, Frederica, 150; visits Prussia (1732), 150–158; meets her sister-in-law, 156; prevents marriage of her father-in-law, 161; meets secretly with Frederick (1734), 163; reaction to her father's illness, 164; visited openly by Frederick, 165, 166; becomes Margravine of Bayreuth, 168; her extravagance, 169, 170; her philosophic correspondence with Frederick, 174, 175; envious of Frederick's friendship with Voltaire, 178;

her ill health, 179; her journey to France and Italy frustrated, 183–185; dissuaded from visiting her father during his last illness, 186, 187; addresses Frederick as "sire," 190; visited by Frederick (1740), 192, 193; visits Rheinsberg and meets Voltaire, 194–196; hears of the battle of Mollwitz, 199; visited by the Marshal de Belle-Isle, 201; her intercession with Frederick asked by Dowager Empress, 202; attends the coronation of Emperor Charles VII, 203–205; gives grudging consent to the engagement of her daughter, 207; entertains Frederick and Voltaire at the Hermitage, 210–214; inaugurates the University of Erlangen, 214; arranges the marriage of Dorothea von der Marwitz to Count Burghauss, 217–219; writes her memoirs, 221–226; pays her respects to Maria Theresa, 223; her quarrel with Frederick resolved, 225, 226; asked to do research for Frederick's history of Brandenburg, 229; paints pastels, 229; visits Frederick at Sans Souci (1747), 230; has an interview with Christian von Wolff, 231; asks Frederick's help for Dorothea Burghauss, 232; writes letter of Folichon to Biche, 233; her daughter's marriage, 233–235; describes Russian troops to Frederick, 234; visits daughter at Stuttgart, 239; visits Sans Souci (1750), 239, 240; detained by illness in Berlin, 240; asks Voltaire to provide her with a suitable companion, 241; chides Voltaire for his lawsuit with Hirschel, 242; tries to make peace between Frederick and Voltaire, 243; wishes she could be of use to Frederick, 247; corresponds with Voltaire, 248, 249; tries to prevent Frederick's break with Voltaire, 253; a refugee from the burnt palace of Bayreuth, 255; consults a faith healer, 256; visited by and visits Frederick, 257; journey to France and Italy, 257–260; meets Voltaire at Colmar and Lyon, 257, 258; sends Frederick a laurel wreath, 260; hears war rumors, 260; hears of Battle of Lobositz, 264; undertakes secret peace negotiations with France, 265; tries to reconcile Frederick with August William, 266; aided in peace negotiations by Voltaire, 266; last illness and death (Oct. 14, 1758), 270–272; memorialized by Frederick and Voltaire, 276, 277; publication of her memoirs, vii.

Wilhelmina of Bayreuth, Wilhelmina's sister-in-law, 144, 169

Wilhelmina of Hesse-Cassel, 248, 301

William, brother of Frederick and Wilhelmina, see Louis Charles William

William, Prince of Bayreuth, Wilhelmina's brother-in-law, 144

Wolden, Counsellor von, 132, 133, 147

Wolfenbuttel, Anton Ulrich von, 292

Wolff, Christian von, 174, 175, 176, 178, 190, 231

Wreech, Colonel von, 137, 151

Wreech, Louisa Eleanora von, 137, 138, 151, 153, 271, 296

Wren, Sir Christopher, 292

Württemberg, Dowager Duchess of, 206, 207, 213, 214, 234, 239

Würzburg, Prince Bishop of, 213

Wusterhausen: 30, 48–52, 61, 66, 74, 91, 109, 122, 135, 187, 230, 247

Xenophon, 212

Zittau, 266, 270

Zorndorf, Battle of, 271